Manning the Nation:
Father figures in
Zimbabwean literature
and society

Manning the Nation:
Father figures in Zimbabwean literature and society

edited by

KIZITO Z. MUCHEMWA AND
ROBERT MUPONDE

Published by Weaver Press, PO Box A1922,
Avondale, Harare. Zimbabwe. 2007
www.weaverpresszimbabwe.com

Published in South Africa by Jacana Media (Pvt) Ltd
PO Box 2004, Houghton, Johannesburg, 2041
www.jacana.co.za

© Each essay the author. This collection Robert
Muponde and Kizito Z. Muchemwa

Typeset by Weaver Press
Cover Design: Heath Manyepa, Harare.
Printed by: Fingerprint Co-operative, Cape Town.

Weaver Press would like to express its gratitude to Hivos for their support in the development of their fiction and outreach programme.

All rights reserved. No part of the publication may be reproduced, stored in a retrieval system or transmitted in any form by any means – electronic, mechanical, photocopying, recording, or otherwise – without the express written permission of the publisher.

ISBN: 978 1 77922 069 1 (Weaver Press)
ISBN: 978 1 77009 500 7 (Jacana Media)

Contents

Acknowledgements
About the contributors

Introduction: Manning the Nation
Kizito Z. Muchemwa and Robert Muponde

Chapter 1: 'Why don't you tell the children a story?': Father figures in the Zimbabwean short stories
Kizito Z. Muchemwa 1

Chapter 2: Killing fathers
Robert Muponde 17

Chapter 3: Of fathers and ancestors in Charles Mungoshi's *Waiting for the Rain*
Neil ten Kortenaar 31

Chapter 4: 'Sins of the Fathers': Revealing family secrets in Mungoshi's later fiction
Pauline Dodgson-Katiyo 46

Chapter 5: The strong healthy man: AIDS and self-delusion
Lizzy Attree 58

Chapter 6: Fatherhood and nationhood: Joshua Nkomo and the re-imagination of the Zimbabwe nation
Sabelo J. Ndlovu-Gatsheni 73

Chapter 7: Mai Mujuru: Father of the nation?
Lene Bull Christiansen 88

Chapter 8: Masculinities, race and violence in the making of Zimbabwe
Jane L. Parpart 102

Chapter 9: It couldn't be anything innocent: Negotiating gender in patriarchal-racial spaces
Ane M. Orbo Kirkegaard 115

Chapter 10: 'Boys': Performing manhood in Zimbabwean drama
Praise Zenenga   127

Chapter 11: 'A man can try': Negotiating manhoods in colonial urban spaces in Dambudzo Marechera's *The House of Hunger* and Yvonne Vera's *Butterfly Burning*
Grace A. Musila   142

Chapter 12: The nature of fatherhood and manhood in Zimbabwean texts of pre-colonial and colonial settings
Mickias Musiyiwa and Memory Chirere   156

Chapter 13: Intricate space: The father-daughter relationship in Zimbabwean literature and culture
Anna Chitando and Angeline M. Madongonda   170

Bibliography   183

This book is dedicated
To all our fathers whose stories have not been told
To all children who have spent their lost years
Looking for lost fathers in graves and prisons of memory

Acknowledgements

First and foremost, the editors would like to express thanks to each other for manfully broaching the subject of manhood at a time when much of the enthusiasm about 'real men' has been depleted by the current crisis in Zimbabwean nationalism and patriarchy. Our tentative probing of the subject in August 2004 at the Zimbabwe Book Fair grounds, amid the noises of bees and hailers, and subsequent intellectual exchanges on the subject, have convinced us that the book has a place in the current struggles in Zimbabwe. Recent events have also convinced us that entrenched interests in Zimbabwean politics do get unsettled with good books, as even a mere biography by Edgar Tekere, one of the fathers of the nation, elicited hostile responses from a sterner father of the nation, Robert Mugabe: 'The machinery is not biographies, the people who vote for us are the ordinary people of Zimbabwe'. (He imagined the book as a missile aimed to unseat him from power!)

We want to thank Irene Staunton of Weaver Press, for her patience with the editors and contributors. With deadlines constantly shifting, some writers dropping out at critical stages in the development of the book, she did not give up. We must also thank Irene and Murray for their constant search for newer subjects, and the sacrifice this entails. May they live to be more than '8 plus 3' years!

Kizito would like to thank his colleague Robert Muponde, a tireless communicator who has managed to establish links across three continents on this book project. Robert thanks Kizito for his very stimulating insights and critical passion and a positive stubborn spirit without which he would not have been able to survive his life-threatening workplace and the deprivations associated with hostile anti-intellectual cultures. It was Kizito's idea to start collaborative research on the subject of 'fathers and fathering of stories' in Zimbabwe.

Our greatest indebtedness goes to the contributors who believed in the project. We thank them for their excellent essays, their time and energy, as well as for the contribution they have made to this growing field of study.

Last but not least, we thank our families in allowing us to invest so much of their valuable time into a project that we hope will turn us into better men and kinder fathers.

About the Contributors

Lizzy Attree is a Ph.D. candidate at SOAS in London studying 'Literary representations of HIV and AIDS in literature from Zimbabwe and South Africa'. Past publications feature in: *Words Gone Two Soon* (Umgangatho, South Africa, 2005), *The End of Unheard Narratives* (Kalliope Paperbacks, Germany, 2004), *Sign and Taboo: Perspectives on the Poetic Fiction of Yvonne Vera* (Weaver Press, Harare; James Currey, Oxford, 2002). An interview with Phaswane Mpe was published in *The Journal of Commonwealth Literature* (2005), and a review of *Nobody ever said AIDS* (Kwela Books) appeared in *Research in African Literatures* (2006). An article on 'Women Writing AIDS' will appear in the *Atlantic Literary Review*. Involved in the literary tours African Visions 2002-05, for the Africa Centre, she also toured African writers as part of Reading Africa for SABDET (Southern African Book Development Education Trust).

Memory Chirere lectures in Literature at the University of Zimbabwe. He has published a collection of short stories called *Somewhere in this Country* with the University of South Africa Press. Together with Maurice Vambe, Chirere edited *Charles Mungoshi: A Critical Reader* (Prestige Books, 2006) a collection of academic articles on the Zimbabwean writer.

Lene Bull Christiansen is a Ph.D. candidate at the Graduate School of International Development Studies at Roskilde University in Denmark. Her research on gender power relations in Zimbabwe is associated with the research programme 'Sexuality, Gender and Society in Africa' at the Nordic Africa Institute in Sweden. Lene holds an MA in Cultural Encounters and International Development Studies from Roskilde University, and she is the author of 'Tales of the Nation. Feminist Nationalism or Patriotic History? Defining National History and Identity in Zimbabwe' (The Nordic Africa Institute, Uppsala, 2005).

Anna Chitando is a lecturer in English and Media Studies at the Zimbabwe Open University. Her research interests comprise children's literature and gender studies. Her publications include (with Ezra Chitando): 'Weaving Sisterhood: Women African Theologians and Creative Writers', Exchange 34 (1), 2005; 'An Investigation into Children's Literature', Zimbabwe Journal of Educational Research 17 (3), 2005; and 'Children's Literature in Zimbabwe: Considerable Creativity and Innovation', Mediaforum 3 (4), 2005. Her current research is on post-conflict transition, the state and civil society in Africa, which is co-ordinated by the Nordic Africa Institute.

Pauline Dodgson-Katiyo is a former Dean of the School of Arts and Letters at Anglia Ruskin University in Cambridge and a former Assistant Dean of the Faculty of Humanities and Education at the University of North London. She lived in Zimbabwe during the 1980s, working for the Ministry of Education and the Institute of Mass Communication at Harare Polytechnic. She has taught at a number of British universities including the Open University, Sussex University, Thames Valley University and the University of Westminster. She has written articles on Zimbabwean and other African literatures and on post-colonial cinema.

Ane Marie Ørbø Kirkegaard is currently working as a lecturer in Peace and Conflict Studies at Malmö University in Sweden. She has conducted qualitative research in Zimbabwe since 1995, and defended her doctoral dissertation in Peace and Development Research at Göteborg University in 2004. Her main field of research has focused on discourses on sexuality and reproduction among black and white Zimbabweans, analysed through feminist and post-colonial theory. Since 2005 her teaching and research has been concentrated on sexualised violence in conflict zones, with a particular focus on a post-colonial reading of masculinity and femininity during conflict.

Neil ten Kortenaar teaches African, Caribbean, and South Asian literature in the English department at the University of Toronto at Scarborough. He is the author of *Self, Nation, Text in Salman Rushdie's Midnight's Children* (McGill-Queen's, 2004) and of numerous articles on African literature, most recently 'Oedipus, Ogbanje and the Sons of Independence' in *Research in African Literatures*, 'Achebe and Modern African Tragedy' in *Philosophia Africana*, 'Parents, Children and Fools' in *Scrutiny 2*.

Angeline M. Madongonda is a lecturer in Communication Skills in the department of English and Communication at the Midlands State University, Zimbabwe. Her research papers include 'Traditional Cultural Practices: Arresting the Spread of HIV and AIDS Pandemic' and 'Islam in Traditional African Societies: Deconstructing the Myth of the Uncivilised Ape.' Currently she is working on a paper entitled ' From the Mouth of Babes: Communicating a Cultural Renaissance through Music – The Rise of the Urban Grooves in Zimbabwe.' Her areas of research interest include African literature and culture, indigenous knowledge systems, HIV and AIDS, and feminist issues.

Kizito Z. Muchemwa is a Senior Lecturer in English and Media Studies at Zimbabwe Open University where he co-ordinates literary studies. He has chapter contributions in *Sign and Taboo: Perspectives on the Poetic Fiction of Yvonne Vera* (Weaver Press, Harare; James Currey, Oxford 2002), *Versions of Zimbabwe: new approaches to literature and culture* (Weaver Press), and *Charles Mungoshi: A Critical Reader* (Prestige Books, 2006).

Robert Muponde holds a Ph.D in African Literature, and is a Senior Lecturer in the Department of English, University of the Witwatersrand, South Africa. His publications include, *No More Plastic Balls: New Voices in the Zimbabwean Short Story* (College Press, Harare, 2000), co-edited with C. Chihota; and *Sign and Taboo: Perspectives on the Poetic Fiction of Yvonne Vera* (Weaver Press, Harare; James Currey, Oxford, 2002), co-edited with M. Taruvinga. His most recent book is *Versions of Zimbabwe: New approaches to literature and culture*, (Weaver Press, 2005) co-edited with Ranka Primorac. His forthcoming book is *A Ground for Action: Childhood in Zimbabwean Literature.*

Grace A. Musila is completing a Ph.D. in African Literature at the University of the Witwatersrand, Johannesburg. Her study examines the 1988 murder of Julie Ward, a young English tourist, in the Maasai Mara Game reserve in Kenya. The study examines the versions of truth regarding the death and the various fictive processes that were enacted in the search for (and attempts to conceal) the truth(s) behind the murder by the Kenyan and British constituencies. She has also written articles on popular culture in Kenya, representations of Africa in Hollywood film and Zimbabwean fiction.

Mickias Musiyiwa is a lecturer in literary theory, African oral literature and culture in the Department of African Languages and Literature at the University of Zimbabwe. He has written articles on Zimbabwean children's literature, women's poetry, novel and oral literature. His current research is on Shona oral literature and Zimbabwean music.

Sabelo J. Ndlovu-Gatsheni holds a Ph.D. in History, is a Senior Lecturer of International Studies at Monash University, South Africa Campus. He is a historian and he writes on African History and Contemporary African Politics covering issues of nation building, governance, nationalism, human rights, peace and human security as well as development. Before joining Monash University, Ndlovu-Gatsheni held the post of Teaching Assistant in the Department of History at the University of Zimbabwe (1995-99) and a tenured Lectureship in History and Development Studies at Midlands State University in Zimbabwe. He is currently editing: *Rethinking and Re-Imagining Nationalism in 21st Century Africa: Ideology, Epistemology, and*

Philosophy. He has published extensively on the contemporary history and politics of Zimbabwe.

Jane L. Parpart teaches at Dalhousie University, Stellenbosch University and Aalborg University (Denmark). She has published extensively on gender, development, urban history and the African elite in Southern Africa. She is currently working on empowerment, gender and violence as well as a book on the urban elite in Bulawayo.

Praise Zenenga holds an interdisciplinary Ph.D. in Theatre and Drama from Northwestern University. He is an Assistant Professor in the Africana Studies Program at the University of Arizona in Tuscon where he teaches courses in Aesthetics of Pan African Theatre and Dance. His areas of research include theatre history, with particular emphasis on community theatre, theatre and non-conventional education, theatre for social change often referred to as theatre for development and popular theatre.

Introduction
Manning the Nation

Kizito Z. Muchemwa and Robert Muponde

Masculinity and fatherhood in the context of Zimbabwe is a field of academic study that has suffered long and unnecessary neglect. To some critics, it is a superfluous and vexatious addition to patriarchal strategies of domination that rams another painful nail into the crucified body of feminism. Gender discussions in Zimbabwe traditionally inhabit essentialist spaces from which emerge descriptions and distinctions that stress ideologically inflected binaries, polarities, and exclusions. Zimbabwean scholarship and research on gender studies is currently skewed in favour of one sex and one gender. To discuss one gender usually implies an adversarial existence of unprivileged genders and a definition through negatives of the privileged one. Like the current nationalist political rhetoric on land, sovereignty, and imperialism, it is characterised by its invariable knee-jerk resort to binarising hate speech and hostile name-calling of the other sexes and genders. Scholarly attitudes of this nature have worked well in an atmosphere of crisis and lack, where society is reduced to the functions of oppositions of colonised and coloniser, race and class, sex and gender, poverty and wealth, patriotism and terrorism, sell-outs and party loyalists, survival and death.

Such critical practices deny the existence of marginalised and emerging masculinities that also seek to unmask the strategies of domination employed by hegemonic masculinity. Another assumption is that Zimbabwean/African feminism has consistently ameliorative agendas that deconstruct patriarchy without wanting to examine ways in which this embedded feminism shares the same nest(s) and reaps the same benefits with hegemonic masculinity.

There are points of convergence. There is need for the complex interlinking of gender studies from a variety of perspectives. Viewing masculinity as embodiment of the ultimate other forecloses the re-territorialisation of gender studies. Debates about gender can only be complete and meaningful when masculinity is brought under close scrutiny as it abuts discussions of other genders. A study of the representations of masculinities, manhood and fatherhood in Zimbabwean literature and society makes it possible to link and enrich productions in various cultural and political fields.

In *Manning the Nation: Father figures in Zimbabwean literature and society*, we view masculinities as sets of ideas that can oppress, repress or liberate, depending on historical and political imperatives. But as ideas and practices, masculinities inhabit, and indeed, proliferate in other genders and sexes as well. They are not a monopoly of one biological sex or social construct. Praise Zenenga and Lene Bull Christiansen, in this volume, demonstrate the pervasiveness of these sightings of multiple masculinities in both men and women, and the systematic attribution of masculinities to particular genders, as well as denial and withdrawal of certain qualities associated with being a member of a particular masculinity, at different times and places in culture and society. Zenenga's chapter is a pained call for suppressed masculinities to find common cause with suppressed femininities in order to unseat oppressive and foreclosing hegemonic masculinities and femininities. Christiansen's paradoxically titled chapter shares with Zenenga some of his concerns, while giving a detailed and nuanced picture of the contradictory discourses surrounding types of femininity that can negotiate patriarchal masculinities and nest within them rather comfortably. Masculinity, manhood and fatherhood are associated with various cultures of performance cutting across many disciplines and spheres, genders and sexes.

The essays in *Manning the Nation* examine the performance and theorisation of masculinity, manhood and fatherhood from the perspectives of literature, history, politics, and social anthropology. What is salutary about these essays is that they depart from imperial and colonial gender constructions of the African Other that persist in different guises and mutations. Characterised by exoticisation and vilification, they provided grounds for administrative, statutory, and media management of African sexuality and manhood. In Zimbabwe, white European genders, masculinities and sexualities never really became objects of critical investigation, before and after black majority rule. Nor was it ever thought a viable project to develop an inclusive critical scholarly practice on the subject. Contributions by Jane Parpart and Ane Kirkegaard unpick the strategies that underpin powerful traditions across divisions of race, ethnicity, and class. What is often occluded, misrepresented, and simplified are finely nuanced masculinities and femininities whose boundaries are constantly shifting, and whose indebtedness to each other is not sufficiently acknowledged.

Most of the contributors challenge the hegemonic strategies that treat Zimbabwean masculinities as homogeneous and univocal. They instead capture the subterranean currents that ripple the beguilingly tranquil surface of the Zimbabwean cultural map. Above all, most contributors explore 'the complex nesting of masculinities within very specific places with histories, supports, threats, possibilities, dreams, and dangers' (Fine and Kuriloff, 2006: 259). Specific to constructions of Zimbabwean masculinities are sites such as traditional culture, colonial history, war, the family, and the body.

The male body

Michel Foucault conceptualises the body as terrain for investing and contesting cultural symbols, values, and power:

> *The body is directly involved in a political field; power relations have an immediate hold upon it: they invest it, train, torture it, force it to carry out tasks, to perform ceremonies and to emit signs* (cited in Epstein and Straub, 1994:14).

Some contributors in *Manning the Nation: Father figures in Zimbabwean literature and society* adopt versions of this Foucauldian critique to examine how cultures invest the body with sex and gender significance that generates specific body semiotics, economic structures, and power relations. Gender at its most intimate and visible finds the body as one of its most important sites. This intimate site is also the most vulnerable since it is also used as a site of dominance, misogyny and othering. Rape, torture, disfigurement, and killing are ways in which recalcitrant bodies are controlled. Although women and children are particularly vulnerable in an uncontrolled and violent patriarchy, men who belong to marginalised masculinities can be feminised through rape and torture. Current political cultures are sustained by the manning of many sites of identity so as to efficiently man women and children and to thoroughly unman other men. The body is a site of menace from which Zimbabwe's stories of sexually and politically vulnerable identities emerge, and it is also from the same site that new strengths can be constructed from a collapse of the menacing male body.[1]

Lizzy Attree's contribution in this volume problematises a hegemonic masculinity predicated on the fixation with an athletic, strong, healthy, masculine body. Disease, decay, hunger and death in the age of HIV/AIDS in contemporary Zimbabwe, and indeed Southern Africa, deconstruct this privileged figuring of the male body. Used as an instrument of domination in reproduction and in the public sphere, it has not benefited from a closer scrutiny of its built-in instabilities and incapacities. There are tectonic shifts in gender and power relations that indicate the temporality and instability of traditional semiotics of the body that are captured in most of the chapters.

Kizito Muchemwa, writing on father figures, shows how fatherhood is related to the performance of hyper-masculinity associated with violence, domination, and biological siring that does not have moral and social legitimacy. Accustomed to disciplining other bodies, the male body finds itself in crisis when confronted by the possibilities opened up by the demise of its virility and physical wellness and the collapse of the life-supporting fictions of its indomitableness. While the ideological imperatives that demand regulation of the bodies of women, children, and masculinities on the margins may exist for the maintenance of a patriarchal economy, conditions for the existence of a narrowly conceived masculinity are consistently being undermined by disease, death, absence and moral and economic uncertainties. Absence, literally and figuratively, is about the forced retreat of the male body from various sites of visuality and authority. Literally, because of the current economic meltdown and political mayhem, a new migrancy on a massive scale is dispersing and re-configuring Zimbabwean manhoods, fatherhoods and masculinities at an unprecedented pace, and will soon be associated with depressed local masculinities, and newer womanhoods and femininities abroad and back home. In the long and often indefinite absence of men, women left behind take on the roles of 'men'. The reverse is true in instances of women leaving men at home as they become international migrant labourers. Men take on the roles of 'women'. Metaphorically, absence is associated with men that have not been allowed to perform their masculinities as they conceive them. These are men who can no longer father their own living stories (children) because of disease and grinding poverty, and therefore are proscribed from manning the nation. This undermining of the popular myth of the male body as strong and healthy and reproductive can only be understood in the context of the forces that have shaped it.[2]

Wars of men

Diachronic and synchronic approaches show how pre-colonial and post-colonial wars and the First and Third Chimurenga are important sites for the historical evolution of Zimbabwean masculinity. War consistently functions as a site of erasure and re-articulation of other sites of masculinity. Families and communities are fractured, erased and dispersed, turning individuals into drifters without allegiance. Outside the war ethic driven by an excess of masculinity, individuals whose gender does not contribute to the war economy are under threat (see also Chris Dolan, 2002: 57-83). There are pressures to discipline, militarise, and transform the male body into an instrument of surveillance and violence. Macho masculinity, in both the public and private spheres, may be understood as a phenomenon unique to the distempers of the Third Chimurenga but its aetiology as already stated can be traced to colonial and pre-colonial times as shown in the chapters in this volume that focus on history.

It is tempting to explain post-colonial violence in Africa using a Fanonian critique in which the colonised reverses the racial pattern of colonial violence as Mamdani's (2000) study shows, but theorising post-colonial violence in Africa reads like a taming and sanitising of black-on-black violence. The deterministic character of the Fanonian critique takes away moral agency and blame from perpetrators of violence. This critique is cynically adopted by violent patriarchy that has nationalised the male body and mind. Most of the contributions in *Manning the Nation: Father figures in Zimbabwean literature and society* attribute current cultures of violence to the insidious ways in which superphallicism predicated on physical power has invaded Zimbabwe's socio-cultural space instilling in women, children, and marginalised masculinities acquiescence, silence, and fear. War and violence as markers of power directly emanate from body semiotics in which the athletic, strong and healthy male body demands the performance of sexual, social, and political dominance. This performance of masculinity is part of a wider culture of spectacle (Mendible, 1999).

The trauma of rape and horrific physical violence has come to dominate post-1980 Zimbabwean fiction, and contemporary literary criticism reflects attempts to interrogate the sites that produce this trauma. War masculinity, celebrated as a cultural and ideological imperative, is the major source of the contemporary crisis of manhood.

The family

The family is the primary site for scripting of gendered identities and it is here that the iconographic investments in the body begin. Masculinities are largely connected to the fatherhood-paternity-manhood nexus where they self-perpetuate. They produce within families relations of anomie, hatred, and indifference. Familial violence marks the dystopia at the heart of the Zimbabwean family romance and *bildungsroman*. Zimbabwean literature has come to be defined by what we would like to describe as a search for utopian families.

Most of the contributors in this volume deal with dystopian families that have been made so by an aberrant masculinity that preys not only on women and children but also on itself. Robert Muponde locates part of this aberrant masculinity in the misfit between siring and fathering, revealing a gap between biology and morality that he subtly negotiates. Gendered identity, as conceived by and determined in the family, can be an ancestral burden at a site that has become claustrophobic as shown in Neil ten Kortenaar's essay. Kortenaar explores in intriguing detail how in Mungoshi's *Waiting for the Rain* children struggle to free themselves from ancestral curses and the entrapment of the family. The family is a dystopian space in which secrets are experienced as atrophying and entrapping as Pauline Dodgson-Katiyo's chapter demonstrates. In her analysis of two stories by Charles Mungoshi, Dodgson-Katiyo unravels the tension that obtains in scripts of identity at both national and familial levels. This tension is largely caused by a father who demands an heir and clone from the son. Such an exacting demand unmans the son. .The father-son relationship is complicated by marriage outside race, ethnicity, incest and xenophobia in 'Empty House' and ethnic cleansing in 'The Sins of the Fathers'.

Fatherhood and paternity nexus

The current crisis of masculinity in Zimbabwean culture and politics manifests itself through the deployment of violence to suppress all other masculinities and police other genders. It seeks to rewrite the history of the country and shape its destiny from a gendered, ethnic, and racial perspective. This brand of masculinity is underpinned by the fatherhood-paternity-manhood nexus taken as a semantic and conceptual synonymy. It is a confusion that deepens a crisis that finds articulation through violence in the public sphere, the family, unreconstructed parenting styles, lack of clarity between siring and fathering, unfulfilled quests for ideal father figures, and the denial of agency to marginalised groups in society.

The theme of manning captures many of the interstices at which themes constellate. The two key meanings of the verb man – 'to furnish with a man or men' and 'to strengthen or put manhood into'– give a sense of the direction discussions about masculinity should take, a direction that requires intricate negotiation. If the business of culture and society is to supply nations with men it is important that the sources, methods, and types of men recruited into the various enterprises of the nation be interrogated. Robert Muponde's chapter, and his work elsewhere (2006), provides instances in which certain fatherhoods and manhoods should never be allowed to stand for the gender, whether marginal, normative or hegemonic. The meaning of strengthening or giving manhood should be viewed beyond the limited scope of masculinity enhanced or distorted by testosterone, steroids, and Viagra. A clearer, more nuanced definition of manhood is urgently needed to address the crisis of manhood that has led to the over-manning of the nation.

Chapters by Kortenaar, Dodgson-Katiyo and Muchemwa on Charles Mungoshi's work, Musila and Muponde on Dambudzo Marechera's work, demonstrate that fatherhood and manhood are nestled precariously on a shaky life-support system, if they have not already placed their societies in the same position. There is a sense of depression and emergency, which only Memory Chirere and Mickias Musiyiwa's chapter on the quest for an ideal father figure attempts to ameliorate. But then, Sabelo Ndlovu-Gatsheni's brave chapter on Joshua Nkomo's posthumous resurrection as Father Zimbabwe, still portrays a rather too cautious egoist, who is depicted as not necessarily any better than his arch-rival Robert Mugabe. The latter presides over the unmanning of the entire folk as well as the burial of heroes year in year out as the chief and sole undertaker of the nation.

The contributions in this volume are not celebrating the demise of manhood but its reconfiguration and possible liberation. Muponde's 'Killing

Fathers' points the reader to this reconfiguration as it unbundles the fatherhood-paternity-manhood matrix to clear the conceptual space for debates on fatherhood. His analysis deploys the parricide trope to revise fatherhood by bringing its biological and social constructions into conflict. Biological fatherhood that emphasises sperm count emerges as unsocialised, morally deficient, and psychologically destabilising. The child as both passive product and victim of biological authoring can only recuperate agency, revise narrative of sacrificial obedience and closure through parricide.

Much as the thrust here is on fathering and childhood, writers in this volume constantly find themselves dealing with mothers and mothering styles. This is inevitably so since mothers cannot be left out of the father-child nexus. Mothers/women also define fatherhood in significant ways. Motherhood and fatherhood often find themselves in an embrace that is difficult to separate as shown in Lene Bull Christiansen's contribution on Joice Mujuru whose iconographic role during the Second Chimurenga and in contemporary politics is brought under scrutiny. Women in politics in other parts of the world who assume leadership positions do not seem to challenge the power men wield. The iconographic significance of such women is often lost in the patriarchal demands of the office of head of government in a patriarchal society.

History and its ceiling

History, it would appear, places a ceiling, to use a phrase from Yvonne Vera's *The Stone Virgins*, on men and women who construct their identities and the discourses that sustain these. Most of the contributions explore the historical roots/routes of masculinity in Zimbabwe and interrogate what Grace Musila describes as 'masculinisation of national history'. Musila argues that Dambudzo Marechera and Yvonne Vera not only subvert this monolithic history of the nation but also subvert normative notions of gender. In *Butterfly Burning* the colonial urban space is viewed as the epitome of colonialism and symbol of Western modernity. While it triggers a crisis in black manhood, it opens up new exhilarating opportunities for black women who, although controlled and constrained by the colonial system and traditional black patriarchy, find in the urban instabilities and insecurities cracks through which to reconfigure black womanhood outside of matrimony and maternity. This rearrangement of ontological signposts in the city leads to an alienation of men that produces violence. This leads befuddled and emasculated men in Dambudzo Marechera's fiction to beat their women to a stain. The excess of violence as a defensive mechanism marks the reaction of 'native' men whose psyches have been challenged and damaged by colonialism and new realities.

But history with its regressions and fast forwards reveals many connections across times and cultures, and the violence of depressed masculinity in colonial times is not very different in severity from that arising out of the post-colonial present and does strangely have several points of intersection with white hegemonic masculinity (see Parpart and Kirkegaard in this volume) that in the past treated it as the primitive Other.

While fatherhood in the West appears to be in decline and there is alarm attached to its presumed demise, fatherhood in Zimbabwe is alive and carried on a resurgent wave of patriotic paternity and patrimony despite legislation that promotes the rights of women. Fatherhood is highly visible and feminism that is tolerated is that which does not threaten the official discourse of fatherhood. Lene Bull Christiansen demonstrates that the iconographic significance of Joice Mujuru can be read as an example of officially sanctioned feminism. In the charged atmosphere of gender ideologies negotiations of a gendered identity become highly problematic raising questions and doubts that surround her fathering/mothering role. Christiansen places her iconographic assessment in the larger context of what she describes as a 'metaphor of kinship [that] can be seen as feeding on 'traditionalist' versions of pre-colonial versions of pre-colonial social structures', a kinship discourse that has given rise to political constructions of patriarchal and matriarchal icons.

Perhaps in the same way that Musiyiwa and Chirere painfully excavate for what constituted an ideal father in pre-colonial and colonial times, in itself a very urgent quest in our depressing times of false 'amadhodha sibili' ('real men'),[3] Anna Chitando and Angeline Madongonda recover a vision of a less dystopian, and perhaps hopeful, fatherhood in Zimbabwean folklore and literature that presents the father as hero in the father-daughter nexus. The psychological growth of the girl child and her gender identity are closely linked to the image of the good father. Their approach shows how dominant conceptions of fatherhood depart significantly from traditional ones.

While *Manning the Nation: Father figures in Zimbabwean literature and society* is not meant to be exhaustive and conclusive, the insights gathered in these excellent essays pose enough questions that should help us to review subjects that, in spite of dominating our lives, and very often endangering and poisoning our politics and economics, are surprisingly taken for granted. It is time we get fathers we *want* (we have agency, vision and choice), not the ones we *deserve* (a question of fate). The same can be said of the nature of society, and how we man it.

ENDNOTES

1. Perhaps the most menacing male body is that which Robert Mugabe presents at his birthday on the 21 February every year. His octogenarian's body is increasingly being presented as a fighting machine with lots of punch; earlier when he was approaching his late 70s, and was faced with a youthful opposition leader Morgan Tsvangirai, his advanced years were converted to horse power; when he turned 82, he conjured a grotesque picture of himself as a 28-year-old inhabiting the body of an 82-year-old; in 2007 when he turned 83, he was quoted in the press as saying he is only 8 plus 3 years old (he is getting dangerously younger at a time when every suffering Zimbabwean wants him to retire!). This is not just denialism, but a very strong tendency in Zimbabwean patriarchal nationalism and politics to seek self-renewal by constantly engaging in violent, militaristic adventures and rhetoric. In the domestic sphere, 'the strong healthy man' is associated with the acquisition of gadgets, more cars, cellphones, and what is now known as 'small houses' (extra-marital affairs).

2. We are sure future studies will examine how Zimbabwean masculinities are configured by sport, schooling, as well as the experiences of land invasions and reform, migrancy, forced homelessness and the current Zimbabwean diaspora.

3. An Ndebele term popularised and abused by Robert Mugabe in 2000 when he created what he called 'A war cabinet' to deal with the opposition and accelerate land invasions.

1
'Why don't you tell the children a story?': Father figures in three Zimbabwean short stories

KIZITO Z. MUCHEMWA

This chapter explores the tensions that inhabit fictional narratives of the nation in the short stories by Charles Mungoshi ('The Sins of the Fathers'), Nevanji Madanhire ('The Grim Reaper's Car'), and Freedom Nyamubaya ('That Special Place').[1] Psychic struggles mark the relations between fathers (real, putative, imaginary and symbolic) and their children, especially sons. The space that separates children from their fathers engenders emotions of endearment strangely mixed with violence. Paternity is used as a trope for scripting identity – both personal and national. Where father figures are associated, directly and indirectly, with the liberation struggle, the gun is an extension of this trope of (auto)biography. This chapter examines – in the 'fathering' of stories of individuals and the nation – the dynamics of continuity in discontinuity and the significance of democratic expression in the creation of father-and-child stories.

The chapter is written against a backdrop of metaphors of national sovereignty produced by cultural essentialists of various persuasions,[2] who have been co-opted by post-colonial ruling elites to legitimate a regime that uses fatherhood to foreclose political debate. The historian Terence Ranger (2005) has identified the production of partisan patriotic history that academics from a variety of disciplines are currently contesting. Here, we seek to critically examine literature's contribution to constructions of nationalist fatherhood and manhood. In current unproblematic narratives of the nation generated by the ZANU-PF government, the father figure serves to provide an uncontested, benevolent authorship of the nation and the state. In a posthumous rehabilitation of Joshua Nkomo and a travesty of the holy trinity,[3] Nkomo is re-claimed as father of the nation, Simon Muzenda reconstructed as its 'soul' and Robert Mugabe offered as the son who interprets and implements its essence.

The three stories selected here provide counter-narratives to the discourse of hegemonic fatherhood, masculinity, and ethnicity as they affect constructions of the nation and its historiography. Absent fathers, tyrannical fathers, weak fathers, true fathers, putative fathers abound in Zimbabwean fiction. Dambudzo Marechera and Charles Mungoshi frame the psychological and cultural terrain in which fathers and their children wrestle for the power to tell stories. This terrain is traversed by a later generation of writers with more nuanced approaches to the relationship between narrative power and gender. Fathering and speaking/writing tropes in constructions of identity manifest themselves at the level of self, family, community, and nation. This imbrication determines the discourse of authorship, authority, and creation in the three short stories. Contrary to traditional story-telling, the origins of the Zimbabwean short story in English has been patriarchal in both authorship and context of creation. Phallic symbols are then deployed to describe the creative process and the stories. The phallus, the gun and pen are often conflated as instruments of writing these texts in articulations of violence and masculinity. Story-telling becomes a violent, masculine, and patriotic act and the authoritarian father figure sees the son/historical narrative as an autonomous text that cannot deviate from a given script. The story-telling urge and atavism associated with sexualised creativity inevitably leads to the exclusion of other story-tellers from sites of narration. Seamless and self-replicating narratives guarantee continuity of the ancestral line.

The three stories discussed here subvert a re-configured official Zimbabwean masculinity that has over-determined fatherhood and nationhood. I want to place the father figure in the context of the re-tribalisation of Zimbabwean society, the obsession with self-perpetuation, self-replication of a militarised masculinity, and narrative closure in narrations of self and nation as articulated by Rwafa in 'Sins of the Fathers', the Grim Reaper in 'The Grim Reaper's Car', and Nyathi in 'That Special Place'. Children struggle with strong, tyrannical fathers to terminate hegemonic narratives leading to de-tribalisation, re-gendering, and re-articulation of nationhood.

Narratives, rituals, and symbols are viewed as cultural productions that reveal power relations in society and telling and performance are the instruments of what Eric Hobsbawm (1983:3) calls 'routinization or bureaucratization' in the invention of tradition that has seen a hagiographic packaging of history, culture, funerals and public holidays. Current cultural interventions by the state in Zimbabwe, which are a quest for legitimation, are manifestations of what Guy Debord (1994) called the 'society of the spectacle'. Spectacle is about performance and visuality of power, a narcissistic admiration of self by those that wield power, an ineffable desire that words and images, like the divine fiat, can be translated into action, and the belief that listening, reading, and viewing are passive activities.

Patriarchy as ambivalent inheritance in Charles Mungoshi's stories
'Shadows on the Wall', Mungoshi's story in *Coming of the Dry Season* (1972), shows the relationship between the father figure and language:

Father is sitting just inside the hut near the door and I am sitting far across the hut near the opposite wall playing with shadows on the wall. Bright sunlight comes in through the doorway now and father, who blocks most of it, is reproduced in caricature on the floor and half-way up the wall. The wall and floor are bare, so he looks like a black scarecrow in a deserted field after the harvest (1).

The extract above illustrates the struggle for the control of psychic space in an ontological and epistemological context constructed by the father. In this structure, dread of the father produces silence in the son who is also shut out from the light. A deconstruction of this imprisoning hut begins when the son re-imagines the father, a process that diminishes the ability of paternal power to menace and paralyse. In a family where the mother is absent, it can also be seen that the putative mother contributes towards the loss of the father's power. A phenomenon not currently explored in Zimbabwean literature is the usurpation of masculine speech, power, and presence by the narrator's stepmother, a woman with 'a strident voice like a cicada's' (6). Her usurpation leads to displacement and emasculation of the father whose 'tough grey stubble looks like the soft unprotected feathers on a dove's nestling' (6). Doubly orphaned by the absence of the true mother and loss of a strong father figure, the son is saddened.

Paternal tyranny in Dambudzo Marechera's *The House of Hunger* (1978) induces speech impediments in the main character as son and narrator. The act of narration itself becomes an act of defiance and subversion of the father's narrative. Linguistic impediments prevent sons from locating themselves in seamless narratives of the nation. In 'The Sins of the Fathers', Rondo's stammer, his inability to write his own story, his reluctance to question the father's ethnic and racial narrative of the nation arise out of an unresolved ambivalence towards his father. Psychologically cowed into pusillanimous silence and acquiescence, Rondo becomes a symbol of Zimbabwean citizenry that dread the violent masculinity of the times.

The three father figures in the story, Rwafa, Mzamane, and Quayle, are drawn from the three major ethnic groups[4] Shona, Ndebele, and white respectively, and compete in the re-fathering of narrative. History binds the three groups in a violent embrace, with each group opting for militarised masculinity that effeminises the other, a process that is found at work in Rwafa's story of ethnic grief and hatred. The story takes the past as both 'still point' and point of rupture. Rwafa inhabits the point that celebrates masculinity with 'a raw lust for blood' as a guarantor of the honour and integrity of the clan. He embarks on a course of ethnic and ideological cleansing in his use of Second Street accidents. Believing in the maintenance of rigid boundaries in the establishment of marital, political, and social relations he is scandalised by his son's marriage. In his eugenics, Rwafa views 'outsiders' as polluters of the purity of the clan/tribe and of the nation.

The biblical echo of the title, 'The Sins of the Fathers', gives an epic, nationalistic, and moral resonance to fatherhood and fathering. The story is about original sin, delayed retribution, divine anger and the moral, political and historical DNA of a nation. The concept of original sin contains the hint of gratuitous punishment and irreconcilable ethnic and racial differences. In a nation characterised by racial and ethnic divisions, Rondo has to contend with three father figures in his search for fresh sites for fathering national narratives beyond race and ethnicity.

Rwafa, the true father, an ex-minister of state security, with the resources of state violence at his disposal, engenders insecurity and fear. He organises road accidents[5] to eliminate personal and state 'enemies'. Rwafa refers to himself as the 'Nyashanu bull', a phallic image of goring, siring, and heterosexual masculinity with a sense of animal territoriality that resonates with current discourses of sovereignty and feminisation[6] of the nation. His messianic sense of manifest destiny, however, threatens the fabric of his text of nation creation: suspicion of other characters, his persecution complex, and his schizophrenia.[7] A victim of both ethnic and colonial history, Rwafa cannot conceive of a Zimbabwean national identity that is totemless and non-racial. Robert Muponde (2004: 176) captures this aspect of contemporary xenophobic nationalism represented by the Third Chimurenga which he describes as 'a recrudescence of powerful urges within the Zimbabwean (read ZANU-PF) psyche to render the idea of nation a taboo and citizenship synonymous with totem'.

Impelled by this sense of ethnic and racial injury, Rwafa's life is one of patriotic commitment that leads him on a crusade against enemies of self, family, and state. He also detests any suspected sources of mis-siring, mis-writing. Miscegenation, for an unreconstructed ethnic nationalist, becomes a metaphor of false writing and false fathering. Rwafa uses images of obscenity, sullying, diluting, and corrupting the purity of the ancestral line to describe his son's marriage. In Mungoshi's fiction, Rwafa is a development from literary predecessors: Samambwa, the Old Man, and John Kuruku in *Waiting for the Rain* are sources of his mania for authenticity, ethnic exclusivity, and anti-racist racism.

The father, as author of narratives, constructs stories of tribal nationalist war heroism, which underpins current discourses of sovereignty. Rwafa proffers a rigid, masculine, and xenophobic warrior ethic as a viable nationalist ideology whose application threatens the viability of the newly formed nation. Emphasising ethnic and violent masculinity in the upbringing of his son, Rwafa rejects alternative masculinities articulated by musicians and men from other ethnicities. Rwafa views these alternative masculinities as effeminate and determines to exclude them from constructions of personal and national stories of heroism. In doing so, he guarantees self-replicating psychological, social, and ideological narratives. Like Faulkner's Thomas Sutpen (Boone, 1997), Rwafa wants to father himself into perpetuity but the biological son turns into a spiritual bastard:

> *His father loved himself so much, he was prepared to destroy his son in his endeavour to have – a duplicate? an heir?* ('The Sins of the Fathers': 145).

Rondo has been psychologically disengaging himself from his father despite the stammer and seeming lack of courage to restore unimpeded speech and healthy cognitive integrity. His defiance of the father's fiat when he marries an Ndebele girl, however may attest to the presence of an intelligence enervated by tyrannical fatherhood. The metonymic significance of his story is reinforced by his place of birth, Old Canaan, Highfield, Harare, the birthplace of Zimbabwean nationalist politics. Immersed by the father in a discourse of tribalism and nationalism, the son who may know better cannot speak otherwise. The matter is further complicated by the fact that Rondo is the immediate material beneficiary of the ethnic nationalism.

On the theme of defective fatherhood Charles Mungoshi works on a subject explored in novelistic detail in Doctorow's *The Waterworks* (1994), which is narrated by the city editor of the *Telegram* who refuses to intervene in the Pembertons' father-son relationship. Augustus Pemberton, the father, is a slave trader, a manufacturer of shoddy goods that he sells to government; he belongs to a cabal of corrupt old men who vampirishly suck life out of the young, an instance of the past parasitically destroying the future. Martin Pemberton, the precociously brilliant, rebellious, and morally alert son, passionately defends public interest and is consequently disinherited for exposing the skeletons in the family cupboard. Disinheritance from material entitlements does not entail total exclusion from patrimony, according to Mr McIlvaine, the narrator and editor, who is reluctant to occupy the imaginative and moral space that legitimately belongs to the materially dispossessed son:

> ... *that's why I never wrote up the story* ... *not because it would not be heard but because it was his* ... *his patrimony* ... *for a writer the story is his patrimony* ... *and he might some day come into it (The Waterworks: 244).*

In the quest for identity, narrative is patrimony larger than material considerations in its ontological and moral ramifications. At both the family and national levels (despite the exclusions by proud and tyrannical fathers) narrative is patrimony that sons and daughters eventually 'come into'. This process of decomposing and recomposing the father's narrative has meaning and value only when the inheritors are not distanced from it through third-party mediation.

In Mungoshi's story this third party mediation is suggested in the actions of Caston Shoko, an investigative journalist with the *Clarion,* Rondo's colleague, friend and alter ego. Like Mr McIlvaine, the editor in Doctorow's novel *The Waterworks,* Shoko views narrative as patrimony. He assumes his friend Rondo to be the legitimate heir to the inheritance of the Second Street accidents, hence his own reluctance to write the story that he would rather Rondo write himself. A number of reasons underline his position. First, he is impatient with Rondo's inertia to assume his narrative responsibility. Second, Rondo lacks the passion and dissident brilliance found in Martin Pemberton, the rebellious son in Doctorow's novel. Lastly, Rwafa, Rwondo's father, exhibits the stubborn pride and tyranny of Augustus Pemberton, Martin's father, who 'bequeaths' a tainted inheritance. However, Shoko finally succeeds in enabling Rondo to accept the burden of narrative that leads to the subversion of official and family narratives. The revelation that there are skeletons in the national cupboard becomes a significant way (among many others indicted in the story) of allowing Rondo to 'come into his patrimony'. His children's birthday party, their deaths, and the subsequent funerals in 'Sins of the Fathers' are the results of unresolved narratives of hatred and violence, Rondo's 'tainted inheritance'. The swift descent from celebration into tragedy, at an allegorical level, expresses the movement of the Zimbabwean nation from independence to civil war.

Caston Shoko's critical perceptivity and iconoclasm deconstruct the narrative of Rwafa's life. The main plot is offered by the author/narrator, Rwafa, as consistent, heroic, idyllic, and beneficent to hearers/readers. It is an historical narrative of nation creation, patriotism, commercial success, and liberation-struggle machismo that admits no deviation from the official canon. The discordant tone and style of the narrative, the paranoia, arrogance, and egocentrism are revealed in Rwafa's harangue (157). Rwafa, as shown in the style and content of his story, is a victim of the history he has authored and distorted. Stylistically, the syntactic and semantic repetitions, the name-calling, the obscene diction, and haranguing are consistent with language use in a public sphere that has been closed to alternative styles and visions.[8]

Mzamane, labelled by the former as a cattle rustler and kidnapper of children because of 'the sins of the fathers', is Rwafa's immediate rival. The latter's drunken outburst carries, at a deeper psychological level, dramatic irony since as the story develops Rondo wishes to switch father figures: 'if he had to choose, he would pick out his father-in-law as his father' (148).

'Why don't you tell the children a story?'

This wish to replace the natural and legal father with a spiritual one is part of the psychic father-son battle in the story. 'When he was with his father-in-law, Rondo always felt that the space around him had expanded', (148) but whenever he is with his father there is a contraction of psychic space. Mzamane is a figure that departs from an idea of fatherhood enmeshed in the past. He nurtures self-authorship, and clears a space for re-writing of national narratives. He stops the bloody outcome of the invasion of the Quayles's farm and provides an alternative solution to land-sharing and distribution. But, significantly, when invited to tell a story at the birthday party and offer a counter-narrative, he politely declines. This is consistent with Mzamane's acceptance and support of the trans-ethnic marriage of his daughter to Rondo. Unlike the ZANU-PF–ZAPU unity accord of 1987, the trans-ethnic marriage goes beyond the tokenism of national galas to reveal the possibility of national re-authoring by a younger generation.

Mr Quayle's fatherhood is not clearly articulated. But in the story his acts of kindness, acceptance, and absence of racism make Rondo unconsciously accept him as a father figure. Caston Shoko, guardian of crossroads, who takes Rondo from political and moral somnolence across the psychological borderline, wants the latter to confront the tyranny and crimes of his father. The contest involves wrestling the two phallic symbols that dominate the story, from the father as the only way of ensuring that inscription of texts, self, nation, and state are not hegemonic and univocal narrations of a single group. Rondo's authoring of an article on the arranged Second Street accidents for the *Clarion*, a state paper, represents an expression of hope against the restrictions of AIPPA, POSA, and MIC.[9] In the article Rondo, beginning at a deeply personal level, confronts the fact that his father arranged to have his daughters and his father-in-law killed; this leads him to accept his father's authorship of 'arranged' accidents. He is thus rudely awakened from the nursery world in which his father is a hero. The ability to write about family taboos heralds the regaining of the power of language to narrate self and others. Caston Shoko adopts the gun as one of the important tropes in the writing and fathering of family and nation allowing possibilities of rupture, parricide, suicide, and termination of the genealogy of violence. This allows for the posthumous re-integration of Mzamane, who had already been accepted by Rondo as a credible father figure.

The fascist descent into anarchy, lawlessness, and amorality have come to dominate post-2002 narratives of the nation, which seek to write out the perceived 'enemies' of a narrow and ethnic nationalism i.e. that which is represented by Mzamane, the Quayles, and Kakuyu. It is they who challenge ethnic exclusivity, paranoia, loathing, and violence as celebrated and narrated by Rwafa. It is he who claims unchallenged possession of authority and legitimacy to author stories and tell them to children. The birthday that turns into a funeral captures the tragedy of the Zimbabwean nationalist epic predicated on violent masculinity, ethnicity and racism, and narrative closure.

The post-colonial father and 'house of hunger' in 'The Grim Reaper's Car'

'The Grim Reaper's Car' differs from the other two stories in its use of narrative voice and metaphor. The story is told by a young girl at the point of her death and this adds special authority to the narrator's innocence and authenticity. Death, according to Walter Benjamin (1992: 93), imbues a dying person's words with authority. In this story, this voice allows the narrator to make unexpected connections and to break political taboos pertaining to official iconographic representations of the president as father of the nation. It also allows for the instability of images and the shifting meaning of icons the public takes for granted. This is a daring strategy used by the writer to subvert the excessive deployment of 'the great' (Simon Muzenda, Joshua Nkomo, and Robert Mugabe) as icons of the Zimbabwe Liberation Struggle. Iconographic constructions are performance acts pertinent to fatherhood and the narration of the nation. Instability of imagery, the narrator's fading psychic integrity, irony, and black humour accompany the sudden transformations that are consistent with the liminality of the child-narrator's consciousness. This transforms the presidential televisual performance into paternal hypnosis, seduction, and vampirism as the narrator dies into an ideological hearse.[10] 'The Grim Reaper's Car' is deconstructive in several ways. Firstly, it counters the official narrative of the nation as given by Rwafa in 'The Sins of the Fathers'. Secondly, it reconstructs and subverts the iconography of the nation and the revolution. Thirdly, it feminises narrative thereby re-gendering it, as in the story 'That Special Place'. Lastly, it inverts the generational hierarchies of traditional story-telling by letting a child tell her story to a hypothetical audience of people of all ages.

Nevanji Madanhire implicitly re-works two metaphors, one of waiting and the other of the house of hunger developed respectively by Mungoshi and Marechera, to re-configure fatherhood in the Zimbabwean post-colonial state. The girl narrator of 'The Grim Reaper's Car' compares fathers – her biological father, an ex-combatant and the president as father of the nation – on the basis of performance and sites of performance. Her comparison equates fatherhood with a masculinity that is determined by the ideological, economic and social pressures of the time.

Hers, in many respects, is a counter-narrative to the masculinised national narrative told by Rwafa. The female site from which she speaks deconstructs patriarchy embedded in the Zimbabwean literary canon. Given authenticity and authority by the act of dying, her narrative ruptures the closure and univocality of the national epic. She views fatherhood as past and present performance. The former reveals two threads: the unwritten subaltern as disclosed in the ex-guerrilla fighter, father of the narrator; and the official representation, as reflected in the president. The militarised masculinity of the subaltern and his past performance sired the post-colonial state that, like the consciousness of the sick narrator, is disintegrating. His present performance represented in changed registers fails: a failure marked by the ex-combatant's invisibility and confinement to the rat-infested urban slum of Tafara. The president's past performance is a retrospective appropriation, extension, and modification of the guerrilla register of militarised masculinity. His current performance is premised on visuality, displacement, and emasculation of all father figures as he separates daughters from their fathers by seducing them into his deathly vehicle of vampirish fatherhood.

> We sometimes watch TV next door. The other day we saw the president... The president fought for freedom, not father. If father is right that he too fought for freedom why doesn't he wear a black suit, a white shirt and red tie? I can imagine our president holding a big gun; like Rambo's. We saw Rambo at the community hall last month. I think Rambo was imitating our president, for how could he shoot so many people if he was not imitating our president (131).

The media – particularly in its electronic form – is ruthlessly exploited to construct and re-construct reality as a managed visual economy, thus glossing over the economic dystopia of the post-colonial state. Zimbabwe is a nation of the observed and observing, the unwilling but captive viewers of ZTV's mono-channel. Enforced spectatorship is instrumental in the emphasis on power as visuality. Father figures that cannot be seen on television are lost to memory, their enforced visual absence ensuring the erasure not only of their personal histories but also the disappearance of their iconic significance.

Public figures, like the president, are engrossed in a register of performance whose emphasis is style. This is a process by which the actor removes self from reality, so creating an alternative reality and re-arranging public conceptions of fatherhood. Embedded in this melodramatic performance is the construction of patriarchal political power and authority that is consistent with the violent patriarchy articulated in Charles Mungoshi's 'The Sins of the Fathers'.

An area that has not received adequate attention in the study of Zimbabwean political cultures is that of power as spectacle (Debord, 1994) and the adoption of the carnivalesque by the marginalised to destabilise its images, symbols, and icons. The ruling party seeks to invade whatever space is available to create spectacles of power and credibility for a captive spectatorship in an environment of mediatised politics. As David Boje puts it, 'Spectacle is a narrative and a theatric performance that legitimates, rationalises, and camouflages violent production and consumption' (2001: 431-58). The president's motorcade, TV appearances, and management of all state occasions are all part of this culture of spectacle. 'The Grim Reaper's Car' takes the first two spectacles as central to the personality cult and iconography of fatherhood in the Zimbabwean post-colonial state. In this carnivalesque narrative the spectator-narrator reclaims visual agency as she re-imagines state-constructed spectacles. In her re-imagination she exposes the lie of the benevolence of masculine power to reveal its vampirish potential. In the performance genre of masculinised politics the narrator juxtaposes two figures, that of the President and Sylvester Stallone, who plays the screen character Rambo, a juxtaposition that blurs the boundary between fact and fiction. Stallone performs muscular white masculinity marked by heterosexuality and exclusion of non-white males and gays.

The appropriation of this white American masculinity is not without irony notwithstanding the convergence of views on gays and violence. The performer of this borrowed masculinity lacks the muscularity and physical presence of the actor. Indeed, arguably, the performance of hyper-masculinity is compensation for a lack of physical stature. The state's cultural appropriation of an American visual register of hyperbole, media hype, bluster and gratuitous violence has travelled from the screen into the public sphere. Policy has been replaced by rhetoric and the conscious exploitation of every semiological system to instil terror. The only remaining policy option is the institutionalisation of violence to appear to solve all problems. Violence takes many forms: incendiary speeches and gory, melodramatic images, commodification of funerals, and single-minded violence in pursuit of an objective, rewarded in the hagiographic construct of 'patriotic' hero. These symbols of excess are consistent with the 'many degrees in violence' the president publicly claims to have.[11] This consistently cultivated visuality ironically subverts the gentlemanly image created by the formal Western dress code the president also adopts for an alternative, less gullible audience.

Patriarchy, paranoia, and persecution in the liberation struggle
In the autobiographical story 'That Special Place' Freedom Nyamubaya uses writing as therapy for emotional damage. She probes dark psychic

spaces in formations of Zimbabwean political and social culture. Here we find rape, torture and murder of those who questioned the liberation struggle's patriarchal structures and practices. By revisiting this past, Nyamubaya prepares for an exorcism of the patriarchal figures who dominated the struggle and extended its hegemony, in different mutations, to the political discourse of post-colonial Zimbabwe. 'That Special Place' articulates the patriarchy, paranoia, persecution, and secrecy that characterised the prosecution of this war. Totalitarian tendencies in current Zimbabwean political culture, though predating the war in the form of indigenous patriarchy and traditional chieftaincy, found reinvigoration and re-inscription during the struggle when the accent fell on the military in the formation of national consciousness and the nation state. Joining the ranks of the guerrilla fighters entailed the ceding of one's right to question and think. A recruit relinquished control, ownership, and privacy of bodily and mental processes in the pursuit of efficient and brutal execution of the war. The ostensible patriotic imperative led to the pathological control of the body and mind by the leadership. To achieve optimum ideological manipulation, traditional patriarchy provided the necessary fall-back position. Military structures were sustained by adherence to traditional patriarchy of deference and subservience to elders and superiors as determined by both chronological age and gender. Liberation war militarised patriarchy demanded filial obedience, fear of outsiders and deviants, and the persecution and elimination of all perceived to be threats to the ideological focus of the war. Evidence that emerges from most narratives of the war, fiction and non-fiction, indicate that the pursuit of a patriarchal agenda, produced paranoia, persecution and fear.

All the above are reflected in intolerance of alternative interpretations of the nationalist dream. Anti-intellectualism and bigotry killed educated guerrillas and their visions of nation creation. Such narratives are shown in the tragic story of Che,[12] the former university student whose decision to become a freedom fighter was premised on his belief in democratic openness, truth, debate, and authentic expression. Such assumptions tragically conflicted with the totalitarian closure of debate, propagandist use of narrative, and the use of deception and intrigue to mask truth Che is a victim of the anti-intellectualism of Zimbabwe's Liberation Struggle and testimony of the savagery with which intellectuals are treated in secretive and pathologically self-serving organisations.

Women and the educated of whatever gender presented a challenge to the patriarchal construction of the armed struggle. 'That Special Place' shows the vicious reaction of the military leadership to the real or imagined threat of an educated military cadre. Indeed, recruits were warned by sympathisers not to disclose their educational achievements. This militarised patriarchal anti-intellectualism is epitomised by Nyathi, the Camp Security Commander, at Tembwe Training Camp. It blighted the struggle and partially accounted for unspoken atrocities perpetrated in Mozambique, Zambia and within Zimbabwe: 'Naively he [Che] had thought that his literacy would be of use to the liberation army. Instead he suffered for it and never even rose to section commander' (227).

Complex and ambivalent motives led many fighters to join the liberation struggle. Some projected their psychological complexes into the prosecution of the war.

He had a loud mouth, and never once do I remember him saying anything constructive or interesting. He used torturous language, and made vulgar jokes about the inmates. Vicious and cruel, he had not even completed his primary education when he was recruited into the liberation struggle. With nothing in terms of brain, he thrived on sadism and intimidation (220).

Nyamubaya's story opens a territory that has not been examined in Zimbabwean history and culture, the psychology of specific father figures and how it has impacted on the construction of national imaginaries. Nyathi has many psychological complexes that distort the narrative of the liberation struggle. He is a paranoid control freak, a sexual sado-masochist with a repressed inferiority complex. His paratactic style, repetition, vituperation and absence of analytic rigour are characteristics of an anti-intellectualism that in various mutations is used to misinform, silence people into submission, and intimidate citizens into telling false stories about themselves. Nyathi, a psychopathic and tyrannical father of the revolution, enjoys inflicting physical violence on his victims.

Nyamubaya re-visits a dark period of the country's history when the violent masculinity predicated on the raping of women insinuated itself as a hegemonic one. Nyathi's ego, big as his penis, seeks submission from female recruits with violence: 'Nyathi had a big black penis whose erection got harder with resistance …' (228). He reads as a sexual pervert for whom the sexual act is synonymous with violence. It is the aberrant sexuality of the rapist, the masochist who finds gratification in pain. His masculinity is predicated on aggression. He lives a fantasy of women who are violated sexually and psychologically. Once a woman is vanquished and ravished, she is discarded and the psychopath prepares himself for the next victim. Incapable of developing a meaningful relationship, he turns himself into a serial rapist whose misogyny will only stop when he is removed from the position that is the source of his power.

The control that Nyathi wields is derived in part from an excessive, unreflective accent on traditional African patriarchy, which has been given a new form of expression in the military structure and ethos of the liberation struggle. African patriarchy clearly describes and assigns gender roles and the subordination of women to male domination is celebrated in traditional discourse. Nyathi's abuse of female recruits is an open secret but the leadership neither debates it nor rebukes him. Silence may result from fear but here it can also be explained by the cultural belief that women are there for the gratification of men.

War is an area of conflict that has a way of rearranging priorities and values, bringing out the best and worst in people, and sadly allowing repressed desires to emerge and proliferate. War simplifies complex issues. It creates a sense of urgency that does not allow for the scrutiny of bad decisions and unethical action. War thrives on secrecy, which allows morons and psychopaths to achieve positions of power and authority, and to brutalise and silence those within their power.

Rape of women, their mutilation, and murder is always prevalent in times of war. Zimbabwean war fiction deals with how these atrocities result in the psychic scarring of both victim and perpetrator. The raping of Mazvita by a combatant in Yvonne Vera's *Without a Name*; the killing of Tenjiwe and the mutilation of Nonceba by an ex-combatant turned dissident in Vera's last published novel *The Stone Virgins*; the killing of 'the woman with a baby on her back' ordered by a Security Commander in Alexander Kanengoni's *Echoing Silences*, all attest to how the gun can be used to write a narrative of sexual violence and domination. The gun becomes an extension of the penis or a prosthetic phallus.

The uncompromising pursuit of masculinity insists that violent dominance of women, blind obedience, bloodletting, and suppression of humane qualities be incorporated into the ethic of the guerrilla fighter. Uncritical acceptance of violently macho father figures allows the power of military authorities like the Camp Security Commander to establish and perpetuate itself. Secretive, vindictive, anti-social, and pathologically ignorant, such figures insinuated themselves into positions of authority by presenting a façade of unflinching support for the revolution and extraordinary patriotism. The few narratives by former liberation fighters consistently refer to this psychopathological figure that traumatised many a guerrilla fighter. The title of security commander is an oxymoron that brings psychic insecurity to victims made to speak and behave in ways that violate their sense of self. This semi-literate figure of terror, invested with so much brute power, is also found in Alexander Kanengoni's *Echoing Silences* traumatising committed revolutionaries.

Psyched into a neurotic state of perpetual vigilance, security personnel seeing themselves as custodians of the revolution, became paranoid. They transformed ordinary, innocent cadres into backsliders and sell-outs. The paranoia justified their exercise of psychopathological power. Forced confessions and false narratives followed by public beatings became routine in the drama of power as we see in *Pawns* by Charles Samupindi.

Women, especially in cases where they would ordinarily be inaccessible to the psychopath, are regarded as chattels of sexual gratification and objects of humiliation.

'That Special Place' is about the emotional struggle between the false father figure of the revolution and the writer. Robbed of the power to authentically narrate and locate self in the political and military space without ambivalence, she had chosen to inhabit herself as writer. By doing so she can confront this ghost from the past and rehabilitate her own damaged personal spaces. She exposes Nyathi's false narrative of the liberation struggle, and re-inscribes the false story that her inhuman and gratuitous interrogation had elicited from her tormentor. The plot of Nyathi unravels when he is demoted and turns out to be a dangerous informer and backslider. The massacre that he instigates, an orgasm of violence, becomes a clear expression of sado-masochistic sexuality. He is a figure of false fatherhood that has come to haunt the Zimbabwean national imaginary and traumatise citizens in the name of a compromised revolution. Nyamubaya's autobiographical return to this 'special place' is a retrospective contestation over narrative so as to redeem the true stories of the revolution.

Conclusion

The three children in these stories emerge from the role of victim to that of agent in articulations of new masculinities and feminisms. They reject the superphallicism celebrated by macho men (*'amadhodha sibili'*)[13] in their patriotic endeavour to write and re-write the story of the country in blood. The connection between narrative and nation has many implications in the post-2001 political and cultural scene that has experienced a massive growth in reconstructed versions of the nationalist narrative dominated by a single father figure and single story-teller who will not tolerate rivals. Mass media in Zimbabwe daily and repetitively reinforces this nationalist narrative which has a vast cast of characters vilified as enemies. In a highly selective and simplistic use of Zimbabwean classical oral tradition, current patriotic myth-making emphasises a homogeneous primordial identity defended by a violent masculinity. Research by Herbert Chimhundu (2006) shows the complexity and balance of the moral and ideological universe as it exists in the Zimbabwean oral tradition. This is masked by the ruling party's current malappropriation of the nation. All official narratives, across all media, and all official performances that pertain to spectacle, generate violent, patriarchal and ethnically inflected versions of the nation.

Apart from creating what Muponde (2004) calls a world of binaries

Zimbabwe's Third Chimurenga discourse is also characterised by linguistic deformations in which words are emptied of meaning or have their meanings inverted. In an age of plagiarism of forms and styles, there is also an appropriation of the discourses of regimes Zimbabwe demonises on a daily basis as evidenced in the post-September 11 world when Zimbabwe cynically used the anti-terror language of the George Bush administration to tyrannise political opponents at home. A terrifying scenario emerges in which there is an obsession with language, form, and style. The world is constantly fractured and reconstructed to fit the idiom of the hour, in which reality fades into the background in the politics of narrative and performance.

ENDNOTES

1. All three stories are published in Irene Staunton's significantly titled collection of 2003: *Writing Still: New Stories From Zimbabwe*. Harare: Weaver Press.
2. Essentialists like Vimbai Chivavura, Claude Mararike, Rebecca Chisamba, and others who regularly appear on television differ significantly from most Zimbabwean cultural workers and artists whose dynamic essentialism operates outside the ambit of the ruling party.
3. Annual musical galas devoted to commemoration of the achievements of Joshua Nkomo and Simon Muzenda and to their posthumous creation of the patriarchal Zimbabwean post-colonial state attest to this aspect. Galas are also part of the current accent on politics as theatrical spectacle.
4. Demographic size is not the sole measure of significance here, especially in terms of the Ndebele and white populations. The writer looks at a group's role in shaping the history, culture, and politics of the country with myths sustained by imperialism.
5. The 1990s saw a rise in mysterious traffic accidents that claimed the lives of politicians and public figures who had fallen out of favour with the ruling party and the leadership. Whether or not they were genuine 'accidents' is immaterial to the belief that they were contrived.
6. Third Chimurenga supporting ex-combatants and many pseudo ex-guerrillas emotively speak of the country as a wife who cannot be rented out to another man.
7. The term may appear too strong here but it appropriately captures the catatonic rigidity, delusions, and divorce from reality that is associated with a ruling party that has malappropriated the nation.
8. Post-2000 official speeches delivered on Independence Day and other important national occasions are marked by name-calling and demonising of members of the opposition.
9. These are legislative and administrative instruments designed to muzzle freedom of expression.
AIPPA – Access to Information and Protection of Privacy Act (2002).
POSA – Public Order Security Act (2002).

MIC – Media and Information Commission. Its officials with great zeal focus on the licensing of media houses and journalists. Its inauguration led to the banning of *The Daily News*, a newspaper whose subscription base and popularity at its height outstripped that of *The Herald*, the state daily.

10. Reference to the Presidential limousine used in his conveyance to and from conferences and the airport whose purchase raised public concerns about profligacy during times of scarcity. This display of affluence is not isolated as there is also a mania for expensive SUVs in the private sector as well (see *Sunday Mail Business* 17-23, 2006 B3 on Phillip Chiyangwa purchase of Hummer SUV).

11. An unashamed invocation of liberation war credentials by the ruling party every time it is threatened by a vibrant opposition. The party deliberately misleads the public by portraying the opposition as a violence-prone entity to be eliminated by extra-judicial measures and state violence at its disposal.

12. *Nom de guerre* used as an expression of re-claiming of power to name oneself against (mis)-naming practices of colonial administrators and missionaries. The nom de guerre protected family of the guerilla against reprisal by the settler regime. It was also an ideological statement of a fighter's political position and ideals.

13. 'Real men', statement used by Robert Mugabe to describe the men who would be appointed to his 'war' cabinet after the flight of Nxosana Moyo in 2001 and increasing signs of disaffection in the upper echelons of ZANU PF.

2
Killing fathers

ROBERT MUPONDE

Introduction

'No one is taking any notice of father,' declares Maureen Green (1976: 1) in her chapter on the decline of the father in the West. There is a sense of moral panic at the rapid decline or disappearance of the father in some western societies, where as John Gillis (2000) notes, 'the sense of failure and loss that surrounds fatherhood is overwhelming,' 'with fewer men entering it and more men leaving it than in past generations' (225). However, in spite of its apparent predicaments, the father figure is thriving, visible and powerful in Zimbabwe. It may be an endangered species or trope, but it is potent in threatening ways. It is interesting to interrogate its powers and influence within the context of a patriarchal nationalism in crisis, or consolidating itself in crisis. The gladiatorial politics endures in the father-son narratives which are replete with metaphors of killing and being killed.

I read two stories by Charles Mungoshi ('The Mount of Moriah') and Dambudzo Marechera ('Protista') as allegories of the unmaking of ossified faiths and loyalties that bind and kill fathers and sons. The stories point to the dilemmas and possibilities locked in the current father-son narratives. They suggest the lines of tension that offer us new ways of thinking about the father figure and its prospects in Zimbabwean literature.

A reading that attempts to revitalise fatherhood is not necessarily patriarchal or backward-looking (Gillis, 2000: 226). It constitutes a quest for healthier, egalitarian, violence-free social life. In Zimbabwe, where the more biological versions of fatherhood and masculinity are grimly insisted upon, we might want to think of what kind of fatherhood we need, or don't need, to 'man' the nation. I must add that: we must think hard too about what kind of childhood might challenge the deadbeat and murderous fatherhood that Mungoshi depicts in his fiction, and the irascible, violent and gullible boyhoods such as in Marechera's 'Protista' that loom chillingly in Zimbabwean nationalism and patriotic history.

'The Mount of Moriah': to kill a questioning son

'The Mount of Moriah' focuses on the relationship between Hama, a crippled young boy, and his drunken, violent, divorced, broke, 'reckless, unstable, unloving and unlovable father' (Zhuwarara, 2001: 67). In the story,

'Hama was tired of his father. Most of the time he was only just indifferent to him' (10). It is a relationship in which father and son are destined to come to blows, or to kill each other literally and metaphorically. With time, 'Hama had learned to forget that his father existed' (10). On his part, when the story begins, the father is being instructed by a medicine-man to prepare 'a very big sacrifice' in order to recover his good luck at gambling, and this involves, as we later discover, the extraction of certain anatomical parts from his son: 'Only his heart, a piece of his liver, his genitals' (12).

The portrayal of fatherhood and fathering in 'The Mount of Moriah' cures us, as critics, of the seductions associated with a critical tropism in which patriarchy is often confused with paternity, and manhood with fatherhood, and vice versa. I would like to look at possibilities of exiting this kind of unhelpful cultural habit by adopting the critical lenses suggested by Gillis (2000: 225-238) and Alice Miller (1990). In the face of the crisis of fatherhood, and manhood, Gillis suggests that we 'denaturalize and degenderize paternity and [...] culturally reconfigure fatherhood as a vocation to which some men are called and others are exempted' (2000: 235) instead of trying to conscript all men to a role 'that many are not suited to and still more do not now have the resources to accomplish successfully' (235). Gillis's suggestion helps us to understand that all men who man our families, communities and nation are not necessarily suited to the role. Miller (1990) suggests how to think our way out of the cultural tropism which reads the son as all submission and obedience, and the father as uncontested authority and faith. She suggests some of the possibilities that tumble into our reach 'when Isaac arises from the sacrificial altar' (137-146), and asks his father critical questions, and when fathers reject the role of Abraham who obeys orders that are 'absurd because they are directed against life' (145). The father figure in Mungoshi's 'The Mount of Moriah' suggests precarious parallels with the biblical image and heritage of Abraham. But unlike Abraham's enduring patriarchal narrative, in Mungoshi's story we are confronted with a fatherhood that is in rapid decline, and is shrinking from both ends. Its past is as bleak as its present and future.

The image of a father who intends to eviscerate his crippled son brings to ruination the ideological braces of patriarchy which conflate fatherhood with paternity. In this story, the father bankrupts the patriarchal idea that a father is a provider, protector and giver of life. He does not only cause his son to lose his left leg in a car accident; he torments and locks up his son in a 'dungeon' (9-10). His paternity is acknowledged by him as accidental: he never loved children, nor himself (7-9). He is constrained into the role of a father by the force of biological necessity. Robert Jensen calls this biological need and pressure 'the imperative to fuck' which is at the heart of patriarchal sex (1998: 99). From biological urges is socially constructed a working definition of what it means to be a man: 'A man is a male human who fucks' (Jensen, 1998: 99). Hama's father's fatherhood is the result of a manhood that has failed to reconstruct and heal from the deeply etched notion and tyrannical practice of patriarchal sex. It is a fatherhood, or rather a manhood, for whom sperm counts more than the social and emotional responsibilities attached to the prospects and aftermaths of penetration and ejaculation.

Hama's father is a paranoid misogynist. He suspects all the women who loved him of chasing after his money. As a man and a father, he is unwilling to pass on his genes and recreate his lineage through children, as patriarchy demands. He is unable to satisfy even one of Lesejane's (2006: 176) five basic rubrics of manly and fatherly conduct in traditional, even modern, society. Briefly stated, these sets of conditions and criteria set up a 'real' man, and therefore real father, as: a custodian of moral authority; a leader with responsibility; a primary provider of material needs; a protector of family; and a role model.

Hama's father is not a custodian of moral authority within and outside his family, nor is he a leader who has final responsibility in the affairs of the family. He has thrown away his family and relatives. The name he gives to his son Hama (meaning 'relative/s') is not a valorisation of the centrality of kith and kin. Rather, it is a primed warning and an invitation to grief and ruin to anyone who wants to claim him as a friend or clansman. Hama, crippled by his father and forcibly cooped up in a 'dungeon,' stands as evidence of the father's death-dealing, rather than of his stature as a protector and giver of life. The father stands alienated, almost a genealogical isolate, only able to connect with his relatives, friends and women via blows and scalding words. He is most alive, and most fearful, when money spins in or out of his hand ('If I don't have money soon I'll be vultures meat!'(8)). He is not a primary provider of the material needs of the family: he is broke and ill, on the verge of becoming 'vultures meat'; and is generally mistrustful of family and friends to the point of being misanthropic. Money, which he sought to define his manhood, had become: 'the sound of breaking crockery and furniture, of belching and vomiting, the stink of beer and stale vomit, the sound of a fist against a mouth so battered it sounded like a wet sponge – and blood all over the place. And the screams and the groans and the moans and the threats' (10). Those who came to visit him, or were invited to parties in his house, risked their lives as he fought them and called them 'parasites' who were after his money and were 'out to ruin him' (10). He is not a protector of the family against threatening forces. He is both the threatened and threatening force, sinking 'into the mud' of debt; tottering from one fight/quarrel to another; the memory of the female prostitute he had picked up (who died in the same accident that took his son's left leg) haunting him; and being eaten by an unnamed illness. He therefore cannot be a role model to any young man, or anyone. Hama's father allows us to see the disconnection between manhood (a signifier of physical maturity) and fatherhood (a socially constructed role which 'stresses the importance of relationships and choice' (Morrell, 2006: 14)). One cannot take up the social role of father just on the basis of being a man (Morrell, 2006: 14-17).

The image of Hama's father upsets long-held patriarchal value systems at the core of which is the untested belief that a boy needs his father, 'the man that fathered him' (Morrell, 2006: 14). As Morrell notes, there are situations when 'living with a father is not in the interests of a child' (2006: 15). Hama's description of his father's house as a war zone and a dungeon means that he sees his life with his father as an inexorable narrative of captivity, privation and danger. The loss of his left leg, the death of the female prostitute as a result of the accident, and 'the curse' (12) that his mother had put on his father, add to the repertoire of risks present in his father's house. But rather out of naivety or sheer indifference to his fate, Hama is unwilling to consider himself the intended victim of the 'very big sacrifice' (12) that his father is planning. His death looks like a foregone conclusion when his father asks him to accompany him to the rural home and assures him that, 'This time there won't be any accident' (14). Hama looks like the ideal offering to his father's gods: already incapacitated by the accident, he cannot escape or resist his fate.

It is at this point, when father and son are travelling in a borrowed car to the place of sacrifice (Hama does not know this!), that we are asked to reflect on the nature of the boyhood represented by Hama. I would like to read his boyhood alongside and against Alice Miller's idea of an ideal Isaac, and an ideal Abraham. This will allow us to see the complex lines of tension in narrative traditions that are construed along the father-son nexus.

Though crippled and unschooled, Hama is not awed by his father's presence, nor cowed by him in any way. He mounts critiques of his father that only a determined foe can muster: they are meant to wrench the figure that hides behind the mask of his father. He finds that the mask is the figure, and the figure is the mask. It is safe to say, before he is killed himself, he has already begun to kill his father by diminishing his figural weight and import. He deploys two complementary strategies to completely destroy his father before he kills him. The first strategy involves the deflation and diminution of the figure of his father. The second involves a combination of elevation and deflation. I will start with the first.

When his father is consulting with the medicine-man, Hama envisions his father as 'visions of money, money and more money took possession of him till he just couldn't sit still, impatient to go out and try out this new medicine' (12-13). His father is a small-minded predator, a despicable common criminal. He is nothing more than a stock figure in generic narratives of robbers, pirates, and treasure-hunters. To be killed by him is to be killed by a common felon. The criminal father is not a worthy adversary. To conjure his potential murderer in those terms helps Hama to think through troubling moral and philosophical dilemmas that ultimately lead to the question of how to be human in times of privation and betrayal. He cannot, unlike Zhuwarara (2001), find solace in glib tropistic readings of the city as 'a diabolic stronghold' in which Hama's father is a mere 'victim of his time,' ill-equipped to survive in the city, 'a poor and lost soul desperate to survive through any means that come his way' (68-69). That kind of reading of the all-powerful and corrupting city is a critical tautology in Zimbabwe. It insists on reading the rural village as a source of happy memories, as compared to the city, and is popularised by Zimunya (1985). It cannot explain why, when scouting for an appropriate location for the murder of his son, Hama's father prefers a rural landscape where his own father used to spend days hunting. Hama's father's spontaneous and monological narration of his clan's history is dominated by the hunting adventures of a fugitive ancestor, who 'was running away from some people – some enemies' (23) in his rural village. So, the founding history of Hama's rural home is marked by disorder and displacement. So is his father's house in the city.

Accordingly Zhuwarara's reading of the city and the father's situation in it misses the agency that Hama's father finally recuperates, or opts for, when he botches the murder of his child. Hama's father opts for life, and goes back to the city to confront his unresolved cash situation, but without having carried out the ritual murder. But that is because Isaac had removed himself from the sacrificial altar, and a new faith in life had to be sought outside the moral gridlock of the narrative of Abraham and Isaac. Zhuwarara's reading of the city, and of the father's existential dilemmas in that city, is via a crude shorthand materialism which seeks to ladle blame for individual moral failings on the configuration of class and society. He is unable to explain why, after reconciling with his son, the father heads back to the city, and what sort of skills he now had to survive in the same unreconfigured 'diabolic stronghold'. Hama's critical comments and meditations are very insightful.

Having reduced his father to a beast, and a felon, he finds his pettiness, nervousness and furtiveness consistent with the image he has built of him. The language of communication between father and son is dead and adversarial: it conjures the numinous and the macabre. Deprived of speech, the father experiences a deeply demeaning crisis of authority. The son is in power, the father is nervous and infantilised by the gaze and resilient presence of his crippled son. He cannot deal with his guilt, the fact that he caused the hopeless condition of the boy. He cannot deal with a questioning son who, mindful of the previous tragic recklessness of his father's driving, asks him whether he now had a driver's licence to be able to drive 'home' safely. 'Conversation with his son seemed to make him nervous. It was like climbing a very high mountain: he was a victim of vertigo' (14). And this man who imagines mountains in speaking to his little crippled son is the same man who is burdened with the task of carrying out a 'very big sacrifice'. This sacrifice conjures mountains too, for Abraham, of whom Hama's father is a parody, had to walk long distances (not travel in a borrowed car) and scale the mountain (not sit on a 'water-polished rock' in the shade of a fig tree at the edge of a shallow pool (17)) to murder his son. The mountain of supreme sacrifice remains unclimbed because Hama's father is not Abraham.

The first person to make us think of Abraham as Hama's father is Hama himself. This is when Hama simultaneously elevates and deflates his father. As they travel along the long road, Hama recalls the song about how God sent Abraham to the Mount of Moriah, with Isaac carrying the faggots that were to be used for the sacrifice. In Mungoshi's story the length of the road invokes the Mountain in the song, and the image of Abraham, 'long-bearded, broad-shouldered, in tattered coloured robes' (16). Hama recalls the pictures of Abraham he had seen, and likes the idea of being Isaac, 'small, eager, smelling of goatmilk cream, his supple boy's back arched under the heavy burden of faggots' (16). He imagines too Abraham's booming, manly, but enigmatic response to his vexing question: 'God shall provide' (16). Hama envisages his father approximating the visionary potential of the biblical Abraham, and himself submissively offering himself to his father's knife. In that sort of narrative of the son dying to please the father, to aid the father's quest and devotion, he is quite in the mould of the 'son of the soil' in Zimbabwean nationalism.

But, luckily, Hama quickly disallows his father the heights of that divine vision by scaling him down to a 'mean, worry-stained face' (16), and someone who 'looked forlornly small' (19). The ruggedness, frugality and forlornness of his father is not that of a man in the presence of an all-powerful, caring God, but a man on whom the god of mammon has dealt an unkind blow. Hama abandons the role of Isaac because, 'His father was a far cry from the self-confident, big-boned Abraham. And if his father couldn't be Abraham, then *he* was not Isaac' (16). He refuses to be killed by a violent, mean-spirited and frail-looking criminal disguised as a father.

As soon as this point is realised, the beckoning symbolism of 'The Mount of Moriah' dissipates too 'in the thirstmaking shimmering blackness' (16) of the landscape. This is the turning point of the story when

Hama, once again, pulls his father's image through the mire. He frees himself of the talismanic power of the ancient patriarchal narrative, 'one predicated on submission, exile, and the sacrifice of the son' (Rahman, 2003: 297) by an overly submissive, unquestioning and divisive father. Rahman (2003) notes that even in the Bible, Abraham the father of submission 'never really manages to establish order in his house,' (296), 'for disorder is written into [his] paternity' (297). In some very uncanny ways, there are parallels with Hama's father's house: the disorder and violence, and the desire to kill a son for some faith in money (in the case of Hama's father) and divine vision (in Abraham's case). But the disorder in Hama's father's house pursues him to the place of sacrifice, where his offering to the god of mammon slips out of his grasp, and exposes his vulnerabilities.

So, even though he is ignorant of his fate, Hama rejects the role of Isaac as natural victim in a vile murder plot. Where Zhuwarara (2001: 68) unthinkingly endorses 'the noble intentions and religious vision and faith of Abraham,' Miller (1990) is critical of the ways in which the victimisation and attempted murder of the boy child has almost been 'accorded the legitimacy of natural law' in spite of the 'monstrousness' of the story (141). She suggests that, 'If we love life more than obedience and are not prepared to die in the name of obedience and our fathers' lack of critical judgment, then we can no longer wait like Isaac, with our eyes bound and our hands tied, for our fathers to carry out the will of their fathers' (143). So, Hama is the first person to reject the role he had imagined for himself, because he does not share the life-denying vision of his father. He is also the first person to discourage us from thinking of his father as Abraham.

Hama appropriates for himself the power of the father, to give and deny, to punish and reward his own father. But like the critic Nyota (2006: 203), who excuses the murder of an only son on the basis of some 'noble and holy cause,' and Zhuwarara (2001) before him, Hama himself is not clear if he would have hesitated to be counted on as a victim if his father had matched the patriarchal stature and unquestioning faith of Abraham. But he does have the imaginative resources to cause his father to say 'Yes to life and No to death' (Miller, 1990: 145). This way he approximates the vision of a new Isaac as imagined by Miller, who 'with his questions, with his awareness, with his refusal to let himself be killed – not only saves his own life but also saves his father from the fate of becoming the unthinking murderer of his child' (Miller: 145).

Having relieved his father of the stature of an Abraham, and of himself as an eager Isaac, Hama proceeds to give a stultifying description of the mundanity of his father's pilgrimage with him to the place of his potential death. They sit on the sacrificial altar, 'a water-polished rock in the shade of a *muonde* tree that grew on the very edge of a pool whose bottom they could not see' (17), and unlike Isaac, Hama is unbound (except by his innocence and disability). Very much unlike Abraham's unperturbed, confident demeanour, Hama's father is literally a distant, shadowy, and menacing, but very frightened and dumb criminal. The lunch he shares with his son before the murder ('bread cut into thin slices with wedges of cheese between the slices, pieces of biltong and two egg-rolls and a bottle of orange juice'(18)) is a parody of the biblical last supper. It is offered rather like the last meal fed to a condemned man by the hangman. In his father's mind, Hama is a dead man walking. But because they share the meal, executioner and unsuspecting victim, 'sipping in turn from the bottle, leaning against the tree' (18), it is not certain at this stage who is going to die. It is like a slapdash show in which the actors have lost the plot and the prompter has passed out. It is not certain when the real action will begin, going by the extreme lassitude displayed both by the reluctant and unimaginative protagonist and innocently languorous, indifferent and inattentive antagonist.

Hama only survives the murder because a *deus ex machina* in the form of a noisy bird in the fig tree, not an angel, distracted him and made him think of a snake, at which point he fell into the shallow pool. He did not see his father come up behind him with a big open knife and a yellow scarf, implements of the murder. But when the father looks at his son's fortuitous escape and his near death by drowning in the shallow pool, his face is 'horror-mottled' and his left hand trembles (20). He does not jump into the water to finish off the son. Franz Kafka would have admired 'an Abraham who would be prepared to satisfy the demand for a sacrifice immediately, with the promptness of a waiter' (in Rahman, 2003: 295). But that prompt closure would close off many possibilities. Hama would not have been able to give life back to his father, nor would the father have been able to narrate his father's story, which is about his heritage as a fugitive, unsociable and misanthropic father. His abrupt homosocial détente with his son, after missing the opportunity to slay him, elicits pity and sympathy rather than condemnation of him as a failed murderer. He is infantilised and disoriented by the experience.

Hama's father can only recount his clan history at the point when he decides to abandon the scene of the bungled murder. That means he can at least be allowed to reconnect with his unreflected past and unsettled childhood. He will be able to pass on some kind of reflected heritage to his son, who all along had only grasped versions of his father's history by eavesdropping through the chinks of the dungeon in which he spent his solitary life. But it is a story of patriarchs, and is as trapping as that of Abraham which Hama conjures and inaugurates into the landscape when he is being led to his slaughter.

It is not clear whether the monological nature of his father's rendition of his past is what will save Hama's life, as he does not partake of its genealogical and symbolic import. Why would a father who fought family and clan all his adult life now want to inaugurate his clan history at the point that his son is exiting another enduring oppressive patriarchal narrative of Isaac and Abraham? The history the father narrates is a history of strife and wandering, and most importantly, the history of a fugitive parent. Hama's father epitomises this history, and its cyclical energies. The place of the bungled murder coalesces and animates in a dramatic way this kind of patriarchal history that traps and ossifies the individual. The place of the failed murder is also the place of failed settlement by his ancestors ('Our home is really beyond those mountains,' says the father (23)). So, in the same way that the story of Abraham could not settle in the 'thirstmaking shimmering blackness' (16) of the bleak landscape, the story of 'that dark time long ago before Hama had been born or was still a baby' (23) does not elicit a response from Hama. 'Hama couldn't think of anything to say to this, so he kept quiet' (23). It shouldn't surprise, because the situational irony is that Hama's grandfather 'used to spend days and days hunting in this area' (23) which his son now turns into the location of the murder of his grandson. As a hunter *manqué*, defeated by the jungle in the city, Hama's father 'raids his own homestead in desperation' (Zhuwarara, 2001: 68). He thus confuses the blood of wild game with that of his loins. There is no redeeming value at all in visiting and soiling the place of ancestral memory and myths with cannibalism.

The past of Hama's father and his father offer no hope, but closure. To achieve substantial beginnings and freedoms, it will take Dambudzo Marechera's boy-son in 'Protista' to kill a father who wants to trap him in a tautological imagination. Alice Miller (1990), imagining Abraham's knife now in Isaac's hands, wonders, 'Would it change if the young were to kill off the old'(143) so as to reclaim their life, or would it perpetuate the same dilemma, this time the old being the victims of the young?(ibid.).

'Protista': to kill a mocking father

'Protista' is a recollection and dramatisation of a mythical boy childhood in which metaphors of journeying and exile work to prise loose the ideologies of nation-narration and belonging that hem in the narrator. Boy childhood in this instance is viewed as a space of experience as well as a place of memory in which the struggle for self-authorship and self-capitalisation is pitted against the grasping, circumscribing and prepossessing narrative of the father, and, by extension, the nation. The father's grasping palm, in which the child's story revolves and is locked, recalls the monocentric vision of the nation as the end and beginning of the self. It is the story of a childhood that is fated to have its independent experience destroyed because it seeks to constitute the urgency of self-search outside what Jameson (1981: 19) called 'the unity of a single great collective story'.

In this story, set in a drought-stricken valley in Lesapi [Rusape], childhood is recalled as a 'ceaselessly unfinished genesis' (Harris, 1992: 15) of the imagination. It is a field of existential attractions which imbues childhood with what Wilson Harris (1992) theorised as 're-visionary potential'. The narrator has been in exile for twelve years and is experiencing stages of personal fragmentation. He recalls the story his father told him when he was six years old. It is necessary to quote the story at length here:

> *a youth rebelling against the things of his father had one morning fled from home and had travelled to the utmost of the earth where he was so happy that he wrote on their wall the words 'I have been here' and signed his new name after the words; the years rolled by with delight until he tired of them and thought to return home and tell his father about them. But when he neared home his father, who was looking out for him, met him and said 'All this time you thought you were actually away from me, you have been right here in my palm.' And the father opened his clenched hand and showed the son what was written in this hand. The words – and the very same signature – of the son were clearly written in the father's open palm: 'I have been here.' The son was so stunned and angry that he there and then slew his father and hung himself on a barren fig-tree which stood in the garden* (128).

The story of the father and the son coheres in the founding legends of the nation which insist on the inescapable nature of its history and forms. To travel outward from the 'fatherland' is ironically to confirm the tenacity of the 'father's' hold on the psyche ('the resilience of human roots'). Ndabaningi Sithole (1977: 18), a founding father of Zimbabwean nationalism, writes about this sense of entrapment: 'The black man belonged to the Soil. It claimed him.' The journeying that the son in the story undertakes is central to the realisation of his rootedness in the 'fatherland' and its myths, and his childlike dependency on his father's authority. At a physical and metaphorical level, the son is immobilised by his inability to escape his hostile roots, whose symbols he recreates in his home of exile. The child maps out his own journeys in rebellion, but he cannot author his own life-story outside the clenched palm of his father. This is because his narrative of adventure and rebellion is performed at the instigation of his father against whom he rebels, if the father is taken to mean a link in the strong chain of a genealogy that claims the son.

Breaking out of the nation-form, the 'fatherland,' is like cutting links with one's biology and history. The desire of the child to found a story ('I have been here') for himself by journeying is a self-siting, self-making symbolic act. But as I have suggested, it lacks authority on its own terms as a narrative of self-making, ironically set off by the father who is the cause of his disenchantment with home, and as a genre of resistance. The son's narrative is entrenched in a binding archetype of the prodigal son and implicitly limits its 're-visionary potential'. The structure and content of his rebellion is archetypally prefigured, and 'tends to build on the way it has been circumscribed by history' (Harris, 1992: 18). Considered in this sense, the child-rebel who wants to re-invent himself suffers a double defeat: that is, in terms both of the form and the content of his gesture.

The story of the rebellious son, as a narrative of symbolic resistance, fits within what Maria Lassen-Seger (2000: 192) calls a 'time out' adventure in which the child takes time away from himself as well as from adult authority. In 'Protista,' he goes to enjoy himself away from home, but the revolt is not sustained. He returns home to tell his father about his adventures. He affords himself the opportunity to try out a new identity, outside adult power circuits, and feels empowered to possess a story and initiate his own return. However, his return conforms to the set patterns of a narrative of seasonal migration, which while it touches on multiple centres, only confirms the enigma and ambiguity of departure and arrival in a genre characterised by circularity and monocentric forces. While 'time out' allows a temporary exit from adult power circuits, and can empower the child in that moment when reality is suspended, it is a paradoxical and conservative literary device. It means not only time away from oneself, 'but a return to the initial order at the end of the narrative' (Lassen-Seger, 2000: 192). In this sense, the 'time out' narrative does not 'only imply that adult authority is interrogated, it also means that that very authority is reinscribed at the end' (ibid.). The impotence and futility of the child's rebellion is magnified by his uneventful journey, his slaying of his father, and his own death on a barren fig-tree. His death is the result of both the frustration and the ultimate tragedy of finding oneself without an original story of oneself in a seemingly foreclosed discourse of self-invention.

As a genre, the story of the boy's adventure fits the structure of many story cycles that confirm communal authority over individual narratives. The journey cycle followed by the rebellious son is already established in folklore.

Home is sanctuary. Its offer of physical and spiritual sustenance is the gravitational pull that ensures that whatever leaves it will ultimately lose its outward momentum and return (Kunene, 1985: 189).

The loss of outward momentum and the ultimate return to roots confirms the son's gravitational pull towards the 'family' which in most national narratives is viewed as a metaphor of 'a single genesis narrative for national history' (McClintock quoted in Taitz, 1999: 29). Writing a story of self-making, as the son in the story under discussion discovers, may require a certain quality of violence on form and genre in order to upset tradition and frustrate its tendency to muffle dissension within its folds. This violence must be a founding violence for newer imaginaries of self to emerge or else self-authoring is an exercise in futility. As the son in this story discovers, his story is already written and told, and his father nurses it for him in trust ('All this time you thought you were actually away from me, you have been right here in my palm.'). The dilemma of the 'son of the soil' equally applies to the position of the son in 'Protista': 'He came from it and therefore he belonged to it. No one comes from where he does not belong. At death he returned to it. No one returns where he does not belong' (Sithole, 1977: 18).

The son as an aspiring author of his own destiny is weighed down by the imponderable and castrating fact of his being already situated, figured and narrated. The barren fig-tree in the story is a national symbol of ritual which is now impotent. The father who is slain by his son is that fig-tree, unable to offer the son life but encirclement in stultifying symbolisms of return and fixity. But the son who hangs himself because of his entrapment in his 'fatherland' is as death-dealing as his father who denies him personal, self-emergence. He is as impotent as the fig-tree upon which he hangs himself. These are the interlocked matrices of the narrator's childhood, which are recalled in a moment of exile and spiritual and imaginative entrapment. The tyranny of roots, as represented by the father's clenched hand, is both imprisoning and suffocating for the son, requiring the resisting subject to stage fictions of suicidal anarchy in a symbolic gesture of self-destruction.

What is implied by this anarchic gesture is the desire to nullify the power of the archetype of the prodigal son or the narrative of 'the return to roots' which invariably suggests itself as the enduring model of experience and imposes an invariant identity. By killing his father, and the narrative that he and his father represents, the son rejects the politics of a narrative which 'reinforces a bias, reinforces its deprivations into a self-righteous cult' (Harris, 1992: 18). The son's gesture only suggests the undoing of a given narrative regime, in which he is subject and victim, but does not install a new one in its place. The significance of his rebellion is twofold: it points to the conditions under which narrative and history are – to follow Reinhart Koselleck's (1985: 198-212) theory on the disposability of history – 'make-able' and 'disposable'. The value of his death is therefore located in the possibilities of text that he opens. These possibilities inhere in Marechera's recollection of childhood as a longing for new form.

Suggested in 'Protista' is the embeddedness of the narrator's childhood in the paralysing riddle of departures and destinations, which replay the 'tautology' (Harris, 1992) of anti-colonial and post-colonial cultural nationalism. The new canon, represented by the rebellious son, 'can be as destructive as the old one' (Rutherford, 1992), represented by the father, in that both emanate from and eddy in the same, unreconfigured narrative politics. The narrator suggests that there is need for a newer kind of childhood which he sees as an interrupted and unfinished genesis. The lineaments of this 're-visionary' childhood are not yet defined, but the feeling that 'all grown-ups are menfish' (133) – cannibalistic monsters – makes the narrator suggest feverishly: 'but remember perhaps there is still a chance that the children – my head!' (133). Childhood in 'Protista' is a recollected trope of creativity and new beginnings, and is viewed as both narrative and a lived space of experience which can be arranged and rearranged to articulate the end of an age of imaginative barrenness and experiential tautology. It is perhaps why the son and the father in 'Protista' are rendered redundant as the barren fig-tree that dominates the mystical landscape.

In 'Protista' is prefigured the deposition of the figure of patriarchal narrative authority, the father, and an abruption of narrative cycles that constitute the space and cosmos from, and in which, the prototype of 'nation' is made. The rupture of the ties that bind son to father(-land) is symbolic of the fissures in the tropes of 'family' and narratives of genealogical continuity and unity which concepts such as 'son of the soil' in Katiyo's *A Son of the Soil* and 'child of war' in Chirasha's *Child of War* suggest.

As I have already intimated, the son's murder of his father is an attempt at self-capitalisation and a desire to clear social and psychic spaces of histories that inhibit motion outside of their fixed orbits in order to grow new narratives in unfettered spaces. In a way, the son who kills his father and himself enters the legends and myths of the valley, in ways that may be considered revolutionary. The son is therefore a 'son of the soil' and 'child of war' in an inverted and subversive sense. He is subversive of the traditions that hold childhood as a compliant political imaginary of eternal cohesion and genesis of the 'nation'. By running away from his father he demonstrates the fault-lines within the edifice of a tradition whose perceptual unity is enacted in the trope of the 'family,' and by killing the father, he loosens the ideologies of tradition that hem in the act of individual will in the interests of community. However, what seems to make 'Protista' a chilling dystopia is the fact that it prefigures an anomic childhood whose present is cut off at both ends: that is it neither has a sustainable past nor a continuing present. It is in a sense, a childhood that contains death in the roots: here is a son who has eliminated both himself and his genealogy. The son's action leaves behind a void which can only be filled by the reconstructive acts of both history and memory.

Conclusion

In both stories, the retreat to a moment in childhood is a symbolic act of self-making. But writing a story of self-making, as the son in Marechera's story discovers, may require a certain quality of violence on form and genre. Without this founding violence, narrative is fraught with the tautology of a culturally framed experience. In both stories boy childhood is presented as a trope of creativity and new beginnings. What is chilling though is the strong sense of anomie when both boys realise that they are caught up in a cyclic narrative of patriarchs. Marechera's boy suggests that the only way to break the father's clenched hand is via murder and suicide. Hama in Mungoshi's story offers the possibility of a transformed life to his father, having unsettled and revealed his father's vulnerabilities. As Ross D. Parke suggests, in certain circumstances, 'Fathers can learn from their children and be matured by them' (1981: 22). But Hama evokes what currently is a Zimbabwean experience of our fathers of the nation: a fatherhood that, like Abraham, is violent, divisive, insensitive and blind, and would like to turn all of the children of the nation into versions of unquestioning Isaacs in the name of some grand vision of sovereignty and freedom. One could imagine too a variant on the father of the nation, Babamukuru, in Tsitsi Dangarembga's two novels *Nervous Conditions* (1988) and *The Book of Not* (2006) being perhaps a benevolent Abraham, turning Tambu into a female Isaac, wanting to sacrifice her in order to fulfil his vision for the homestead. When she could not fulfil her role as an ideal Isaac, an instrument of his vision for the homestead, she ceases to exist in his heart, and is disowned by him. It seems painful, but justifiable that he is paralysed at the end of *The Book of Not*, and Tambu recovers a sense of her own bearings. However, in spite of its dystopic nature, boy childhood in Mungoshi's and Marechera's fiction is shaped into founding iconic material for self-writing and substantial new beginnings in the way we imagine father figures and growing up male in Zimbabwean literature and society.

3

Of fathers and ancestors in Charles Mungoshi's *Waiting for the Rain*

NEIL TEN KORTENAAR

Charles Mungoshi's one English-language novel, *Waiting for the Rain*, although published in 1975, in the middle of the Zimbabwean War of Liberation, and set around the same time,[1] ignores politics almost altogether in order to focus on a single and singularly dysfunctional family.[2] Three generations of the Mandengu family live together on a homestead in Manyene, near present-day Chivhu. Tongoona, the head of the household, lives with his wife, a daughter and three young sons, his parents and his mother-in-law. The family is extended vertically in time but not laterally in space: Tongoona has but one wife, as his father had before him, and the children on the homestead are all his own. Tongoona's elder brother, although he lives in the vicinity, is not part of the family. The family constitutes a closed, self-sufficient entity with 'The Father and the Mother of the House' at the centre (136), and its mistrust of outsiders is so deep as to resemble paranoia. In terms of setting, *Waiting for the Rain* is even more confined. The novel retells the events over the three days that the two adult sons return home, Lucifer from the city and Garabha from his wandering in the rural areas. The narrative never travels to another homestead, let alone to the city, and the second half of the novel does not venture from the homestead at all. When, on the last page, Lucifer drives away, the novel cannot follow him and must end. It feels as though the homestead and the nearby road are surrounded by a vast space of darkness, and so they are. In that darkness, however, there are mountains, a plain, a forest and a desert, aspects of a dreamscape visited on occasion by Lucifer, Garabha, and their paternal grandfather, called simply Sekuru or the Old Man. In these phantasmal landscapes, the dreamer is the sole human, but there are other presences, inscrutable and ominous. It is the looming presence of the ancestors that makes it impossible to consider Tongoona's household a nuclear family.

The hostility of this phantasmal landscape reflects the Mandengus' sense of their immediate surroundings. Although, in the course of the novel, the Mandengus receive visits from neighbours and even host a party for the village, the family regards all outsiders with suspicion. This is a family that 'rarely borrowed fire' (81), and only pretends to show warmth to extended family in order not to give cause for more enmity. In another context, for instance, the contemporary world depicted in Tsitsi Dangarembga's *Nervous Conditions*, Tongoona's older brother, Kuruku, would be the *babamukuru* or Father of the Family. In this novel, however, Tongoona and his wife mistrust Kuruku and blame his wife Rhoda for the long-ago death of an infant son (74). They fear that the success of Lucifer, about to go overseas, will invite the hostile attention of the paternal uncle and his family.

If things continue as they are, Tongoona's branch of the Mandengu family will come to an end with the current generation, which seems determined never to marry. The thought of children fills Garabha, the eldest, with 'a vision of black ants tearing away at a helpless buck that is still kicking with life having fallen and broken its leg' (85). His sister Betty, pregnant as a result of an adulterous affair, is a partial exception to the sterility of the younger generation, but her pregnancy is primarily a form of filial rebellion. Her desire is not for a lover or even a child, but a form of suicide: 'She is quite aware that her chances of coming out of it alive are ... bleak, but a rope around her neck wouldn't have been wiser either' (38). Later we learn from Matandangoma, the spirit medium, that Betty's child will be stillborn (145).

All three adult Mandengu children want to escape the painful world they grew up in, the sons by leaving and the daughter by having an affair without her parents' knowledge. Their desire to escape, however, contributes to the decline of the family; and the mutual recrimination and the misery that result add to their own torment. The two sons carry the family with them wherever they go. Lucifer has accepted the sponsorship of a Catholic priest to travel overseas, and his current visit home is a farewell. He is only concerned, however, with getting away, not with getting somewhere, and he fears that the experience of travel will merely confirm the established pattern of his life (70). Even as he sloughs off 'the leprous skin of his country' on the last page of the novel, Lucifer's thoughts are with the home he leaves behind and not the world he is going to (180). The novel is not interested in the world outside family and does not actually believe there is one.

Critics rightly attribute the desolation of the Mandengu family to the experience of colonisation. In twentieth-century Rhodesia, Africans have been thoroughly dispossessed and relegated to marginal lands, the only land that whites do not covet, land that cannot support the population. Parents cannot bequeath land or status to their children. Young people leave, but there is nowhere for them to go. School-leavers like Lucifer cannot find work, 'not in this country ... at this time' (79).

Rino Zhuwarara (2001) reads *Waiting for the Rain* alongside a nationalist narrative of resistance and decolonisation and maps the three Mandengu generations against Rhodesian history as the pre-colonial, the colonial, and the post-colonial. The Old Man fought in the First Chimurenga, the Shona war of resistance to the British in the 1890s, and is a link to a valuable tradition. The grandsons Lucifer and Garabha now represent alternative courses of action in the age of the Second Chimurenga, the liberation struggle of the 1970s. The past, which represents authentic Shona values, has been submerged under colonialism but will reassert itself in Zimbabwe. Zhuwarara dismisses the middle generation of Tongoona, a former member of the B.S.A. Police and a convert to Christianity, as unworthy and regrettable.

Zhuwarara reads generational succession in terms of a national history already known, and he locates in the family a core of identity that will redeem national history. He assumes that the family preserves an essential character that paradoxically skips a generation but is nonetheless passed on and will reassert itself. We could reverse the terms of this paradox and it would still be true: Zhuwarara's nationalist reading values cultural continuity, but he assumes that the life choices of the young adult males are what really matter. Nationalist critics emphasise the youngest generation in part because they identify with it and in part because they seek in the text moral lessons that can be imparted to their own students. The assumption is that the value of the novel is how it can assist the critics in teaching others what those others need to learn.

Such an allegorical reading is legitimate: everywhere nations imagine themselves in terms of family, and kinship is deeply affected by political understandings. The Mandengu family, however, should not be reduced to an allegorical figure for something else assumed to be already known. In Mungoshi's novel, family is itself the primary field of experience and the ground of identity and security. Kinship, not nation, is what matters most to all of Mungoshi's characters, even to those who wish to escape the hold that family has on them. The climax of the novel is the revelation of a series of ancestral curses remarkable for the way they attribute the misery of the Mandengus to the family's own past.

The novel barely alludes to national history and then only with deep ambivalence. Sekuru, who fought in the First Chimurenga is skeptical about his grandson John and those currently fighting for liberation because they are tainted by the Westernness they oppose (32). The novel perversely depicts the liberation war as an experience of fraternal betrayal rather than of heroism. Kuruku and his sons are the novel's only nationalists, and as we have mentioned, John, the only son not in jail or in exile, has betrayed his brother to the police in order to gain access to his brother's wife. A nationalist speech that Zhuwarara (2001) quotes with approval is delivered by

Kuruku while drunk. In the same alcoholic breath with which he boasts of his defiance in wearing the *ngundu*, a skin hat outlawed by the Rhodesian government, Kuruku attributes blackness to the curse of Ham (63)!

Waiting for the Rain is not about the war but it is about colonisation: it documents how oppressive historical forces have harmed the family and how the family understands and copes with those forces. Zhuwarara (2001) is interested in ancestors only as symbols of resistance or of a lost cultural wholeness, but in *Waiting for the Rain*, the ancestors are alive and act on the world, and the unhappy members of the youngest generation are all subject to them. Tradition is not something that once existed, has been submerged, and will re-emerge. Instead tradition is at work in the present and governs the relations among the three generations of the Mandengus, including the middle generation that Zhuwarara despises. Zhuwarara, who affirms the continuity of Shona culture by excising Tongoona, implies that some things that a son inherits are more properly his than other things he inherits. Florence Stratton (1986) argues that fathers in Mungoshi's work 'have been rendered impotent by the usurpation of their masculine role in society by the colonial "masters"' (15), and that Tongoona, in particular, 'provides an image of the shattered Shona sensibility' (14). That is a fair reading, but it is a mistake to regard Tongoona's woundedness as his irrelevance. In the world ruled by ancestors, it is precisely wounds that are passed on.

Waiting for the Rain features two etiologies of the present: the first based on personal memory and centred on the man who is the father; the second centred on the ancestors, who serve as a collective memory (of the family not the nation). The educated Lucifer shares the impulse informing most modern novels that understands the adult in terms of the child he was. His return to the homestead brings back memories of his painful childhood, but he believes that in that pain lies the secret of his present misery. At the same time, he feels he 'should have been born elsewhere – of some other parents' (162). The modern alienated intellectual is divided into psychologist and the object of psychological study. That division corresponds to one in Lucifer's childhood. As a boy, he sought only to make his parents happy, a seemingly impossible task given the family's deep poverty: 'When I grow up, I shall buy my parents a big house and a beautiful car.' This was his childish acknowledgement of any sacrifices he felt his parents were making on his behalf when he was still a boy' (76). All he wanted was a kind word from his father: 'And not knowing how to balance the one kind word or deed against the hundred-and-one scoldings and hidings [...], he would cry, condemning himself as the worst sinner on earth, full of repentance and resolutions to be worthy of such parents in the future' (76). Young Lucifer's desire was attached to a single love-object, his father, but that love went unreturned and the boy blamed himself. Freud would diagnose the adult Lucifer's condition as melancholy. When the object of his love rejected his love, the boy did not transfer his desire to another object, but turned it inwards. Lucifer narcissistically identifies with the father with one part of his ego, and, with another part, criticises and reproaches himself. The result is a devastating internal split.³

As an adult, Lucifer's relations to his parents have changed but not improved. Now it is they who need acknowledgement from him, and he who is unwilling to provide it. Lucifer's habit of reading has become 'an unfailing source of pride' to Tongoona (43), but the ironic corollary is the son's shame at his father's backwardness. Lucifer 'feels resentful, then embarrassed, then just saddened at his father's lack of self-confidence' (44). The same conditions of poverty that the boy Lucifer wanted to relieve in order to win his parents' love now make it impossible for Tongoona's love to satisfy the young man. Lucifer wishes 'he had a different father,' but the 'thought is so cruel that he immediately suppresses it without examining it carefully' (43). Shame feeds guilt: as always, Lucifer manages to sever his attachment to his father only by turning both love and hate inwards.

In the course of Lucifer's visit, Tongoona announces that he wants to pass on 'the burden of Father of the Family' to Lucifer and not to his elder brother, to whom the title would by rights fall (151). The act of bequeathing the title asserts Tongoona's own claim to be Father of the Family, the title is his to bestow. The love he feels for Lucifer is a self-love: he projects his self forward onto descendants in order to receive confirmation of his self. Like Lucifer as a boy, Tongoona needs a Father to ratify his own status. Lucifer, however, rejects the proffered title. He feels his parents 'would make him something more than what he really is' (72). He does not want to be the Father; he wants a Father. When he stands up to Tongoona, he expects and almost wants his father to punish him, since that would prove his love. When the slap does not come, Lucifer realises that 'Never again will his father raise his hand to beat him': 'Somehow the slap of his father's open palm now seems to him infinitely easier to bear than this responsibility of his independence' (43-44). 'Independence' is a charged word in 1975 in Rhodesia, where the white settler regime has issued a Unilateral Declaration of Independence and a struggle for Zimbabwe is underway. Lucifer's 'independence', however, is something he has but does not want. It is the measure of his lack of a Father whose love he wanted and could not find.

Lucifer and Tongoona both want the other to be the Father who will confirm their own place in the world and both are disappointed. They internalise the disappointment and reproach themselves. Tongoona, too, is haunted by a great ambivalence: proud that his son is going overseas, he is 'afraid that the boy stays away from home because he, the father, has nothing to give him' (44). This ambivalence, part identification, part hostile distancing, is the complement of the son's own melancholic self-division. Lucifer studies psychology as avidly as he does not just in order to understand himself, but also to stave off other orders of experience which fill him with fear. When he comes home he is haunted by dreams of witches (52), which he hopes his reading will help him escape. Modern psychology empowers by naming experience: Garabha, for instance, achieves a distance from his mother when he is able to label her 'hysterical' and as suffering from 'Uncoordinated nerves' (103). But Freud is not sufficient to explain Lucifer. Lucifer's memories of childhood are the only scenes of a character's personal past that the novel shows, and they betray how close Lucifer is to the implied writer. But the narrative reminds us that the other characters, who do not have a past or do not think about it, have other ways of understanding. In particular, they have 'Those-Long-Gone' (63).

Waiting for the Rain, in which, as Flora Veit-Wild (1992) writes, the narrator himself 'functions as a psychotherapist' (289), opens with a dream in which submerged images rise to the surface: 'broken images, faces half-hidden among other faces, flittingly glimpsed in passing and only vaguely remembered' (2). Desert gives way to plain, which in turn becomes a forest and 'the mulchy damp of millions of years of rotting leaves and creepers and the stench of decay' (2). If dreams represent features of the unconscious, as Freud would have it, this particular unconscious is unusual in that it is shared among several dreamers. The Old Man awakes from the dream (4), but there is a second presence in his dream, addressed as 'you,' who also dreams the dream. The dream landscape is inside 'him,' but 'you' are inside the landscape. 'You' and 'he' keep changing places. It is not clear whether the Old Man is dreaming 'you' or 'you' are dreaming that 'you' are the Old Man: 'Things are happening here and there and whether you can see them or not you can't certainly say the Old Man doesn't see them' (1). This second dreamer may be Garabha, the player of drums, because 'you' are making noise with 'cracked little tin toys' which threatens to block out the sound of the Old Man's drum (1). But 'you' may also be Lucifer who later has a similar dream of 'faces he has seen before but he cannot give any of them names' (154). Lucifer dreams that Matandangoma tells him the story of Magaba who followed a strange bird to the Big Plain and to his death. Or 'you' may even be Garabha's address to Lucifer, for when the elder brother has a foreboding that Lucifer is following the voice of the strange bird, he slips into the second person: 'Only to realise in the end that you have been traveling towards this place: The Plain of Skulls' (164).

The phantasmal dreamscape, which resembles the space where Oedipus confronted the sphinx, is the realm of the ancestors. Ancestor worship in the novel has in common with modern psychology the assumption that the present cannot be understood without the baggage from the past and that family is the major site where the present is formed. As Richard Werbner (1991) found among the Kalanga, 'The present was an effect caused by the past. Hence to know the past down to the circumstantial details of who said what to whom, when, and where was to anticipate, to gain forewarning of characteristic actions by family members'(83). The past of the ancestors is not the past of personal experience but the past of the people closest to one. Pace Freud, it is impossible to imagine personal experience that has not been shaped by the experience of others. If one is shaped by parents, they, in turn, have been shaped by their parents. Each generation passes on to its children its traumas and neuroses.

The ancestors in Mungoshi's novel are not a monolithic category representing something called tradition, whether considered the repository of all value or a debilitating remnant of superstition. Instead there are faultlines, divisions among the ancestors, and different modes of access to them. Tongoona claims the title of Father of the Family and the authority associated with the clan founders, but his son Garabha, the wanderer for whom he has nothing but contempt, is able through his drumming to become Samambwa, his great-great-ancestor and the Founder of the Tribe.

When Garabha seeks to understand himself and his relation to those around him, he does not return in memory to unhappy episodes of childhood, as Lucifer does, but he enters the ancestral dreamscape through his drumming. Drumming is never a solitary activity, though Garabha makes the spiritual journey alone. At the communal get-together hosted by the Mandengus in honour of Lucifer, Garabha drums and reenacts the story of Samambwa. He travels far from this world and can look back on those left behind with the Founder's eyes: 'he can now see them – the people: helpless, dancing, begging, grovelling for mercy' (128). Samambwa's story resonates with Garabha's own peripatetic existence. Samambwa, too, was a loner and a wanderer who 'couldn't live with people any more': 'He was a hunter and all he had were his dogs and nothing more; no family, no tribe, no law except the law of survival and the family of wild animals, trees, rivers and mountains' (128-29). The errant ways of the prodigal Garabha thus receive the sanction of the deepest tradition, and the current decline, which seems to mark the end of the family, resembles the moment of the family's origins! Matandangoma proclaims that Garabha is Samambwa reborn (130), and his grandfather is confident that, despite his anti-social fecklessness, Garabha 'is home' and that his restless searching is actually a sign that 'the House is in order' (165).

When Garabha drums his way to the ancestors, he does not meet Samambwa; he becomes Samambwa. His performance re-enacts a story that 'the Old Man has often told him' (128). The Founder, no longer accessible in person, has become his story. The story no doubt varies according to the needs of those who retell it, but we can say nonetheless that Garabha enters a story already constituted: it has a familiar beginning, middle, and end. When Garabha comes to the end of the story, the moment when the Founder left the world 'to be with his people who had gone before him,' a moment which also marks 'the beginning of the present generation' of the family (129), his drums fail him. The subsequent generations of ancestors are not accessible to Garabha through the drums. They have not yet become stories.

There is an important distinction between the distant Founders of the clan and the dead whom the family knew personally. Sekuru invokes the blessing of the ancestors thus: 'I speak to you my Father, Mandengu. Pass it on to your Father Nhema and all those who have gone before us, those in the hills of Manhize, and on to him who came alone from the North, Our Big Father, and ask him to pass it on to Him who dwells in the Heavens ...' (175). This patrilineal chain links Mandengu, Sekuru's father, through Our Big Father, Samambwa, directly to God the Father. However, the chain of fathers includes only three nameable generations. As Iona Mayer points out with regards to the Gusii, 'effective genealogical memory peters out at about the level of grandfather or great-grandfather and this is the reason why genealogies of commoners tends to be four or five generations in depth' (in Hammond-Tooke, 1985: 314).

Others in the immediate region of Manyene also worship the clan ancestor Samambwa and retell his story. Hammond-Tooke (1985) observes, however, that 'the widespread folk model of "descendants of a common grandfather" (often great-grandfather), limiting effective tracing to two generations beyond Ego, would seem to have set very definite limits for expansion. Fission occurred when the groups became larger than this' (316). Tongoona's family extends backward to include Samambwa, the Founder of the Tribe, but, as we have seen, no longer includes Kuruku, Tongoona's older brother, now head of another family. Werbner (1991) finds that it was common among the Kalanga 'for brothers to gain their independence and live apart by their mid-fifties, having reached an age when, no longer labour migrants, they had adult and married children and were themselves on the verge of elderhood' (112). Regardless of how usual the pattern, it is nonetheless traumatic. Werbner writes, 'No one [...] took the emerging split as a matter of course, as if it were natural and unavoidable. Everyone, even those expressing relief that at last they would live by themselves, saw it as an injury to the family which was a matter of blame' (112). The fissure in the family, although the inevitable result of family dynamics, explicitly contravenes the ideology of unity and raises deep anxieties, which are, in turn, given expression by the ancestors.

Alongside the Fathers, who are shared with many households, there is another class of ancestor, by no means as exalted: the dead whom the living once knew personally. Hammond-Tooke (1985) explains that 'Although each section invokes all the dead members of its particular clan at every ritual killing (through the symbolic use of its founder's name), the particular ancestor causing the misfortune is always drawn from the limited clan section genealogy and is identified through the exact genealogical connection and also, usually, known in life' (317). When Tongoona's family consult the spirit called the Doctor through his medium, Matandangoma, in order to understand what is wrong in their own home, they receive news not of the Founder Samambwa but of a son of Sekuru and brother of Tongoona now dead. That brother was known as Makiwa (white men) because, long before Lucifer, 'he ran away from home to the white men's towns when he was still young' (138). The death of Makiwa did something to the mind of the white man who had adopted him and who was responsible for the accident that killed him (139), yet Makiwa also seeks placation from the family that he himself had left behind and whom he punishes for having forgotten him.

By virtue of his death, Makiwa is a 'Father of the Family' (139; capitalised in the text) as his own father, Sekuru, is not yet (because he is still alive) or is no longer (having surrendered that title to his son Tongoona). Ancestors like Makiwa function as the hypostasis of the wrongs that have occurred within the family. Family dynamics give rise to feelings of hurt; death then makes those wrongs irreparable; and the fathers (which I spell with a small 'f' to distinguish them from the Founding Fathers like Samambwa) dwell on those unassuageable wrongs. Theirs are the faces who appear to Lucifer and demand 'pay back' (154). As in Freud, the deepest sources of the self also pose the greatest threat to the self.

The Mandengu family curse is over-determined. Makiwa's bitterness cannot be the original cause of the family's current ills for it leaves unexplained why he had to leave in the first place and why he died. Makiwa, who started the pattern of filial rejection of the homestead, did not cause the pattern. It seems there has always been a curse on the family. Makiwa presumably poses a problem at this particular juncture because he is an instance on the level of the ancestors of the crisis posed by Lucifer's plan to go overseas, but it is impossible to say of the ancestral wound and the present crisis which is cause and which effect. The ancestors share with the spirit forces of Western psychology, Oedipus, Eros and Thanatos, superego and id, an almost limitless interpretability (they can mean almost anything and are read differently by different experts in different contexts), coupled with an almost complete ineluctability (they cannot be avoided). This makes it difficult ever to make peace with the ancestors, but also means that the interpreter is not without power, the power imparted by interpretation itself. Makiwa and Samambwa were both self-destructive wanderers who left family behind and who died alone. These ancestors do not represent communal values but the danger and the potential that young adult males have always presented to the community. Family has always relied on individuals who broke new paths. But individual restlessness and ambition also threaten the value of equality that holds the family together. Individual ambition arouses jealousy and suspicion both within and without the family. And family, in turn, poses a threat to strong male spirits, who feel its demands for sharing and its suspicion of ambition as intolerable constraints. The example of Samambwa suggests that the individual who does not merge his individuality in the family can nevertheless be integrated in the family. To join Samambwa, as the Old Man does through his story and Garabha through his drumming, is to be filled with the deepest rhythms of life, to recognise that the conflict between the young man and the family fulfils a pattern underlying all family relations. Makiwa's great bitterness is precisely that he is not remembered, he does not have a story as Samambwa does. His life and death are not accessible through Garabha's drums. Samambwa, who was as unhappy while alive as Makiwa, is now safely part of a story, but Makiwa still walks in the present and has a power to hurt. It is also still possible to listen and speak to him (through Matandangoma), as one cannot speak to Samambwa.

Lucifer and Garabha's alienation is nothing new. Makiwa would be at peace, we are told, if Lucifer were to take his name. In other words, Lucifer would be obeying the wishes of the ancestors if he were to call himself 'White Men'! The family tries to contain the threat that Lucifer's planned trip represents by fitting it into a story. The Doctor, speaking through Matandangoma, never refers to Lucifer by name but calls him the 'Wandering One' (143) or 'Traveller' (144). In part, this renaming is to deflect the attention of hostile spirits from him, but it also serves to locate him within a familiar story: if the Wandering One and the House are both to be secured, the former must be shown his home and the latter must be cleansed (143).

The division of the ancestors into Fathers and fathers resonates with the distinction I made earlier between actual fathers and ideal Fathers. The title of Father of the Family that Tongoona wants to pass on to his younger son implies a line of Fathers that excludes his own father and his older son. At the very moment that he accuses Garabha of not paying him filial respect, Tongoona insults his own father: 'I have told you again and again that the only advice that you can give at your age is to your belly' (111). Tongoona asserts his rights over his sons but expresses the same contempt for his own father that his son Lucifer feels for him. Sekuru replies in kind:

'You are a fine father, aren't you? Is there anyone else in the whole world who has got it hanging in a bunch between his legs except you?' (111). Stratton (1986) blames Tongoona for the family's misery: 'by entrusting the welfare of the family to Lucifer, who is already alienated from the familial scene, he is sealing its doom' (14). But Tongoona, who chooses the younger son to be his heir, is only doing what his father did before him when he 'put his hopes for the future of the Family' in Tongoona rather than in his elder brothers (7). Sekuru now 'feels Tongoona will betray the Family' (7), but making the wrong choice of an heir is what defines this family. When Tongoona chooses Lucifer over Garabha, his father objects: 'You want to disinherit the eldest son while he is still alive?' (152), forgetting that he himself did exactly the same. Tongoona responds, 'Father, I am a man now ... ... Just for this once let me be the father of my own children and leave the deciding of who of them shall do what to me. Garabha ran away from school against my wish and since then he has taken it upon himself to flaunt (sic) every one of my orders' (152). Tongoona does not listen to his father's advice because his own son did not listen to him and thus proves he does not deserve to lead the family! In *Waiting for the Rain* all fathers are treated with contempt by their sons and respond with bitter recrimination. Kuruku, who has not accepted his own father into his house, denounces the world that teaches his sons 'that the name "Father" is just an empty shell to hide nothing between the legs' (64).

Tongoona despises Garabha because he sees in him his own despised father. He sees what is there: grandfather and grandson are kindred spirits. 'In his young days,' Sekuru, too, 'would go for days on end without eating anything, playing drums and singing – and the women followed him' (49). Old Japi says, 'If my husband were dead I would say his spirit sits in that boy' (49). Radcliffe-Brown (1950) writes of generational succession in Africa, 'In the passage of persons through the social structure which they enter by birth and leave by death, and in which they occupy successive positions, it is not, properly speaking, children who replace their parents, but those of the grandparents' generation who are replaced by those of the grandchildren's generation' (28). One result is 'the merging of alternate generations': 'A man with his "father's fathers", his "son's son," and his "brothers" in the classificatory sense form a social division over against his "fathers" and "sons," who constitute another division' (29).

Sekuru, who has abdicated paternal authority and is without respect in his son's household, now has some of the spiritual powers associated with the ancestors whom I have called the Fathers: especially the power to travel to the Big Plain, the power to read others' thoughts, and the power to bless. Garabha has the same spiritual powers: the ability to play the drum and so become the Founder, and the ability to feel what another is thinking, especially his grandfather and his sister. As we have seen, however, Fathers like Samambwa have less direct power over events than do the fathers like Makiwa. We cannot but feel that Sekuru and Garabha are closer to the ancestral Fathers because they are without responsibility for others. On the other hand, Tongoona, who claims to be Father of the Family, that is, to have the authority of the clan Fathers, is actually closer to the ancestors I have called fathers with a small 'f', wounded spirits who continue to wreak harm on those who knew them.

Among the three adult generations in the Tongoona household, the elderly who no longer wield power and the young who do not yet wield power are allied against the middle-aged wielders of power. Zhuwarara (2001) suggests that this conjunction reflects the impact of history on the colonised. But it seems also to be a recurring pattern: every male who lives into old age can count on spending one third of his adult life in a position of power, and two-thirds in a position without. If we imagine the three generations of Mandengus as embodying the age grades of youth, maturity, and elderhood that each cohort must pass through, then nothing is more certain than that Tongoona, the current Father of the Family, will himself eventually be displaced and become a seemingly irrelevant elder like his father. Indeed, we can see that decline already in the way Lucifer treats him.

Although, in *Waiting for the Rain*, sons reject their fathers in every generation, this is not Oedipal succession, because the sons do not then introject their fathers in their psyches in order to become fathers themselves. If we use the distinction I have made between Fathers and fathers, we can say that, in the Oedipal model, sons reject Fathers in order to become Fathers, whereas Mungoshi's characters reject their fathers because the latter are not Fathers. Whereas Oedipal succession implies a linear progression, generational succession in Mungoshi's novel is cyclical and doubled. As successive generations are driven apart, alternating generations are brought closer together. Among the Mandengus, the pendulum of patriarchy requires two generations to perform the return to an original point that the Oedipal model accomplishes in half a lifetime.

In Mungoshi, the amplitude of the intergenerational pendulum makes the conflict between 'self' and 'other' characteristic of colonialism (and nationalism) into a function of generational succession. The feared other is recognised as already part of the self, as close to the self as one's own parent, and the self is in turn discovered to be terrifyingly other. Kuruku, the spokesman for nationalism, tells Lucifer a confused story about why he is black: the young generation, says the uncle, are the Sons of Ham and cursed because they laughed at their fathers' drunkenness (63). Kuruku transposes racialised terms for 'self' and 'other' deployed by the colonisers on to generational relations: sons are 'black' because they reject fathers. Sons, of course, feel the opposite is the case: their fathers, who have been colonised, have made blackness into something shameful. Colonisation emasculates the Father of the Family, and Lucifer wishes 'he had a different father' (43). Post-colonial sons may seek a Father in the previous generation, as Garabha does, or like Lucifer, they may look to the coloniser, especially a missionary, to adopt them. Lucifer addresses the white priest who sponsors his studies overseas, as 'Father' (179). We suspect that Lucifer's experience will end as unhappily as Makiwa's. Matandangoma predicts that Lucifer will live overseas with a black veil forever over his head (138), and Lucifer dreams of a journey that ends 'on the brink of nowhere' (153).

Father and son relations in the novel also involve another category of 'self' and 'other', every bit as significant as race, and that is gender. Tongoona is determined to make men of his sons and discourages his wife's close relations with them. Lucifer remembers his father insisting, 'He is a man, not a woman. Don't spoil him with these female softies' (75). Matandangoma, however, pronounces Tongoona himself weak and says, 'A woman should have been given what you carry between your legs instead' (150). The figure of the dreaded other, suspected to be the truth of genetic inheritance, is associated with women. Another way of describing the oscillation between fathers and Fathers is to say that each generation of males assumes the quality of maleness for itself and attributes femaleness to the other.

Women do not share blood with their husbands or children and belong to another patrilineage. Tongoona explains to his son that his mother may become a source of danger to him when she dies: 'Anything [...] that any member of this family has done to her and she didn't like it – everything has to be paid back by you or any one of this family' (159). Women bring into the family a third kind of ancestor, neither the Fathers nor the fathers. Hanging over Tongoona's family is an ancestral curse belonging not to the Mandengus at all but to the family of the maternal grandmother, Old Mandisa. The Kandengwas were guilty of a murder several generations before, and since, as part of the curse, Mandisa has lost all her children but one, the only people left who can expiate the crime are the family that her daughter has married into, who have otherwise nothing to do with the crime. The curse is carried into the family by women; it is also women who 'pay for it' (149). If the whole family is not to be destroyed, a woman must serve as appeasement: either Betty, the unmarried adult daughter, must be sent away to find the family that suffered the original wrong and join them as compensation or a virgin scapegoat must be sacrificed.

The two eldest generations of Mandengus decide to ask Matandangoma to use her power to harm Rudo, the daughter of their neighbour and enemy, in order to remove the curse. They summon Lucifer, the designated heir, to hear their decision, but this last is a meeting that the novel does not record. Readers can be sure that Lucifer feels the horror that they do, but his response will have been characteristically passive, limited to distancing himself from the unfairness of the curse and its requital. At Lucifer's departure the next day, he tries to break all links by leaving behind the protective medicines his family have prepared. When he sees Rudo, whom the Mandengus are conspiring against, and she waves to him, Lucifer hurriedly 'turns back and starts running towards his parents' home' (163). He feels powerless to intervene and wants only to avoid involvement.

It is not clear how Lucifer could intervene: he is faced with a power, be it of the ancestors, of an entire culture, or, as he feels it, of superstition, that is much larger than he is. But Lucifer's response is cowardly nonetheless. He feels the curse which requires that the family decide which woman will suffer as a kind of contamination of himself. We can measure Lucifer's failure by contrasting it with the feeling that Garabha has for his sister, Betty, who suffers the family dynamics more directly and more severely than her brothers. Lucifer cannot talk with either of his siblings, although they are his fellow victims. He feels his sister's presence in his room as an accusation, filling him with 'shame' and 'guilt' that he then redirects at the accuser (51). He never recognises her suffering. Garabha and Betty, on the other hand, think alike, can read each other's minds, and are free to tease each other. Garabha the wastrel brings home a necklace for his beloved sister. The sight of her calloused hands stabs him in the heart: 'In a flash he sees her whole life in those hands and his gift of beads seems too small. He will never be able to do enough for her, he feels' (88). His reaction allows us to judge Lucifer. Lucifer fails not because he turns his back on family but because he turns his back on those who suffer most from family.

Waiting for the Rain could be read as a warning to the post-colonial nation of the perils of cutting oneself off from all neighbours and extended family. The feared others, kept so resolutely outside the Mandengu family, return in a different form to disturb the family from within. But, I emphasise that family is not merely a metaphor for nation, and it is a mistake to focus critical analysis solely on political ideology. The post-colonial condition involves all aspects of the self and the psyche. The ancestors in the novel are as real as those other great spiritual forces, the elements of psychology and Zhuwarara's nation. What Peter Geschiere (1997) writes of African witchcraft could also be said of ancestors: they express 'the frightening realisation that aggression threatens from within the intimacy of the family – that is, from the very space where complete solidarity and trust should reign without fail' (212). Werbner (1991) writes, 'The powerful assumption was that [...] that 'one is killed by one's own person, not someone coming from afar' (85). Family has the capacity to inflict the deepest wounds precisely because it is where one looks for security and trust: 'It is those closest to our hearts who are the worst thorns,' says Tongoona, speaking more wisely than he knows (160).

I do not mean that we must respect the Mandengus' worship of ancestors in some absolute way: they are distinctly disempowered by some ancestors. I am arguing that the critical solution is not to reject the ancestors as remnants of superstition standing in the way of modernity nor to celebrate them as repositories of authenticity to which people must return; the goal must be, as in psychology, to become conscious of and so to reduce the space occupied by the ancestors and thus to win a space of freedom from them. In other words, the major interpretative task of a novel so heavily dependent on the ancestors is to understand how the ancestors work. To consider the Mandengu family on its own terms is not to accept the inevitability or validity of patriarchy, let alone of colonialism, but to seek to understand how this particular form of patriarchy functions and how colonialism is experienced in this place.

Mungoshi occupies an unusual position in the African literary canon. Commonly recognised as 'Zimbabwe's most accomplished writer' (Malaba, 1997: 301), he is little taught outside Zimbabwe. He does not fit the usual paradigms, which hold that Africans are concerned first and foremost with the nation. But Mungoshi has much to tell us about family, the preserve of some of the strongest values and the cause of the most deeply penetrating anxiety and pain. If we critics accept as our task the analysis of the literary imagination, then family would play an important position in our analyses and Mungoshi would occupy the canonical position he deserves.

Endnotes

1. Maurice Vambe (2004: 53), taking his cue from the novel's lack of political awareness, says it is set in the 1950s, but several details point to a later time: the radio reports coups in independent African republics (*Waiting for the Rain*: 31), and Kuruku's nationalist sons are in exile in Zambia (ibid: 69).

2. The writing of this article was assisted by a grant from the Social Sciences and Humanities Research Council of Canada.

3. I invoke Freud not because psychoanalysis tells us a universal truth or even the truth about Lucifer, but because modern psychology underwrites Lucifer's return to his personal past. He is proud of 'his knowledge of modern psychology' (52), and this presumably is what he reads in his room throughout his visit home. The significance of a term like 'melancholia' is not that it explains Lucifer, but that it is how Lucifer understands himself.

4

'Sins of the Fathers': Revealing family secrets in Mungoshi's later fiction

PAULINE DODGSON-KATIYO

A recurring theme in Mungoshi's work since his early short stories in English has been the effect of fathering on sons. In his exploration of the relationship between adult sons and fathers in his later short fiction, Mungoshi portrays dominant fathers who turn their sons into fearful men, lacking in confidence and insecure in their work and marriages. This paper analyses two short stories, 'The Empty House' (1997) and 'The Sins of the Fathers' (2003) and examines the ways in which they reveal unease around generational conflict, national identities and the promotion of masculinity in Zimbabwean society. In my analysis of 'The Empty House', I show how the diffusion of the father/son relationship among various themes results in a satire on aspects of post-independence Zimbabwe, but avoids a more focussed representation of the contradictions in a society in transition. In my analysis of 'The Sins of the Fathers', I argue that the representation of the two fathers as politicians with different visions of Zimbabwe allows Mungoshi to move between the familial and the national in an exposition of the legacy of the liberation war.

'The Empty House'
The antagonistic father/son relationship in 'The Empty House' is embedded in a number of other themes which offer a satirical take on contemporary Zimbabwean culture. These include male infertility, art as commodity, and the outsider's search for African authenticity. 'The Empty House' appears to be set in the early 1980s when Zimbabwe was a transitional society, open to foreigners interested in working in the 'new' country. The story suggests that this openness was a mask, disguising residual conflicts within a society that had not yet come to know or understand itself.

The father in 'The Empty House', Mark Maneto is a self-made man, a successful businessman 'who had also found God through his own personal efforts' (Mungoshi, 1997: 84). He regards as treacherous his son Gwizo's rejection of business in favour of painting as a career. Maneto's disapproval of his son is so severe that he refuses to talk about Gwizo in public, silencing people who question him with, 'What son are you talking about?' (83). Gwizo's choice of career is a decadent foreign imposition, 'Art, among Maneto's people, was a foreign thing, a disease, something you didn't want to be associated with. It was like syphilis or some mental aberration' (83). Maneto's view is in keeping with his nationalism since, in the years before independence, painting was seen as an individualist, indulgent art form, mainly practised by whites. According to Williams, painting 'suffered more from the isolation of UDI and sanctions' (1991: 72) than sculpture or craftwork and did not focus on social reality. Gwizo's espousal of an individual form of artistic expression makes him a latter-day adult version of Lucifer, the alienated boy in Mungoshi's *Waiting for the Rain* (1975), whose art is described by Muchemwa as lacking social purpose, as the discourse 'of an individual artist who does not draw inspiration from ancestral springs' (2006: 48). Maneto, like Lucifer's father, Tongoona, worries that his son will not earn a living from his Western-inspired art. For him, Gwizo's painting is mere child's play.

Maneto's views on gender are also traditional. He considers that his two daughters, taken together, are of less significance than a son and he adheres to the belief that 'only sons were entitled to inherit their father's wealth' (84). This position is put to the test when his elder daughter, Synodia, graduates as a civil engineer. At first, he suggests that she give her degree to her brother but, as time passes, and 'his views on girls – and women in general – mellowed' (84), he thinks about leaving part of his business to Synodia. She too remains unimpressed by everything that Gwizo does, agreeing with her father's view that her brother is a failure, a man who is marrying late and has no property or money.

Gwizo constructs a different identity for himself from that of other members of his family, not only through his art but also through his relationship and subsequent marriage to Agatha MacFarlane, a white American who has come to Zimbabwe to discover African life. However, although he has committed himself to the role of painter, Gwizo is more ambivalent about his relationship with Agatha, 'He felt rebellious, adventurous as if he were headed for a place from which he would never return' (85). Yet when he eventually, and reluctantly, takes Agatha to visit his family, Gwizo fears that she has been caught in his father's 'snare'. Agatha sees Maneto as culturally authentic, 'so *alive*' (87) and believes that being associated with him is buying into traditional culture. Gwizo, too, thinks this must be what people find attractive in his father. Wondering what is meant by charisma, he speculates that, 'if his father had it, then it must be the smell of an old man's sweat – something akin to soil' (86).

Gwizo's family is divided in their reaction to Agatha. His mother will not even say her name. Her fear and suspicion is based on past family history. She tells Gwizo that he will be the second member of the family to sleep with a white woman – the first, his great-grandfather was hanged for allegedly raping one. When she hears this, Agatha compares it to the history of inter-racial sexual relations in the United States, 'Everything looks so like a bad replay of everything at home' (87). Two histories lie behind Mrs Maneto's story and Agatha's response. The first is the history of what was colloquially known as Black Peril in Southern Rhodesia when the Criminal Law Amendment Ordinance of 1903 made it a capital offence for a black man to assault a white woman. According to McCulloch, 'As many as twenty men were executed for sexual crime and another two hundred were jailed. Such assaults were perceived not just as an attack upon the body of a woman but as an attack upon the white community itself' (2000: 4). Gwizo has no knowledge of this history, only remembering that his father swears 'on the head of Chigiga Maneto whom the whiteman hanged' (87) but Agatha's dismay suggests that, although she knows the second history, the controversies around inter-racial sex and rape in the United States, she prefers not to deal with it. Instead she wants to immerse herself in what she sees as 'innocent' practices, learning Shona and visiting Gwizo's grandmother in rural Bikita.

Gwizo and Agatha's relationship is fraught with difficulty. When she argues with him in public, ominously, he feels 'like strangling her' (88) and when she expresses dissatisfaction with his city life, which does not fit in with her image of Africa, he suspects that she is treating him merely as a commodity she has found on her 'great romantic safari through Africa' (88). However, after Agatha has become Gwizo's agent and his paintings fetch high prices in the international art market, Gwizo and Agatha marry, although 'how it happened, Gwizo would never be able to explain' (89). Gwizo fears Maneto's disapproval. When Agatha carries out a traditional daughter-in-law ceremony, Maneto refuses the bath water and oil she offers him. During the ceremony, Gwizo is aware 'of the dark hawkish figure of the Old Man standing and glooming in the dark background, making the shadows darker, hurling curses at the shame and ignominy with which his own son had seen fit to crown his days and nights of labour' (90). Agatha, though, takes control of the situation, knowing that she can bring Maneto round and get him to work with her.

As Gwizo and Agatha's marriage begins to fall apart with Gwizo drinking heavily, suffering a loss of creativity and remaining childless, Maneto reveals his mercenary side. Whatever his original feelings about Agatha, Maneto now sees her as an entrepreneur who will make money for the family; she becomes his secretary and he works with her in her art export business. Maneto crudely tells his son that he is useless without Agatha. Maneto's nationalist agenda gives way to a politics of accommodation as he tells Gwizo, 'The trouble with you young people is that you take our politics too much to heart and then ask all the wrong questions. There is such a thing as compromise' (96). Gwizo's marriage to a white foreign woman and choice of career as an artist had suggested that he preferred modernity to tradition but now he appears lost as the black radical artist Ranga and his seemingly nationalist father Maneto get what they want from Agatha while he takes refuge in a politics of crude racial antagonism, telling Agatha that she is afraid to have his baby.

When Agatha does become pregnant, who fathers her child appears not to be an issue for her. However, it is an issue for Gwizo. Agatha may be enacting her perverted version of a Shona remedy for a husband's infertility, *kupindira*, the custom of asking a brother or friend to impregnate the wife of an infertile man, without that man's knowledge. However, in Shona tradition the child belongs to the husband's family since *roora* has been paid for the wife. Given that no bride price has been paid for Agatha, she can respond to Gwizo's persistent question 'It's his, isn't it?' with the words 'No, Gwizo. It's mine' (104). This insistence denies Gwizo fatherhood and further infantilises him. Having previously produced art which his father considered child's play, he now produces neither art nor children and his wife has looked elsewhere for both. The traditional authority of a father over his son has become distorted as Maneto usurps Gwizo's role as breadwinner and biological father in his family, preventing Gwizo from taking on an adult role.

Instead of confronting his father, Gwizo displaces his anger on to Agatha. In Gwizo's mind, his wife has become the castrating 'monstrous feminine', her appropriation of Shona tradition being akin to Blanche Goodfather's fierce attraction 'to the lights of the savage, the earthy, the primitive' in Marechera's *Black Sunlight* (1980: 4). It could be argued that Agatha's appearance in the lives of both men has increased the antagonism between father and son. However, towards the end of the story, the antagonism is only on Gwizo's side. For Maneto, his son quite simply no longer matters. Since Agatha's baby is a boy, he believes he has found his heir in the next generation. In the denouement to the story, it is as if Gwizo recovers a macabre form of his art, far removed from the creativity that Agatha wants him to rediscover in the landscape. Gwizo is 'fascinated with the play of his fingers, feeling the familiar itch slowly awakening'. Agatha stands at the window 'with that wonderful light round her' (104). If Gwizo is about to strangle Agatha at the end of the story, then, he renders her into *nature morte* in this tableau-like final scene.

The underlying tensions in the story remain unresolved. There is little to explain how the strongly traditionalist and nationalist Maneto becomes the pragmatist who admires Agatha's business acumen and chooses her as the mother of his putative heir, despite previous worries about the colour of his potential grandchildren. Agatha's foreignness becomes the pivotal force in the story, taking over from the father/son conflict. Her outsider status makes it possible for Maneto to have a sexual relationship with her, even though she is his son's wife. Zhuwarara refers to Agatha's impregnation by her father-in-law as a 'brazen violation of social convention and taboos' (2001: 110). However, her cultural difference means that she has not been fully recognised as Gwizo's wife (People said 'It wasn't quite a marriage' [89] and they came to the ceremony to laugh) and Maneto feels as free to have an affair with her as with his previous secretaries. Gwizo's marriage has brought the 'curse' of the ancestor on the family but, unlike the ancestor's story, it remains a familial tragedy rather than a representation of contradictions within wider society.

The Sins of the Fathers'

'The Sins of the Fathers' is also concerned with who does or does not belong in Zimbabwe but the story is set in the 21st century and deals with race and ethnicity *within* Zimbabwean society. Mungoshi, in an interview with Mai Palmberg, commented on the critical reception of his early work. He explained that, in the years after independence, his major novel, *Waiting for the Rain* was criticised for lacking historical and political content and not contributing to the liberation war. However, in recent years this view has been revised and now, 'a criticism of the present seems to have been written already in a book many years ago, which was then stamped as being ideologically empty' (Mungoshi, 2004). As Mungoshi hints, the changing critical response to *Waiting for the Rain*, has as much to do with the way critics' ideological positions have changed since the 1980s (in line with growing disillusion in Zimbabwean society) as with the content of the book. I would agree that Mungoshi's earlier work sheds light on the political malaise in contemporary Zimbabwe. However, 'The Sins of the Fathers' does appear to be different from his other work. Its political content is quite explicit and, in making the father a member of the ruling elite, Mungoshi offers a critique of the state of the nation.

'The Sins of the Fathers' begins enigmatically. Rondo Rwafa and his father are sitting alone in the yard of Rondo's house. Rwafa does not know that his son, 'who'd never handled a gun before' has one in his jacket pocket and that 'by the end of the day he would shoot – or not shoot – his father' (Mungoshi, 2003: 137). The reader is presented immediately with what needs to be resolved by the end of the story but, as the story unfolds, we also expect to find out why Rondo would want to kill his father. It is soon apparent that Rondo's father-in-law, Basil Mzamane and Rondo's two young daughters have died in an accident. As the story progresses, it gradually emerges that Rwafa has ordered the killing of Mzamane, his political adversary.

Rondo's uncertainty about the present is embedded in his memories of both the recent past, the death of his father-in-law and daughters, and in his memories of his father during his childhood and young manhood. Even when Rondo remembers details of his father's domestic life and his own painful relationship with him, Rwafa is seen as a public figure, a patriarch within a wider society. From the beginning of the story, Rondo's relationship to his father is juxtaposed with the latter's political role; Rwafa is 'his father, the ex-minister' (137) and this parallelism is maintained throughout the story. Rwafa 'as Minister of Security, seemed to have pursued his duties so zealously that he hadn't been able to distinguish Party from family' (145). Rondo, as a child, develops a stammer when he cannot answer his father's questions, just as many others did when questioned by the minister. The threatening speech Rwafa makes at his grandchildren's birthday party reminds Rondo of an incident from his childhood when a neighbour beat him for stealing mangoes; then his father arrived and started beating Rondo himself. Rondo remembers his mother running from one man to the other, begging them to stop. He realises that 'at that early age ... he must have understood what *powerlessness* meant' (158). Even after the children's deaths, Rwafa's status turns the rituals of mourning into photo opportunities as people come to the house to be seen with the nationalist politician and gain political preferment.

Like Maneto, Rwafa has always wanted Rondo to develop in his own likeness. His wife, Selina tells him, *'You are always in the shadow of your father'* (140) and it is this stunted development which has emasculated him. His father arranged his job on a newspaper where, although the other staff laugh at him, they are afraid of him because he is Rwafa's son. Knowing his colleagues do not respect him, he plays the fool that they and others think he is. Although Rondo has stood up to Rwafa in marrying an Ndebele woman, he feels insecure, knowing that Selina thinks she is more a man than he is. Rondo believes his wife sees herself as morally superior, passing judgment on him. Rondo is always on the defensive and has left decision-making to his wife.

After the children's funeral, Rondo wants his wife to tell him what *she* thinks of his father so that *he* knows how he should feel and think about him and how he should handle him. Selina avoids doing this, 'she hadn't said anything at all about anything' (142). Unlike Rondo's speech, which is hesitant, never quite reaching the point and not completing thoughts or sentences, Selina's silence about her father-in-law and the accident is, to adopt a phrase from Coetzee's *Foe*, 'chosen and purposeful' (1987: 142). Selina knows that it is time for action, not speech. Rondo's hesitation reveals that he is belatedly trying to understand who his father is and what this means. Rondo does not understand why he has always been afraid of Rwafa. He has always believed that his father is right because he is 'too diminished to think otherwise' (145). His father is seen as a super hero, 'Yet he couldn't tell in exactly what sense' (145). Rondo appears to have repeatedly blanked out any specific knowledge or memory of his father's role in the liberation struggle or government. There are references to how his mother 'of course ... knew' (143) and his mother 'could have told him' (145) but Mrs Rwafa is afraid for her son and is herself a victim of patriarchal oppression. Rondo's colleague, Caston, asks him if he knows what his father does and he just shrugs as if it is of no interest to him. However, when Caston tells him that the accident is 'a typical Second Street accident', Rondo 'in that moment accepted that he had always refused to think about why his father left the house in the morning and what he did before he returned in the evenings – or the following week, for that matter' (147).

Gagiano, writing on *Walking Still*, has referred to the dark epiphanies Mungoshi's characters experience when 'difficult or even tragic realisation' (2006: 144) dawns upon them. Rondo experiences several dark 'near epiphanic' moments in the story when he realises that his blindness has been a contributory factor in the deaths of his father-in-law and daughters. Under Caston's insistent probing, he comes to see that 'the accumulation of events and the history behind them had made him so numb, he was almost a zombie' (148). Rondo remembers a 'seemingly insignificant thing that had happened' after it was agreed that the children could travel with Mzamane. His mother had asked if anyone had seen where her husband had gone and 'remembering it later, Rondo was not sure that this should have been ignored' (159). When Selina joins him in the garden after his father has returned to the house, Rondo tells her, 'I feel as if I have been asleep all my life' (141).

Ironically, Rondo's awakening comes only after the death of his father-in-law. Mzamane is Rondo's ideal father. When he is with him, Rondo feels that the space around him is expanded and he will be allowed to do anything he likes. It is Mzamane who encourages Rondo to think for himself and, through his stories and consideration for others, gives him an ethical education. However, the story is not just about Rondo's preference for one style of fatherhood rather than another. Through the representation of Rwafa and Mzamane, Mungoshi rehearses different versions of Zimbabwe, specifically around questions of inclusion and exclusion.

Rwafa can be seen as an exponent of what Ranger (2004) has described as patriotic history, a history delineating an unbroken continuity from the 1896 uprising to the Second Chimurenga of the 1960s and 70s. This history emphasises the primacy of ZANU-PF's version of the liberation struggle, marginalising the role of ZAPU and ZIPRA[1] and seeing land reform as the prime motive for the struggle. Challenging this position is seen as a betrayal of the country's revolutionary history. From 2000, a new period in Zimbabwean history has emerged, the Third Chimurenga in which war veterans have played a violent role in the expropriation of farm land and diverse groups of Zimbabweans have been vilified as totemless people, undeserving of a place in the nation. In his interview with Palmberg, Mungoshi links the Second and Third Chimurenga:

> ... *It's interesting how we say third and second Chimurenga when the people are really the same people who are afraid, who fight, who are greedy, who hate their own or who twist, the same old – who love. I mean, they loved in the second, now they still love, they hate, and it's always about people who don't deliver, isn't it?* (Mungoshi, 2004)

The genesis of 'The Sins of the Fathers' predates the Third Chimurenga. Mungoshi worked on the story for many years but could never quite finish it.[2] Reworking it, in mid-2003, he was able to draw on contemporary political events.

As Ranger has shown, patriotic history divides the nation into revolutionaries or sell-outs (2004, 223). Rwafa is quick to brand both his son and Mzamane as traitors. Moreover, Rwafa, whose lineage is derived from the Nyashanu dynasty of Shona rulers, is locked into a history of ethnic conflict dating back to the nineteenth century when Ndebele and Shona engaged in skirmishes and wars with each other. Rondo's mother explains to him:

> *Your father is Zezuru-Karanga and, once-upon-a-time, they were raided by the maDzviti-Ndebele. Well, in those days or even in these days, if you have a war, you have a war. It does bad things to people's minds. So they will always remember the pain of the scars rather than the relief of the healing. Your father,* mwanangu, *is one bombed-out battlefield of scars. And his deepest scar is that he cannot forgive: not just his enemies.*

You. Me. Anyone (144)[3].

Rwafa sees Rondo's marriage to an Ndebele woman as shameful. He does not attend the wedding and refuses to forgive him for this act of treachery, 'It was as if his son had been written out, written off, disappeared' (144). When Rwafa makes his virulent speech (ostensibly to children) at the birthday party, he condemns 'effeminate, spineless sons of the family who marry into the families of their enemies, poisoning the pure blood of the Rwafa clan' (157). When he has Mzamane killed, he is killing an old personal and political enemy, but it is not clear whether his granddaughters are collateral damage or whether (consciously or unconsciously) he is ridding his family of the taint of Ndebele blood. However, what Rwafa represents is not nationalism but quasi-nationalism. In *Tears of the Dead*, Werbner explains that recruitment to the two liberation armies, ZANLA and ZIPRA was on a regional basis and that this resulted in polarisation with each army being seen as either predominantly Shona-speaking or Ndebele-speaking. According to Werbner, 'The nationalist struggle thus fed and in turn was fed by its antithesis, the polarisation of two quasi-nations or super-tribes, the Shona against the Ndebele' (1991: 159). Werbner argues that this quasi-nationalism cannot be explained simply as a remnant of pre-colonial society or as a consequence of settler divide and rule policies. Rather it develops within the new nation state:

> *Quasi-nationalism, like the nationalism with which it breeds, is a movement of ideas and practices that wins its often cruelly violent moments within the formation of the nation-state in the twentieth century. If energised by a myth of being prior to the nation state, of revenging old scores left as unsettled from ancient hostilities, quasi-nationalism is none the less made in and by the struggle for power and moral authority in the nation state* (159).

In 'The Sins of the Fathers' Rondo and Mzamane accompany Rwafa on what they think is a duck-shooting expedition but what is, in fact, an attempt to evict the white Quayle family so that Rwafa can take possession of their farm. Rwafa has arranged for them to be followed by a truck occupied by armed youth, brandishing weapons and singing *chimurenga* songs. Rondo sees these young men as different from himself. Listening to them singing, he wonders whether they see the beauty of the country as he does. As their singing becomes more menacing, 'There was something elemental in it, the naked, unashamed raw lust for blood' (151). Rondo knows the songs they are singing but wishes they would use the peacetime words, not those sung during the war. The young men, though, may have undergone a training programme which required them to repeat the war songs.[4] As Rondo's party travels in tandem with the truck, 'the air acquired the dark colour of old memories' (152).

The war and old memories, though, resurface in Mungoshi's text in another way, in Caston's insinuations of 'Second Street accidents', an indication that there are ways of getting rid of political opponents in contemporary Zimbabwe and, by extension, in the Zimbabwean past. Mzamane's murder is redolent of the allegations around the deaths of the ZANU leaders, Herbert Chitepo and Josiah Tongogara. As White (2003) has shown, anxieties around their deaths refuse to go away and continue to haunt ZANU-PF.[5] The continuing allegations and the anxieties they create contribute to 21st century debates on the writing and ownership of history and, in doing so, feed into contemporary discourses on the right to speak and act for the nation.[6]

White argues that among the reasons why views on Chitepo's assassination and Tongorara's death are still so important is because they raise questions about leadership and legitimacy:

> As topics of conversation and press conferences, and as ghosts, both men were portrayed as more heroic, more charismatic, and more judicious figures than they had ever been considered in their lifetimes. Chitepo and Tongogara have been reinvented as men who would have been president of independent Zimbabwe had they lived. The persistence of talk about Chitepo and of talk about and visions of Tongogara literally left a trace of the idea of Mugabe's illegitimacy ... Chitepo and Tongogara come back, as it were, to show that the president is unlawfully in his office (2003: 96-97).

Perhaps what this persistence suggests, put simply, is that there are (or were) alternatives. In Mungoshi's story not only is Mzamane the ideal father, he also represents the ideal leader (at least from the older political generation). Mzamane is also idealised. He represents an inclusive version of Zimbabwe in which, its people, regardless of ethnic origin, can co-exist and prosper peacefully, respecting and learning from each other. His folk stories speak of integration, of what people have in common; he defends Mrs Quayle from the violence of the youths and in his singing of the Oliver Mtukudzi song, '*Todini? Senzeni?* /What Shall We Do', he suggests his awareness that it is AIDS and other post-independence issues that now need to be addressed in Zimbabwe. In telling the youth that he is 'in the same work, same rank' (153) as Rwafa, he claims legitimacy for his own leadership.

As in many of Mungoshi's Chekhov-influenced stories, there is a degree of ambiguity – of things left unsaid – in the conclusion. Instead of shooting his father, Rondo hands him the gun and invites him to kill himself. Rwafa tells Rondo and Selina (who has entered the room without Rondo seeing her) to leave and then shoots himself with his own pistol. Selina is seen holding a gun, given to her by Rondo's mother. Primorac states that 'some of Charles Mungoshi's short stories possess the uncanny quality of lending themselves to a plurality of reading, all equally persuasive' (2006: 124) and, at first reading, 'The Sins of the Fathers' appears to be such a story. One could argue that Rondo is weak in not being able to kill his father and that Selina intends to carry out the killing because she and his mother expect him to fail. The final sentence, 'Rondo bent his head in silence' (160) would seem to support this interpretation. My preferred reading, though, is that there is a *rightness* in the way that Rwafa dies.

Rondo's last words to his father, 'I thought you'd do this thing better than me. After all, this is the story of your life' (160) are deeply ironic. Rwafa, having belittled Rondo throughout his life for his alleged lack of masculinity, continues to jeer at him just before his death. After Rondo has handed him a piece of paper (this may be his 'confession' written by Rondo or it may be Rondo's indictment of him) he sarcastically asks Rondo if it was written by one of his more intelligent friends and then searches Rondo's face for 'a foothold of manhood' (159). In not killing his father, Rondo refuses to accept his father's definition of manhood and in 'indicting' him, he shows that he now knows the life story of 'his father, the ex-minister'. The representation of Rwafa is, of course, biased towards the negative. The reader can speculate that, in his commitment to the liberation struggle, Rwafa might have been heroic, might have made good strategic decisions and would certainly have made sacrifices. However, his story is now part of an 'ugly' history and he belongs to the past, not the future. The priority for the middle generation of Selina and Rondo is to save the children, including the youth militia, not to avenge them.

Conclusion

In 'The Empty House', the theme of Mark Maneto's hold over his son is eclipsed at the end of the story by Gwizo's confrontation with Agatha. The difficulty in concluding the father/son relationship lies, in part, in the lack of consistency in the attitudes and positions adopted by Maneto. There is little to explain how the traditionalist and nationalist Maneto becomes the pragmatist who admires the Western expertise of Agatha. Maneto's use of his daughter-in-law can be seen as a satirical representation of the type of hypocritical man who will loudly advocate cultural purity while reaping the commercial benefits of collaborating with the 'enemy'. However, this representation seems slight and superficial when weighed against the themes of cultural identity and conflict that keep emerging in the story but which are left undeveloped. Given the rapid changes that have taken place in Zimbabwean society and politics since the story was written, it now seems like a historical piece and, despite the violent ending, there is something curiously innocent, at least on the surface, about its representation of a society in transition.

In contrast, 'The Sins of the Fathers' convincingly shows the tragic effect of perverted masculinity, tribalism and the political corruption of an unchanging nationalist ideology. The success of the story lies in its use of a self-effacing man as focaliser. The reader follows Rondo's trajectory and, with him, slowly and painfully uncovers the truth about the accident. Gagiano has asked whether Mungoshi's work is realist (2006: 132). In its use of Lukacsian types to reveal the underlying forces at work in Zimbabwean society, 'The Sins of the Fathers' can be seen as realist but there is also something here other than realism. In this, perhaps the darkest of Mungoshi's stories to date, the reader wants a sense of an ending, to know what happens after the Chekhovian pistol shot. Mungoshi does not, of course, provide this. However, in leaving the reader with the question 'what will happen next?', 'The Sins of the Fathers' is a literary intervention in a continuing political debate.

ENDNOTES

1 The military wing of the Zimbabwe African National Union (ZANU) was the Zimbabwe African Liberation Army (ZANLA). The military wing of the Zimbabwe African Peoples Union (ZAPU) was the Zimbabwe Peoples Revolutionary Army (ZIPRA). In 1980, the political party ZANU became the Zimbabwe African National Union (Patriotic Front) (ZANU-PF).
2 I am grateful to Irene Staunton for this information (e-mail of 4 September, 2006).
3 Musiyiwa and Matshakayile-Ndlovu, in their analysis of Shona literary representations of the Ndebele, quote Mutswairo's definition of *madzviti*, a derogatory term for Ndebele warriors, 'the lazy, lousy, wandering, greasy, stinking locusts' (2005: 77).
4 In 2001, the government set up youth militia camps intended to indoctrinate young Zimbabweans in patriotic history. Ranger has shown how the militia camps were intended to train young warriors who, unlike their parents and school teachers, would return to the liberation struggle for inspiration: in effect, 'the revolutionary spirit would skip a generation' (2004: 219).
5 When Chitepo was killed by a car bomb in 1975, the Zambian government set up a Commission to investigate his death. Its findings implicated some of the ZANU leadership, including Tongogara, but the Commission's methods were generally regarded as flawed, thus casting doubt on its conclusions. There is still no certainty as to whether Chitepo was killed by the Rhodesians or by members of ZANU. Tongogara was killed in an apparent road accident in 1979. He was said to be in favour of uniting ZANU and ZAPU and much speculation followed his death. In 2001, two government ministers, Moven Mahachi and Border Gezi, the organiser of the youth militia, were killed in accidents. There is no evidence that these were not accidents. However, 'accident' has resonances in ZANU-PF history.
6 White explains that the Report of the Chitepo Commission (1976), previously unpublished in Zimbabwe, was serialised in the independent newspaper, the Standard in what she describes as 'the anxious space' (2003: 100) between the parliamentary elections in 2000 and the presidential elections in 2002.

5

The strong healthy man: AIDS and self-delusion

LIZZY ATTREE

> *Historically, men, unlike women, have not needed to explore their own body image, because their relation with the world is not mediated by the body... Indeed, in order for men to preserve the hegemony of male power, it has been essential to keep the body at a safe distance, even if it cannot be rendered completely invisible. The body is always there, but rarely accorded (by men) its place as a fundamental structuring principle. Indeed, in order to retain their power, men have collectively refused to interrogate their bodies, which have thereby become unhealthily protected from public (and often private) scrutiny. Illness changes all that and makes the body urgently present, albeit in a state of deterioration and decay* (Worton, 2004: 157).

The nuanced presentation of conflict and perceptions of illness in selected short stories from Mungoshi's *Walking Still* (1997) and Kanengoni's *Effortless Tears* (1993), seek to establish a world in which war and violence are no longer the markers of power. The disruption of conventional gender roles is linked to the fragmentation of the nation and disillusionment with national structures, but Mungoshi's focus on individual stories symbolises and evokes new struggles. In contrast Kanengoni's focus on the brutality of war and its effect on the family exposes alterations and scars in the national psyche. By questioning the consequences for communities that abandon the land to join the liberation struggle, or are forced to commit patricide to express loyalty to a cause, Kanengoni unveils the barren heart of a nation whose masculinity has been usurped by a greater power: fear. How do men reclaim their lives and define themselves in these circumstances? Can masculinity survive with integrity when under pressure to survive in any form? Who are the heroes and saviours now? By comparing stories by these two great writers against the background of HIV/AIDS, it is possible to see the extent to which the depiction of the health of the individual male disrupts conceptions of a stable patriarchal masculinity that in turn upholds the hegemony of male power in the nation.

I would argue that part of the definition of a father figure relies on the identification of a son or daughter with a 'strong healthy man'. According to Freud the father figure is the first logical means by which we seek to identify masculinity in our formative years and yet Oliver Sacks might say that in the absence of a father figure or due to neurological damage, we could equally identify a hat stand with the masculine authoritative phallus that shapes our formation of self and identity. In other words the creation of gender norms is arbitrary or at least the accepted definitions of what constitutes masculinity in a patriarchal society is governed by the language and culture in which we live. I will bypass Lacan's abstract formulations of psycho-sexual development, to concur with Sacks that 'the study of disease and identity cannot be disjoined' (1986, x). This prompts the question: how does one formulate the masculinity of a father figure when that figure is absent, ill or dying? The male body is inextricably bound up with notions of masculinity and physical performance, sexual or otherwise; the body provides the dominant foundation for the initial separation of the sexes. Clichés such as that the female is the weaker sex are of course inaccurate, (particularly in Zimbabwe where women bear the majority of labour in the average household), studies of genetic diseases show that the 'X' chromosome is far less vulnerable to hereditary disease than the male 'Y' chromosome. However the myth of the 'strong healthy man' lingers in the imagination as the defining, if not the basic aspiration of men in most cultures. In Zimbabwe this is further linked with the hegemonic rhetoric of heroism that is deeply associated with violence and which valorises men in the context of the Second Chimurenga as 'war veterans' or 'sons of the soil'.

Above and beyond the social disruption of war, and in a quite different context Michael Worton evinces that:

> *As soon as the social structure is shaken, as it has been through such different phenomena as the creative challenges of feminism and the ravages of AIDS ... traditional certainties about masculinity begin to dissolve and the male body becomes the site of interrogation rather than of affirmation and confidence, and this means that masculinity needs to be increasingly recognised as a personal narrative or representation. However, this personalising of the body is no privatisation, no appropriation or imposition of power through secrecy and willed invisibility. It is a staging of difference, a play of and with representation that entails a repositioning of the question(s) of gender outside the traditional binary oppositions of male/female and heterosexual/homosexual* (Worton, 2004: 157).

In the case of Mungoshi's and to a lesser extent Kanengoni's short story collections it seems possible that their unique approaches to the construction of masculinity may be rooted in the 'shaking of the social structure'. Disruptions caused by colonialism, war, feminism and AIDS have undermined traditional understandings of gender roles and re-positioned the male body at the centre of a number of their narratives. I would argue that both writers play with representations of masculinity, favouring the personal, placing idiosyncratic, individualised narratives at the heart of their fiction.

The 'staging of difference' that Worton exhorts us to examine (in analysing a re-construction of gender) can be played out both in the external realities depicted in fictional narratives and in the psyche, such that interior monologues and perceptions are as important in both texts as 'actual' events in each story. The shaken social structure can also result in a fragmented sense of reality, such that a distorted view of the world is evoked by characters such as Paul in Kanengoni's 'Things We'd Rather Not Talk About'. By interrogating the vulnerability of the male body to damage or infection, whether externally or self-inflicted, and the consequences, both authors de-stabilise conventional notions of gender exemplified by 'the strong healthy man.' I will attempt to demonstrate my theory by analysing two of Mungoshi's stories from *Walking Still* 'Did You have to Go that Far?' and 'Of Lovers and Wives' and three of Kanengoni's stories from *Effortless Tears* 'Things We'd Rather Not Talk About', 'Men' and 'Effortless Tears'.

Throughout *Walking Still* Mungoshi eloquently problematises the apparently clear cut relations between men and women. In 'The Hare', 'The Empty House' and 'The Wedding Singer', real domestic and sexual power is shown to be in the hands of women who through family structures cleverly manipulate men into new positions by the end of each story. In 'The Empty House' this manipulation suggests a violent end for Agatha at the hands of the drunken, lazy but cuckolded artist Gwizo, ending with the spine-tingling lines 'Gently, his fingers encircled her neck' (104). In 'The Wedding Singer' the woman scorned by the promiscuous 'virginal' groom, sings of her ominous intentions towards both his new wife and the child she is carrying that will prove the groom's deceit and infidelity. Whereas these stories end with funerals pending, 'The Hare' begins the collection with a tale that ends on a disconcerting, polygamous but generally well-adjusted reconciliatory note. All three stories demonstrate the male characters are unaware of the implications of their behaviour and the machinations of female life around them.

The stories I will focus on contain much more self-aware male characters who undermine accepted constructs of masculinity in entirely different ways. 'Of Lovers and Wives' tells the story of Shami, Chasi and Peter, who, at first glance, have negotiated a *Jules et Jim* style love triangle to suit the needs of each person. However it soon becomes obvious that Shami has been unaware of the depth of the relationship in which she shares her husband Chasi with Peter. By choosing to focus on a loving depiction of homosexuality Mungoshi breaks all social and literary taboos in Zimbabwean culture[1] and flaunts a heart-breakingly poignant narrative in the faces of those who would deny same sex love relationships moral or emotional legitimacy. 'Did You have to Go that Far?', takes on three families from a child's perspective unmanning both fathers and sons in the process. The ability of the characters in this story to develop and change is anathema to a fixed notion of masculinity. One such discourse that has been entrenched in sexist masculine language is the discourse framing AIDS in Zimbabwe. I would argue that this hegemonic discourse is located in static ideas of Zimbabwean masculinity and acts as a defensive response to the threat of change.

Though *Walking Still* was published in 1997, misogynistic and indeed militaristic attitudes towards AIDS have apparently changed little as Retired Brigadier General David Chiweza brutally reminds us in *The Herald* on 27 July 2006 when he advocates mandatory HIV testing by any means necessary:

> *HIV must be stopped at all costs. To refuse to recognise and apply the minimum necessary force means the job remains undone. It means people will continue to infect each other ... The arguments for the use of force can be traced back in our history. When Rhodesian Prime Minister Ian Smith said there would be no black majority rule in a thousand years, the stage was set for the choice between the use of the necessary force to bring about independence or to remain in a perpetual time warp ... God is more interested in the fruit than the person or method that brings the fruit* (Chiweza, 2006: 10).

presumably 'God' would feel the same about rape, finding value only in the child, the 'fruit', regardless of the violent method used to bring about this progeny? It is the ZANU-PF ideology of the enemy-within that has been sublimated from White British and Rhodesian ideology, and is perhaps a natural human tendency (i.e. to formulate an 'other' in order to define your own identity) that I wish to highlight in Chiweza's rhetoric. He has apparently, as Fanon predicted, uncritically appropriated the hostile language and the mentality of the colonisers Zimbabweans once fought to liberate themselves from.

The legacy for linguistic framing of disease with metaphors of war, invasion and resistance is not uncommon particularly in relation to AIDS, as Sontag has documented in both *Illness as Metaphor* (1978) and *AIDS and its Metaphors* (1988). However Sontag is right to point out the flaws in such language, as 'the move from the demonization of the illness to the attribution of fault to the patient is an inevitable one.' (Sontag, 2002: 97) Although in Zulu culture the use of war metaphors has been relatively successful[2] as an educational medium in KwaZulu-Natal for example, it is the way in which those suffering with AIDS are associated with 'AIDS: the enemy' that has led to stigmatisation and ostracism that makes this language so dangerous. It also appeals to a largely masculine audience, who identify with the 'warriors' required to fight the disease, and does little to dissociate women (often seen as carriers of HIV, and subsequently subjected to enforced virginity testing) from 'the enemy', thus 'military metaphors contribute to the stigmatising of certain illnesses and, by extension, of those who are ill.' (97) The failure to associate compassion with those suffering from AIDS and the resulting distancing from and abstraction of those who are ill as enemies to be defeated, leads to misunderstandings and miscommunications of the dangers and risks associated with HIV infection. It is the binary 'them' and 'us' approach to HIV that has failed to eradicate the disease from both South Africa and Zimbabwe to date.[3]

Chiweza's tautologous, contradictory, self-defeating argument is particularly badly written, and he falls into all the traps that a violent nationalistic hyper-masculine, war-based rhetoric sets itself. His argument is self-defeating because to believe AIDS is 'other' and can be removed (by force) is to misunderstand the nature of the disease, which is transmitted in intimate sexual acts, often of love, and is intrinsically internal and undetectable in its initial manifestation and remains bound to the individual, from which it cannot be separated. The individual does not become less human once he or she is infected with HIV. To advocate destruction of the other is to advocate the ultimate destruction of oneself. It is the same trap that resists the acknowledgement that 'the strong healthy man' is vulnerable to infection and disease. The violent connotations of the 'Embryo Effect Strategy' (which is not explained) seems to suggest that HIV can be forcibly removed from 'our people'. At a time when vilification of those with AIDS is widespread, his solution to the pandemic seems analogous with utilitarian murder when he states:

> *The Embryo Effect Strategy is simply the principle of the minimum necessary force to kick HIV out of our people. Anything less is time wasting. Excessive is better than inadequate force and optimum force is the ideal.*

He places mandatory HIV testing alongside the 'heroic' land redistribution project[4] and Operation Murambatsvina,[5] which not only puts the infected in the same category as the apparently disposable whites ('the land had to be redistributed' and the 'dirty rubbish' of the poor 'litter is not needed in the city') but he also genders the debate. The 'embryos' and 'eggs' that he claims 'cannot be cracked with cotton wool' acquire a distinctly eugenic feel when he concludes that although the person 'who uses a hammer to crack an egg is ... in serious error ... History is more likely to forgive the one who erred in excessive force than the one who failed outright to do the job.' Which is like saying we must absolve the back-street abortionist who sterilises or kills the desperate women who visit him, (because at least this halts the spread of AIDS), rather than counsel and treat the pregnant, HIV-positive women who need ARVs and Nevarapine because they have been raped, infected and impregnated.

I am relieved the Brigadier General is retired, and yet his signature 'Till next week' haunts me with the threat of impending violence if I have not been tested in the meantime. Chiweza appears to advocate the necessary destruction of the people (particularly women) before the 'enemy' AIDS can be defeated. Perhaps that's what war and its rhetoric always amounts to? If it is not caught early and beaten into submission, presumably annihilation is his preferred solution to the potential devastation and suffering of wider infection. Castro had the same militaristic idea when he tested the entire Cuban population for HIV and confined to sanatoriums those whom he found to be positive.[6] Those who were HIV positive were treated as AIDS patients even if they did not actually become ill for many years. Meanwhile those who still remained vulnerable to infection were not educated with transmission and prevention information.

Suddenly the title of Mungoshi's story 'Did You have to Go that Far?' seems a pertinent question to ask when faced with cruel, inhuman cultural responses to possible infection with HIV. Staged on the micro-level the title refers to the threat of violence and its consequences. Admittedly the story touches on HIV and AIDS only briefly (naming the disease only as AIDS throughout) but it is in this illustration of the fear and confusion around the disease that wider cultural assumptions about masculinity and its relation to health are represented. Two young friends, Damba (the narrator) and Pamba overhear their mothers discussing their new neighbours: Mrs Gwaze and her son Dura. Their mothers' gossip leads the boys to believe that their neighbours are infected with 'the new disease' (52). This is based on the hearsay that 'her husband died mysteriously' (52) and their assumption that this must be because 'She has a disease. That's what killed him' (52). They quickly jump to also condemning her skinny son 'Look at that son of hers, do you think he will survive? ... He looks very sickly'. Having overheard, the boys' perceptions are understandably guided by this information, so that when Damba points out 'a frail boy ... in thick glasses and a very smart school uniform.' (52) Pamba soon quips 'He does look as if he is going to die soon, doesn't he?' The children's constructions of both health and difference, including the gendered element of both (which is prejudiced towards the illegitimacy of a single mother) are clearly influenced by their observations of their parents' words and behaviour. The power of rumour to create 'truth' based on misinformation is deftly observed.

Dura's masculinity as defined or limited by the other boys is based on the fact that he is a 'sickly' child and he does not fight but cries when provoked. His father is also absent and the source of the boys' taunts is 'Where is your father?', which is again clearly gendered in its presumptive blame of his mother for her husband's disappearance in their song 'Dura's mother, Dura's mother, ... Where did you put Dura's father?' (55). The trial and conviction of Dura as HIV positive is proven entirely on his physique, which for a boy his age is not strong and healthy looking enough. After claiming that she will just tell her son the truth, Damba's mother displays her ignorance or perhaps her failure to tackle a difficult issue directly in her 'explanation' of the 'truth of AIDS'. She first asks Damba if he knows what AIDS is? When he says 'people die from it.' She concords, adding 'Young or old, they die from it. Now listen very carefully. Keep away from the new people that have come to live next door.' (53) When Damba queries her and seeks confirmation of their suspicions by asking 'Have they got *AIDS!*' she parries confusingly 'I didn't say that' as if saying it would implicate her in some way, not only in spreading an unsubstantiated rumour, but also in naming such a deadly disease out loud. This is her way of telling the 'truth'. She continues 'just keep away from them if you don't want to die. Especially the son. You can see how thin he is?' (53) Not only is this a form of misguided but understandable protection of her son, it is also cruel in its admonition to isolate, even ostracise a sickly young boy. AIDS cannot be caught through casual contact, and although this is not pursued in this story, the lack of compassion towards anyone who appears weak or unwell displays a Darwinian tendency towards the survival of the fittest. The human ability to imagine and empathise with another person's pain is one of the traits that distinguishes us from animals. The boys are learning early on to disassociate themselves from signs of frailty and weakness.

Not only is Dura labelled with a disease that cannot be spoken of based on his puny size, but AIDS is fixed in the boys' imaginations as a disease that can be caught by proximity to an infected person: 'Pamba's mother told him the same thing. Pamba's mother *actually* said they had AIDS, and ordered Pamba not to go near the boy.' (53) The sexual element of the disease has been ignored completely, (presumably partly due to their age) although we can see by Damba's commentary on his eavesdropping that 'The women on our street – and anywhere else for that matter – didn't like women with children without visible husbands.' Of course the assumption is that this single mother will poach their husbands. Women are shown to have internalised a form of sexism that assumes male infidelity is inevitable.

The women not only assume a single woman will need a man, but they do not query why Mrs Gwaze is on her own or where her husband is. Not only is it possible that she doesn't have a husband either through death, divorce, abandonment for any number of reasons, or rape, but it also assumes that her position as single is isolated and unsustainable for survival in their neighbourhood. Intriguingly when Mrs Gwaze leaves at the end of the story Damba reports seeing 'a strange man at the wheel and Mrs Gwaze sitting beside him,' raising the possibility that Dura's father is still alive and has merely been away, or that Mrs Gwaze has a new partner.

As with the 'poisoned' chicken, Damba's 'dark epiphany' (Gagiano, 2006) by the end of the story reveals to him that as he grows up things are not always as they seem, Damba has learnt to interrogate the received notions of superstition and masculinity that he has accepted until now. Not only are appearances deceiving: Dura's thinness and vulnerability did not mean that he was HIV positive or indeed a sensitive boy without feelings who could not retaliate in kind, but the words of those he trusts describing those appearances can also be misleading '"The woman is a witch! A witch!" Pamba's mother was almost screaming ... "You see how thin that son of hers is? He shares his food with a huge python she keeps in a trunk in one of the rooms."' (57) It is not only Mrs Gwaze's status and the appearance of her son, but their comparative wealth which disturbs Mrs Dengu and fuels her jealous accusations of witchcraft: 'what do they need a house as big as that one for?' In this way Mungoshi not only allows Damba a series of epiphanies, but through Damba's elliptic child's perspective the reader also glimpses that there are wider, adult concerns governing the behaviour of the women in this community towards their new neighbour. Mungoshi also cleverly satirises belief in 'muti' and witchcraft by demonstrating the childish and foolhardy nature of those (both children and adults) who believe in its effects. However the power of this belief is still shown to have deadly consequences. The manipulation of language, the power of description, the fear of death and the belief in the power of language to define reality is the equivocal truth we are left with.

Whether Dura is HIV positive is hard to discern and not a central issue as the story unfolds, but he is admitted to hospital with a 'severe attack of pneumonia' (81) after Damba has pushed him into the river. Whether infection with HIV is the cause of his general weakness and ill-health is shown to be irrelevant compared to the vulnerability of the three boys to language. Their weakness is their ignorance rather than physical prowess. It is Pamba, the strongest, most vindictively physically violent of the three boys who dies, and yet Dura, whose assumed 'victim of AIDS' status is shown to be a misnomer for his apparent physical weakness. As readers we initially expect Dura to die by the end of the story, but it is his clear mental cunning that has cruel and perhaps unforeseen consequences for Pamba who foolishly believes in the 'poisoned' chicken that he stole and ate. For all his bravado Pamba is easily manipulated and seems only to see the bad in people, perhaps because his father does too.

The children have learnt their violent/unaccountable behaviour from their peers and from their fathers, who are frequently absent, always at Party meetings, and often come home drunk. The distinction between Pamba and Damba's fathers affects the boys and their fate. Damba eventually blames Pamba's father, as does his wife, who leaves him after her son's body is found. His failure to go out looking for his son highlights his negligence as a father, having preferred to go drinking than watch over his family. Then, having beaten his wife in her hysterical grief, he creates another single woman out on her own, Pamba's mother: 'walked out and walked down the street without looking back, or saying anything to the people who looked at her from their gates on our street. I never saw her again.' (81). She becomes the very thing she was so afraid of in Mrs Gwaze and yet was so reluctant to blame a man for. Damba's father on the other hand is kinder and more attentive and Damba is shown early on to already have a conscience that reflects a healthier emotional upbringing, still reliant on male power, but displaying a more nuanced version of masculinity.

A less innocuous exposition of involvement in the Party is staged in Kanengoni's 'Things We'd Rather Not Talk About' in which the relatively minor fear of violence (although it does result in the accidental death of Pamba) is thrown into sharp relief by the damaged, haunted suffering of Paul, who in a state of medicine-deprived paranoia relives the moment in which he was forced to kill his own father by the youth leader Amos or face certain death himself. Patricide in a patriarchal society is the ultimate crime, and in this instance it destroys the basis on which existence and identity is founded. Kanengoni illustrates Paul's vulnerability to severe trauma resulting in physical or mental ill-health, which has cyclically violent consequences. Violence is reinterpreted in the light of this re-contextualisation of masculinity – reconfiguring the motivation of violence into a response to castration or emasculation. This is further evidenced in the final story in the collection, 'Men', in which a husband's violence towards his wife is clearly shown to result from the frustration towards the abusive treatment he receives from his employer. Emasculated as a domestic worker he reasserts his masculinity by first cheating on his wife by getting drunk with a prostitute, realising 'He hated himself' (113) before beating his wife when she gives him cold food because he has failed to bring home money to buy paraffin. The story ends with Joramu's impotent cry:

How many times must I tell you that I am the man of this house? And how long will it take you to understand that? I will repeat it over and over again for you today: I am the man of this house. I am the man of this house. I am the man of this house! (114).

Like Pamba's father this husband is shown to be incapacitated and emasculated by alcoholism, a theme that recurs frequently in *Walking Still*. Although I have not space to illustrate it at great length at this point, alcoholism is also a disease that would fit with my theorisation of the re-conceptualisation of 'the strong healthy man'. Colonialism, war and poverty are potential root causes of the high incidence of alcoholism in places like Zimbabwe, however in each of Mungoshi's characters wider factors are not foregrounded, rather personal stories are staged to reveal each individual's unique weakness or susceptibility to such a debilitating illness.

A wholly different emasculation is staged in Mungoshi's 'Of Lovers and Wives' the title indicating the order of preference between the two. Undermining the most adulterous assertion of masculinity, the lover in question is not another woman, but a man – a double negation of both masculinity and femininity. Indeed, it is the fact of Chasi's homosexuality rather than his infidelity which is the issue in this marriage, both to his wife and those that might condemn him from the community. As Annie Gagiano points out it is an awkwardly achieved story 'somewhat coarse-grained in its texture' (Gagiano, 2006: 140), but Mungoshi exposes a fundamental flaw in the masculinity founded on or defined by the male's role as husband and father. He reveals the superficiality of such a socially sanctioned role – the deeper, primary position of 'lover' over 'wife' and thereby over 'husband' simultaneously undermines the 'natural' (Mungoshi, 1997: 108) sexual basis for marital union, placing it in direct opposition to the emotional and sexual love of a man for another man.

The human reaction when things are not 'right', they don't 'fit', when life isn't within our control, when someone is ill or behaving abnormally, can be to feel alienated. Shami drunkenly expresses this when she says 'I've been pushed to the periphery, to the place where the light ends, to the edge' (109). She is no longer at the centre, indeed the socially and religiously sanctioned heterosexual concept of marriage is no longer at the centre of this story. Perhaps Peter is more genuinely Chasi's wife? Anthony Chennells has identified the existential dilemmas in Mungoshi's work as 'alienation' which he writes 'takes many forms and can be transcended in many ways' (35). Alienation from the body is one of the forms an identity crisis can take. Whether symbolically or literally, the condition of the body can become emblematic of an identity crisis. The ability of the diseased or weakened state of one's own or another's body to reflect and encapsulate one's own fears of pain and mortality is a striking feature of both Kanengoni's and Mungoshi's fiction. The mere perception of abnormality is enough as

Mungoshi brilliantly illuminates in 'Of Lovers and Wives'. It is Chasi's body that gives him away to Shami 'You were calling out his name, smiling.' And when Shami quizzes Chasi on Peter's physical, sexual health: 'She had once asked Chasi if Peter was all right – biologically' (106) the irreverent laughter this generates soon silences her, though she does not understand the irony of their response.

Kizito Muchemwa notes that the tendency to root identity in the body is a form of Kristeva's notion of the 'abject' (Muchemwa, 2006: 41), but limits its reach to the construction of racial and ethnic identities or identification. This theorisation can be extended to perceptions of the 'abnormal', sick or diseased body in direct contrast to gender normification along the lines of 'the strong healthy man'. The ideal man, as we have seen, should not be absent, weak, sick, display paranoid delusions, express or enact love for another man (gayness is treated in many parts of the world as an illness to be cured), be a gay father, or die in a non-heroic fashion. But when the body is used as the 'fundamental structuring principle' it seems the body refuses to be contained in reductive structures.

By the end of her story, one cannot help but feel sympathy for Shamiso, who, notwithstanding her unbelievable blindness 'had loved Chasi so much that she had accepted Peter as part of her life without question.' She not only deluded herself, but learnt to live with the painful deception and loss of love; her husband has always been in love with Peter: 'she had found Chasi already in – a spade is a spade – Peter's arms when she married him' (106). But the affair is not condemned. Once she has poured out her heart, it is Peter who seems to do the honourable thing and leave; it seems he 'drove' himself into the Mupfure River, perhaps out of guilt for Shamiso's pain, to which he was apparently an unwitting accomplice: 'Peter couldn't believe she hadn't known' (106). The cause remains ambiguous: whether it was an accident, or the strain of hiding an illicit love from the rest of the community, it seems they both believed that 'There is no other way.' (110). When all of these possibilities finally take their toll, the 'natural' order of the world is finally restored. In the process fixed notions of masculinity have been challenged.

Confirmation of this restoration of the 'natural' order comes in the final paragraph when the narrator confirms 'There could be no question about the rightness of certain situations, under certain circumstances,' (111) which as a resolution, is as much a compromise as the marriage itself. It also proves that 'rightness' is not an absolute truth, but subject to different contexts. Sadly it seems Shamiso did love Chasi, but not as deeply as Peter, so when she consents to what amounts to a separation after Peter's death 'Shamiso felt that that too had its own fitting rightness.' Perhaps it would have been more honest, or more respectful to have separated earlier, but of course this would have been impossible for Chasi if it had been to live with Peter. As we have been shown on numerous occasions, women without husbands or men without at least one wife, are considered suspicious in the patriarchal masculinity of Zimbabwe. When these structures also require children to cement the bond between man and wife and confirm the primacy of the patriarchy, legitimating the marriage itself, we must ask what models of masculinity these children imbibe and inherit? The resounding ambiguity of this tale leaves both masculine and feminine identities in perpetual flux.

Interestingly, Mungoshi's tale does not raise the subject of HIV infection as a possible consequence not only of the infidelity, but of a 'deviant' sexual relationship. I would not normally make what could be conceived as a stereotypical correlation between homosexual narratives and their frequent association with AIDS if it was not to make the more specific point, that in Zimbabwe, not only are there very few fictional narratives about homosexuality in general,[7] but there are *none* which relate homosexuality to AIDS. Kanengoni's 'Effortless Tears' demonstrates one of the key reasons why this is the case when he uses the event of a funeral to broach the subject of AIDS. AIDS in Zimbabwe is spread primarily through heterosexual transmission and it is this well-known fact that is still not tackled with any change of behaviour that the author laments in this story.

The rapid heterosexual transmission of HIV was apparently so obvious in 1990 when the story was first published in *The Herald* that it was given the less enigmatic title 'The Writing is on the Wall'. The author believes the story, published as 'Effortless Tears' in 1993, is still pertinent today almost twenty years after it was written:

> *there is a degree of openness now ... because I do not think there is any family that has not been affected by now ... there are tragic stories of entire families wiped out with just a single member or two remaining ... But I find it very interesting actually that even in that acceptance, people still don't want to say AIDS.* [8]

Kanengoni opens the first published story on AIDS in Zimbabwe with the second sentence: 'Almost everyone there knew that George had died of an Aids-related illness but no one mentioned it' (71). He goes on to explode the dominant, patriarchal response, which is to deny the truth of what has happened. First 'The preacher told the parable of the Ten Virgins' (73). Second, George's Grandfather 'mourned the strange doings of this earth ... such were the weird ways of witches and wizards that they preferred to pluck the youngest'. Third, George's father 'talked of an invisible enemy that had sneaked into our midst and threatened the very core of our existence' before fourth and finally George's wife, who was 'beyond weeping', speaks of 'a need for moral strength during such critical times'. The narrator admits 'We were not weeping for the dead. We were weeping for the living' (73) thereby acknowledging what everyone else has failed to, that George's surviving wife is also infected with HIV.

The dominant masculine patriarchal voices in this story are shown to be impotent and fearful of the truth as it would involve changing their entrenched concepts of masculinity. For example, the narrator criticises his uncle's cowardice as 'He never mentioned the word 'Aids', the acronym A.I.D.S.' (73) and yet this disease has killed his son. After the funeral the village chairman of the Party speaks, as does George's younger brother and the Methodist lay-preacher, all men, all without mentioning AIDS until 'inevitably, Aids came up. It was a topic that everyone had been making a conscious effort to avoid' (75) and yet even when it comes up 'Everyone referred to it in indirect terms: that animal, that phantom, that creature, that beast.' We have seen in 'Did You have to Go that Far?' that such evasion is fertile ground for confused misapprehension. The narrator reveals that the favouring of euphemisms 'was not out of any respect for George. It was out of fear and despair.' The constant evasion of a subject that would undoubtedly force all of the men present to change their own ideas of acceptable behaviour causes a rupture in the narrator's conscience: 'Something in me snapped.' And yet he does not break the silence in the reality of the story itself, but in writing the story and identifying this silence Kanengoni, via the narrator, instigates change. He uses an alienated stance to destabilise the notions of masculinity that remain disrupted in the event of the funeral itself, in the fabric of the narrative that frames the story. In particular he draws attention to the decimated physique 'that thread, that bundle of skin and bones' (74) of his dead cousin, equating the guests' refusal to view George in his coffin and acknowledge the deterioration of his body with the silent refusal to say AIDS or acknowledge that it could have been George's 'Mr Bigstuff' style that caused him to contract the deadly disease, which he has certainly passed on to his wife. The inability to condemn what amounts to murderous behaviour, is identified as misplaced support of the *status quo* and tacit consent to the death of the people: 'soon there will be no one to bury anybody.' (75) The failure to address the flaws of such fixed notions of masculinity is shown to be a threat to humanity as a whole.

To conclude, 'the strong healthy man' can be said to embody the potent lethal warrior, the strong labourer, the authoritarian father, the loyal son, and the promiscuous beer-drinking Party member but in these stories these hitherto valorised categories have been disrupted with the alternative strengths of wisdom, empathy, sensitivity, understanding and love. The broad spectrum of these unstable, moveable identities, perpetually in flux are what comprise masculinity in Zimbabwe today. A logical outcome of the continued reliance on a dominant hyper-masculine discourse, is total destruction. By beginning the process of 'un-manning' the Zimbabwean nationalist driven construction of male identity, these writers deconstruct one-dimensional notions of masculinity, unveiling compassionate, multi-faceted layers beneath 'the strong healthy man', such that it is not that he is no longer strong, but that this strength need not be one of force and indeed may lie in recognising his weaknesses. If the body is taken as the 'fundamental structuring principle' then the frailty of this body must be acknowledged. A new heroism lies in an individual taking responsibility for his own health, that of his wife and children and in doing so, the health of the nation. This would undoubtedly contribute to a form of women's liberation in Zimbabwe but which, while under the control of the unreconstructed 'strong healthy man', has little room for survival. The 'staging of difference' in fiction is part of the essential beauty of literature to imagine other worlds, to bring possible and impossible worlds into existence. More recently published anthologies such as *We Are the Herb* (2001) and *Nobody ever said AIDS* (2004) demonstrate that writers are now tackling and imagining the issue of AIDS more directly. Each human being contains at least one world. It is essential to uncover the versatility, and illimitable nature of these ways of being in order that we are not resigned or confined to our fate, kicked into submission, as Chiweza would have Zimbabweans 'kick HIV out of our people'. There is strength in weakness; after all, why not fear death, who does not die? Facing mortality, the vulnerability and susceptibility of the human body to disease, and changing one's attitudes in order to deflect the power of fear, can be the only way to survive.

ENDNOTES

1. Its publication is only pre-dated by Madanhire's *If the Wind Blew* (1996) by one year, of which Drew Shaw exclaims 'This articulation of gay sexual preference on the pages of mainstream Zimbabwean literature is a milestone. Moreover, it confounds stereotypes because Hebrew is not only black and gay but also classically masculine: good-looking, fit, strong and virile – an 'ordinary' man' (Shaw: 280).
2. This year's UNAIDS Epidemic Update suggests that HIV prevalence among young people in South Africa may be stabilising but life expectancy in KwaZulu-Natal has fallen below 50 <www.unaids.org > (11).
3. Approximately one in five adults in Zimbabwe is living with HIV. Life expectancy in Zimbabwe is 34 for women, 37 for men (11) A large proportion of South Africans do not believe they are at risk; approximately two million South Africans living with HIV do not know that they are infected and believe they face no danger of becoming infected. <www.unaids.org> (13).
4. In November 2001 the Zimbabwean government amended the Land Acquisition Act to allow it to allocate land without giving the owners the right to contest the seizures. The reclaiming of white-owned farms by force in order to

'redistribute' land to the black population was violent and has been largely unsuccessful in redistributing wealth; the resulting political instability and neglected, uncultivated land are cited as the cause for the current economic crisis in Zimbabwe, which with inflation at over 1200 per cent (at the time of writing) is the highest in the world.

5. Murambatsvina, meaning 'clear away the rubbish', was a government initiated clearance of housing instigated in May 2005. The choice of name contained echoes of Gukuruhundi, meaning 'to blow away the chaff', which is the name given to the massacre of 20,000 civilian Ndebele people by Mugabe's 5th Brigade in 1982, justified as necessary to quell dissidence and protect the formation of the new nation of Zimbabwe.

6. For more on Cuba's controversial policies towards AIDS in the 1980s and 1990s see Leiner, 1994. Kruger also usefully elaborates on the colonial ideology of divide and rule that via medical discourses we can see has been re-appropriated in modern Zimbabwe. He quotes Haraway: 'Expansionist Western medical discourse in colonizing contexts has been obsessed with the notion of contagion and hostile penetration of the healthy body, as well as of terrorism and mutiny from within. This approach to disease involved a stunning reversal: the colonised was perceived as the invader' (Simians, Cyborgs, and Women, 223) (Kruger, 1996: 40) demonstrating the double-speak that enables the colonisers to fear invasion from those they have invaded.

7. For more on homosexuality in Zimbabwean writing see Shaw, 2006 and Epprecht, 2004.

8. Interview with Kanengoni 4 August 2006.

6

Fatherhood and nationhood: Joshua Nkomo and the re-imagination of the Zimbabwe nation

SABELO J. NDLOVU-GATSHENI

Introduction

This chapter explores the metamorphosis of Joshua Nkomo from 'father of dissidents' into the 'founding father' of Zimbabwe in the context of posthumous, politically motivated rewriting of the roles played in the struggle for independence by departed Zimbabwean nationalists (White, 2003). The focus is on the metamorphosis that took place in the period 1980-99, involving three levels of representation which are shot through with instrumental deconstruction and reconstruction processes. These deconstructions and reconstructions include Nkomo as the opposition leader of Patriotic Front-Zimbabwe African People's Union (PF-ZAPU) marked by his reduction to a 'father of dissidents' who was bent on destabilising Zimbabwe. Nkomo carried this negative representation until a time when he decided to dismantle PF-ZAPU in the wake of unprecedented state-sanctioned political violence that engulfed the Matebeleland and Midlands provinces and the second electoral defeat of PF-ZAPU by ZANU-PF in the general elections of 1985. This culminated in the Unity Accord of 22 December 1987 and the official swallowing of PF-ZAPU by ZANU-PF.

This move by Nkomo to unite with ZANU-PF fell neatly into Robert Mugabe's drive for a one-party state. He was soon represented by the president as a typical example of a selfless nation-builder who favoured peace and unity over and above personal political ambition. That he was the 'father of dissidents' became water under the bridge and the new Nkomo moved onto the centre stage of Zimbabwe mainstream politics, firstly as Senior Minister in the President's Office and later as the Second Vice-President of Zimbabwe, a position he held up until his death on 1 July 1999. The day he died, a third representation of Nkomo as 'Father Zimbabwe' and a 'Hero of Heroes' soon emerged as a result of political engineering by Mugabe who was comfortable with the dead. Mugabe became an advocate of a necrophilic imagination of the nation which was based on a sanitised and reinvented past. After Nkomo's death, and for the first time, Mugabe acknowledged that Nkomo was the founder of the nationalist liberation struggle and posthumously accorded him the long-contested and denied status of 'Father Zimbabwe'. Nkomo became the key symbol of national unity in Zimbabwe.

This chapter is therefore a study in representation, hegemony and commemoration, all predicated on the use of Nkomo in the re-imagination of the Zimbabwean nation. It is partly about how nationalist heroes are used by ruling elites for political renewal, and forging the nation and national unity as well as power consolidation in the midst of a political and economic crisis.

Nationalism and founding fathers

Ernest Renan (1990) defined a nation as a soul and a spiritual principle founded on sacrifices. In Zimbabwe, the two co-vice-presidents of the country were given different statuses at death in the narration of the nation. Nkomo was remembered as the 'Father of the Nation/Father Zimbabwe' and Simon Muzenda was described as the 'Soul of the Nation'. While these two nationalist politicians were being elevated to the centre of the national pantheon, heroes like Josiah Tongogara, Herbert Chitepo, Jason Moyo, Alfred Nikita Mangena and others were gradually being excluded from the post-colonial historical record. New heroes like Border Gezi, Cain Nkala and Chenjerai Hunzvi associated with the Third Chimurenga were being written into history, particularly the narrowly defined 'Patriotic History' (Ranger, 2004). The complex politics of 'creating national heroes' is well treated by Norma Kriger (1995).

The idea of the 'creation of national heroes' dovetails with Benedict Anderson's (1983) popular concept of nations as 'imagined communities'. Nations just like heroes are not pre-existing entities but are imagined and created. Forging a nation includes the instrumental use of the media, the educational system, administrative regulations, propaganda, sometimes outright lies and carefully selected fragments of history. This theoretical intervention by Anderson is very useful in understanding the articulation of hegemonies in and through media where the reconstructed legacy of Nkomo is today repeatedly used in order to invoke the idea of him as the 'father' of Zimbabwe. The re-imagination of the nation has taken the form of a family epic where Mugabe is the practical creator of what Nkomo founded and is the leading ideologist and articulator of Zimbabweanism. This is clearly laid out in the book *Inside the Third Chimurenga* (2001) consisting of Mugabe's 'enlightened' speeches.

At death Nkomo was useful for purposes of re-imagination of the Zimbabwean nation in ways favourable to ZANU-PF's hegemonic purposes. Numerous obituaries and televised oral reflections emerged, competing to re-situate Nkomo in the long struggle for independence and the general political history of Zimbabwe. Leading intellectual commentators of various persuasions immediately embarked on instant analyses of the politics of the day in the context of Nkomo's political career and death. Nkomo became a political saint, a torch-bearer of the liberation struggle, and a selfless freedom fighter whose legacy was to be emulated by every patriotic Zimbabwean. The current conception of the Zimbabwean nation is as a system of representation articulated in and through history and media. Nkomo's political career has been redefined into a macrocosm of the whole struggle for Zimbabwe.

Triple metamorphosis of Joshua Nkomo

The context of the triple metamorphosis of Nkomo took place within the continuation of what Masipula Sithole (1999) described as 'struggles within the struggle' mutating into 'struggles after the struggle'. As I have noted elsewhere (2006: 345-96), nationalist rivalry took the form of personality clashes thus making the whole nationalist struggle assume the form of factions, internal governments-in-waiting and externally based governments-in-waiting. Besides personality clashes, the use of tribalism and ethnicity led to numerous splits as well as proved and alleged assassinations. These occurrences prompted Sithole (1999) to describe the nationalist liberation struggle as 'a revolution that ate its own children'.

The first level of representation of Nkomo covers the period 1980-87 where he was portrayed as the enemy of Zimbabwe bent on using his ex-Zimbabwe People's Revolutionary Army (ZIPRA) combatants to destabilise the country and topple the ZANU-PF government. All this was taking place against the background of Nkomo, the leader of PF-ZAPU, who had lost the first independence elections to Mugabe. This period saw some disgruntled ex-ZIPRA combatants 'going back to the bush', introducing what became known as the dissident era in Zimbabwe. This portrayal of Nkomo as 'father of dissidents' set the stage for a systematic, violent campaign against PF-ZAPU, Joshua Nkomo and ZIPRA combatants, which became known as the Gukurahundi (a Shona term for the Storm that sweeps away the chaff, paving way for the normal rainy season), and was marked by the massacre of about 20,000 Ndebele-speaking people. Nkomo and his largely Ndebele supporters were the 'chaff' that needed to be swept away. K. P. Yap (2001) focussed specifically on the politics of 'uprooting the weeds, power, violence and ethnicity' in Matebeleland in the period 1980-87. Alexander et al (2000) and Ndlovu-Gatsheni (2003) also engaged with the issue of violence in Matebeleland and the Midlands in the 1980s.

The violence against PF-ZAPU, demonisation of Joshua Nkomo and attempts at writing ZIPRA out of the liberation struggle, was taking place at a crucial time of nation-building by ZANU-PF. Nation-building took the form of power-building and legitimacy-seeking processes. It looked as if winning elections was not enough as a legitimacy builder for Mugabe. ZANU-PF faced four main challenges, namely a defeated Father Zimbabwe with a military force able to destabilise the new republic; the competing armies of ZIPRA, ZANLA and Rhodesian forces, which needed either to be demobilised or integrated into one national army; white-controlled state institutions, and a white-owned private sector. In Nkomo and PF-ZAPU, ZANU-PF faced a strong counter-hegemonic force based in Matebeleland, a fertile ground for alternative sovereignty derived from the pre-colonial independent Ndebele state. The whites on the other hand constituted a sub-hegemonic force that was not yet properly demobilised and in whose hands the economy was still placed and whose military force was still intact.

ZANU-PF's nation-building efforts slanted heavily towards what Kriger (2003: 75-77) termed 'a party-nation and a party-state' where it sought to make itself and its guerrillas (ZANLA) the base of the nation and the state. This was indicated by promotion of ZANLA, party songs, symbols, and slogans as national and state business rather than party politics. The national broadcaster soon highlighted the contributions of ZANU-PF and ZANLA to the liberation of Zimbabwe to the exclusion of PF-ZAPU and ZIPRA. Despite the proclamation of the policy of reconciliation and the creation of a coalition government including PF-ZAPU and Nkomo as the Minister of Home Affairs, ZANU-PF worked hard to seek ways of representing Nkomo, PF-ZAPU and ZIPRA as enemies of Zimbabwe. This involved down-playing the contribution of PF-ZAPU and ZIPRA to the liberation of Zimbabwe.

The first opportunity to move openly against PF-ZAPU, ZIPRA and Joshua Nkomo was availed by guerrilla faction fighting, which pitted ZIPRA and ZANLA against each other in Chitungwiza, Entumbane, Ntabazinduna, Glenville and Connemara Assembly Points (APs) between 1980 and 1981. ZANU-PF leaders quickly apportioned blame on PF-ZAPU leaders whom Eddison Zvobgo, a ZANU-PF stalwart described as 'rabble-rousers and political malcontents who were still licking their wounds as a result of having lost the elections ...' (*The Chronicle*, 11 November 1981). The second opportunity was availed by the arms caches in PF-ZAPU-owned properties near Bulawayo in 1982. This incident led to the crumbling of the veneer of Government of National Unity (GNU) forged in 1980.

Nkomo was dismissed from the government in 1982. On 10 March 1982, ZIPRA's two wartime commanders, Dumiso Dabengwa and Lookout Masuku, were arrested on the grounds of plotting to topple the ZANU-PF government. Other PF-ZAPU cabinet ministers were withdrawn from the coalition government. ZANU-PF indeed took advantage of the situation to completely discredit Nkomo. What followed were witch-hunts within the army forcing terrified ZIPRA cadres to flee to the bush, where they were labelled 'dissidents.' Enos Nkala, a leading anti-Nkomo, ZANU-PF politician, told a rally in Bulawayo that the party's task 'from now is to crush Joshua Nkomo' whom he castigated as a 'self-appointed Ndebele king' (*The Herald*, 4 July 1980). In the midst of sporadic detentions of ZIPRA, PF-ZAPU leaders, disappearances of civilians from Matebeleland and murder of many others, Nkomo was represented as Dzimudewere (a Shona diminutive vulgarisation of Nkomo's large stature as a big, boring and useless Ndebele political figure), implying a Ndebele tribal leader bent on destabilising Zimbabwe because of power hunger. ZANU-PF slogans became openly hostile to ZIPRA, Nkomo and the Ndebele-speaking people. The slogans included Pasi ne Machuwachuwa (Down with ZIPRA), Pasi nevanematumbu (a Shona slogan meaning, 'Down with those with big stomachs', a reference to Nkomo's big stomach), and Pasi neVadzvinyiriri (a Shona slogan meaning, 'Down with oppressors', a reference to Ndebele raids on the Shona in the nineteenth century). This slogan is quoted in *The Herald* of 7 November 1980.

The move to deconstruct Nkomo, PF-ZAPU and ZIPRA can be summarised as: First, PF-ZAPU and ZIPRA were said to have made a very minimal contribution to the liberation struggle. Nkala put it in these words, 'They contributed in their small way and we have given them a share proportional to their contributions' (*The Herald*, 4 July 1980). PF-ZAPU was said to have committed very few of its trained forces to the front, keeping the bulk of its well-trained personnel in Zambian camps for purposes of staging a *coup d'etat* once ZANU-PF was in power (Brickhill, 1995). Second, Joshua Nkomo's nationalist credentials were attacked. He was described as a coward who always escaped imprisonment by going overseas; a vacillating politician who continued to negotiate with Ian Smith up to 1976; a man who only reluctantly embraced the armed struggle. Another ZANU-PF politician Edgar Tekere went to the extent of telling a rally that he had been trying to depose Nkomo since 1961, confirming the long history of nationalist rivalry and power struggles. He went on to mock Joshua Nkomo in a rhetorical manner saying, 'Do you know what war is, dear Nkomo?' (*The Herald*, 4 July 1980)

ZANU-PF's plans to crush Nkomo culminated in the deployment of the notoriously violent Fifth Brigade in Matebeleland and the Midlands regions ostensibly to deal with 'dissidents'. Its operations turned out to involve hunting down of PF-ZAPU leaders, indiscriminate attacks on Ndebele-speaking civilians, and killing of ex-ZIPRA combatants. The full-scale details of the operations are given in the Catholic Commission for Justice and Peace (CCJP) and The Legal Resources Foundation's (LRF) publication, *Breaking the Silence: Building True Peace: Report on the Disturbances in Matebeleland and the Midlands 1980-1988* (1997). What needs to be added is that the intention of ZANU-PF was to destroy once and for all Nkomo's support base and to force the Ndebele-speaking people to support ZANU-PF. This was confirmed by the forcible distribution of ZANU-PF party cards in Matebeleland and the Midlands (Ndlovu-Gatsheni, 2003). Those people found without these cards suffered at the hands of the notorious Fifth Brigade. Wartime ZANLA *pungwes* (a Shona term for night vigils during which ZANLA guerrillas politicised people and, together with the people, they sang liberation war songs as a morale booster) were inaugurated in Matebeleland and the Midlands, characterised by demonisation of Nkomo and valorisation of Mugabe. The coercive construction of a 'party-nation and party-state' was premised on the deconstruction of Nkomo's legacy and stature. This deconstruction had begun since the nationalist split of 1963 and it reached its zenith in the 1980s when ZANU-PF acquired control of the state.

The politics of self-representation and self-construction

Nkomo's book *Nkomo: The Story of My Life* must be read as part of his self-representation. It was written while he was in exile in Britain in 1983. It forms a part of political self-construction in the midst of hostile deconstruction. In the book, Nkomo re-claims the Father Zimbabwe title through some historical justifications, and careful and selective mapping out of personal contributions to the liberation of Zimbabwe. The book is also a rebuttal of criticisms leveled against him by his opponents. Nkomo (1984: xii) clearly states that:

> *This book is not a history – one day, if I am spared, I may contribute to the writing of one with a happy ending. Instead it is the personal record of a life that played a part in history, and it is also the work of an active politician who wishes to see things change for the better in the lives of the ordinary people in his country. I have been called 'Father Zimbabwe'. Whether I deserve that title is not for me to say. But by a dozen years in prison and half as many in exile I believe I have earned the right to speak for freedom while it is still endangered – this time not by far-off colonial rulers, nor by a settler population who will, I hope, now play their full part as citizens of a new nation, but by my former colleagues in the liberation struggle.*

He added that 'the leaders of the party that won (by unquestionable means, but let that pass for now) our first elections believed that I symbolised the national unity that they rejected. So I became the focus of their anger, perhaps of their envy' (ibid.). There is no doubt from these excerpts that Nkomo wrote from the perspective of a bitter politician who felt persecuted after working so hard for the country. He clearly states that he was called Father Zimbabwe and justifies it on the basis of his detention and exile years. Nkomo thought perhaps he was being persecuted because of 'envy' that he symbolised the totality of the struggle for Zimbabwe and that he stood for the national unity that ZANU-PF rejected the very day they broke away from ZAPU in 1963. His opening remarks in the book set the tone for the importance of the title Father Zimbabwe in nationalist rivalry prior and after independence.

Nkomo represented himself as a cultural nationalist and a man of the people who symbolised and cherished African traditional norms and religious beliefs. He became a member of the Kalanga Dawn Society (KDS), Matebele Home Society (MHS) and Southern Rhodesia African National Congress (SRANC) and his politics included appropriating Kalanga, Ndebele and Shona territorial symbols. Terence Ranger (1999) observed that among the Kalanga-speaking people in Kezi, Nkomo was a Kalanga and he behaved as such, among the Ndebele in Bulawayo, Nkomo was an Ndebele and he behaved as such, and among the Shona in Harare, he was a Zimbabwean. In his book, he described himself as a 'native son' and provides details on his African roots and his attraction 'to the traditional religion of our people'. This culminated in Nkomo visiting the Dula Mwali cult shrine in the Matopos Hills in the 1950s. This shrine has been used by pre-colonial leaders as a source of legitimacy and was consulted for divine advice. Nkomo's visit was to ask Ngwali (Ndebele term for mountain God) to assist them as nationalists to get back the country from the colonialists and to get blessings for the nationalist struggle.

One sees Nkomo's claim to be Father Zimbabwe taking him to a point where he appropriates ritual powers so as to mythologise himself as the true inheritor of a chain of power that stretched from pre-colonial times only to be disturbed by colonial rule. Nkomo portrays himself as a keeper of national ritual secrets that other nationalists did not even know. Nkomo's ritualisation was further cemented in 1962, when a Shona spirit-medium presented him, on behalf of the freedom fighters of the 1896-97 uprising, with a ceremonial axe, a symbol of resistance. He was also given the title Chibwechitedza (a Shona term for slippery stone). Nkomo was described thus because he was said to be adept at hiding from the colonial police and indeed he evaded arrest many times. Nkomo includes a picture of the spirit-medium handing over the ritual axe to him.

Until his death Nkomo associated himself with Matopos Shrines (Njelele) and carried a short knobkerrie wherever he went as a symbol of African traditional culture. He was very careful not to reduce the struggle for independence to a war between blacks and whites. He preferred to speak of a struggle against oppression rather than against whites. One is led to suggest that perhaps he was conscious not to repeat the Ndebele King Lobengula's mistakes as advised by the Dula shrine. When he returned from exile in 1980, he went to the shrines for a ritual ceremony and to report that the struggle was over and the country was now back with its original owners (Ranger 1999a). These shrines were and are still revered by traditionalists who believe that Ngwali resides there. At times of natural disaster and crisis like drought, the shrines are visited for divine advice. They are today largely visited for rain-making ceremonies.

Throughout the struggle for Zimbabwe, Nkomo kept the option of negotiations open. In his book, Nkomo emphasised the fact that he was forced by circumstances beyond his power to take up arms against white-settler belligerence and their refusal to embrace the peaceful option. Nkomo gives details of his education, harassment by settler police, his travels, negotiations with the settler government, exile life, how he ran ZIPRA, ZIPRA strategy, the Lancaster Conference negotiations, betrayal and post-colonial problems. He takes care to explain issues such as overseas trips and warns that they were not always comfortable. Nkomo (1984: 75) goes to the extent of saying by 1957, 'I was still the only ANC leader with a passport.' He justifies why he was the only one who attended to ANC (African National Congress) business outside Rhodesia. He was at pains to explain why he traveled outside the country so frequently, in order to counter his opponents' view that he was escaping detention. Thus his book is full of detailed objectives, as well as information about the problems he met while popularising the Rhodesian crisis.

Nkomo also includes details of his acquaintances and contemporaries, those whom he met and worked with in the struggle against colonialism. The list includes Kwame Nkrumah, Tom Mboya, Nelson Mandela, Sir Seretse Khama, Holden Roberto, Kenneth Kaunda, and many others. His intention was to alert his readers to his rightfulness to the leadership of Zimbabwe, like other continental leaders who assumed power at the departure of colonialists. One is also given the impression that Joshua Nkomo is projecting himself as a supra-nationalist who ranks alongside luminaries of the broader pan-Africanist struggle in Africa.

Chapter 10 of Nkomo's book is even more important in that he explains how he acquired the first guns that were brought to Rhodesia and how this was the first step in the direction of armed struggle. According to Nkomo the first arms for the liberation of the country entered Rhodesia in 1962. They were 24 semi-automatic assault rifles, with magazines and ammunition, plus some grenades. Nkomo sourced these from Egypt. The importance of this detail must be interpreted as a counter to ZANU-PF claims that they inaugurated the armed struggle in Zimbabwe and their attempt to present the death of seven ZANLA guerrillas at Sinoia in 1966 as the beginning of the armed struggle.

Nkomo explains the 1963 split in ZAPU along purely tribal lines, plus the interference of Julius Nyerere who 'had a special problem with me personally'. He squarely blames Washington Malianga and Leopold Takawira for influencing younger politicians like Robert Mugabe to split the party (Nkomo, 1984: 109-119). In other words, Nkomo projects himself as a symbol of unity and his opponents as tribalists who were just power hungry.

The last sections of Nkomo's book detail how he worked for unity and how Mugabe frustrated all his efforts. He bemoans the untimely death of General Josiah Magama Tongogara whom he saw as similarly committed to unity (Nkomo, 1984: 201). The popular view is that Tongogara was a victim of political assassination. One can interpret Nkomo's openly expressed admiration as a consequence of a shared political victimhood. It could be that Nkomo was using this instance to question ZANU-PF's political innocence even when it came to their own rank and file. The advocates of unity became victims of ZANU-PF violence and dirty tricks.

By discrediting such machinations within ZANU-PF, Nkomo projects himself as a real statesman and a true nation builder who was also a victim of power-hungry politicians. This projection is evident in his statement that, 'To me the most important fact appeared to be that we had fought the war on the same side, negotiated as one, and been victorious. It seemed a great disservice to the people of Zimbabwe to launch their independent history divided by party quarrels, not united by national feeling' (Nkomo, 1984: 203).

When Nkomo came home in 1980, he modeled himself as a real statesman as he began to talk of the war that was over, the need to forget the past, reconciliation and collective nation-building. Even when he lost the elections, he refused to be a 'Savimbi of Zimbabwe'.

In his last chapter, Nkomo grapples with issues of governance in postcolonial Africa in general and Zimbabwe in particular and concludes with a plea for national reconciliation. He wrote two letters to Robert Mugabe containing a call for a process of reconciliation. His last words were those of an optimist and nation builder par excellence. Nkomo (1984: 252) made these closing remarks:

> *It is not too late to change all that, to muster the collective energy of our people and build the new Zimbabwe we promised through all those long years of suffering and struggle. During my brief exile in 1983 I appealed in this sense to Prime Minister Robert Mugabe, calling as a start for a national conference of all the country's interest groups, under his chairmanship, to begin the process of reconciliation. He did not answer then.*

> *Perhaps in the interval between writing this book and its publication he will change his mind and reply constructively. For my part, I shall continue working to that end. Long Live Zimbabwe!*

Nkomo left the Prime Minister with a challenge to either choose the path of violence and chaos or reconciliation and nation building. For his part he had made his wishes clear to his readers. He gives the impression of being a committed nation builder. One can say his efforts were rewarded in the form of the Unity Accord of 22 December 1987. That way Nkomo maintained his credentials as Father Zimbabwe and gained a lot of sympathisers and supporters.

The post-unity accord period saw Nkomo serving the country loyally. He clearly presented his understanding of unity as a process rather than an event. Together with Mugabe, Nkomo traveled around the country selling the idea of unity to the mainstream Zimbabwean population. Mugabe and Nkomo had photographs taken together with their hands raised high; the local people, regional leaders and the international community hailed them as statesmen and nation builders. It seemed Mugabe also enjoyed being associated with such statesmanship. In reality his celebration was of victory over Joshua Nkomo. Thus in the post-unity accord period ZANU-PF did not waste time, the gospel of unity preached by Nkomo was seized and appropriated as a justification for the one-party-state agenda in Zimbabwe. The 1990s were dominated by debates on this topic and on democracy in the country. The main contours of that debate were well captured by Ibbo Mandaza and Lloyd Sachikonye in their book, *The One-Party State and Democracy: The Zimbabwe Debate* (1991). Joshua Nkomo decided to keep his mouth shut on this issue, leading Mugabe to lament that he was a solo voice in the push for a one party state in Zimbabwe.

During Nkomo's tenure as Vice-President of Zimbabwe, he concentrated on development issues and the fight for economic empowerment of black Zimbabweans. This was indicated by his move to lead a Zimbabwean delegation to the West to solicit for investment. He became very vocal against land imbalances in Zimbabwe. He was the first person to warn about a second revolution as long as the land remained concentrated in the hands of few whites and a few blacks. He noted that 'In order to avoid a conflict between the blacks and the well-to-do who are mainly whites, Government has to deliberately assist the disadvantaged blacks' (*Horizon*, 1993: 7).

Nkomo warned the whites about the inevitability and the danger of a black economic revolution as long as they refused to share resources with the black majority: 'They are immigrants to this country and if young blacks remain at the stage where they are today they will say *'makabva kupi imi? Nyika ndeyedu'* (Where did you come from? This country is ours). But it must be *'nyika ndeyedu tese, varungu nevanhu vatema'* (The country is ours, both white and blacks) (*The Financial Gazette*, 28 January 1993).

Brian Raftopoulos (1996: 9) noted that Nkomo became a leading spokesperson for the aspiring black bourgeoisie in Zimbabwe. He dedicated his last days to talking about the need for land reform. However, he also emphasised the need for national unity. The politics of black empowerment were seized upon by ZANU-PF to justify its violent and chaotic fast track land reform programme in the 21st century.

'Josh Will Never Die'

The veteran nationalist, Dr Eddison Zvobgo stated that: 'It is true that all of us die, but some truly don't die. It will never be possible for Joshua Nkomo's name to vanish from our history. Josh will never die' (*The Financial Gazette*, 8 July 1999). The death of Nkomo opened an opportunity for ZANU-PF to reflect on issues of patriotism, national sacrifice, heroism, liberation politics and fatherhood of the nation.

The burial of Nkomo raised crucial political issues pertinent to the development of Zimbabwe as a nation. His wife and relatives wanted him buried in the family cemetery in rural Kezi district where his grandparents were buried. Mugabe and ZANU-PF vetoed this decision arguing that Nkomo did not belong to the Nkomo family. He belonged to the Zimbabwean nation, and should therefore be buried by the state at Heroes Acre. Already the expropriation of the dead had begun. For Mugabe and ZANU-PF, Nkomo was a son of the soil, 'a national property', over which the state had power to decide where his body should be laid to rest.

ZANU-PF did not rest on its laurels as it quickly and selectively appropriated the political in Nkomo's life and legacy for hegemonic purposes. Five days were dedicated by the state to mourning his death. Politicians fell over each other to describe Nkomo in celebratory tones as Hero of Heroes, Father Zimbabwe, King of Zimbabwe, Umdala Wethu (Ndebele word for our beloved old man), illustrious son of Africa and a symbol of the totality of national liberation and patriotism. The issue of national unity under ZANU-PF was hammered home vociferously and those perceived to be against this vision of the ruling party were 'othered' into enemies of the nation. A reconstruction of Nkomo's legacy was very useful to the ZANU-PF political project to renew nationalism and efforts to immortalise itself in the Zimbabwean body politic; and political space as the only authentic political force legitimately carrying the historic burden of liberation; a party with noble emancipatory and patriotic traditions carried to their logical conclusion far ahead of the Movement for Democratic Change (MDC), a force that was considered an enemy of Zimbabwe sponsored by British and

American imperialists.

Announcing his death, Mugabe declared that 'The Mountain has fallen' and added that 'It is a loss so keenly felt by all of us, by all Zimbabweans who saw in the Vice-President a father-figure, a founder of our nation. The giant has fallen and the nation mourns' (*Zimbabwe News* 30 (6), July 1999). Nkomo was accorded the status of a nation builder after his death. Mugabe set the tone of Nkomo's nation-building career by stating that 'you must identify those virtues that made him (Joshua Nkomo) a national model, a supra-nationalist. He became a man of all the cultures of the country' (ibid.).

The *Zimbabwe News* of July 1999 editorial column carried the title: 'Farewell dear Father', stating that:

> *The death of Cde. Joshua Nkomo must give birth to national rededication to those ideals that made him a national hero. To act otherwise would be betrayal of not only Cde. Joshua Nkomo, but all those in whose footsteps he walked such as Ambuya Nehanda, Sekuru Kaguvi, uMzilikazi KaMatshobana, and Lobengula the Great.*

Nkomo was now being included among political and religious figures who had graced the Zimbabwean landscape in pre-colonial times. The title Father Zimbabwe, which Mugabe had once worked so hard to deny Nkomo, was now posthumously accorded to him. The president accepted that Nkomo pioneered the country's liberation struggle, at a time when people did not know what road to follow and how to put ideas together. He even confessed that he was inspired by Nkomo to join the struggle for independence and that Nkomo was indeed 'a true Father of the Nation'.

The editorial in the *Zimbabwe News*, quoted above, also confessed that, 'There are some amongst us who did not see the greatness in Cde. Joshua Nkomo when he was still alive. They should not be ashamed to admit that theirs was an impaired vision. There are those amongst us who recognised the greatness of Cde. Nkomo in his lifetime. Let them help those who were misguided to tow the correct line.' This appears to be a regret and apology by those who abused Nkomo.

Even Ndabaningi Sithole who led the dissidents that formed ZANU in 1963 admitted that Nkomo was a pragmatic politician. Perhaps Sithole's positive evaluation of the former's political legacy reflected the changed views of a man who himself was eventually driven from ZANU-PF. He was accused of sponsoring dissidents who styled themselves as Chimwenje ('fire') in post-independence Zimbabwe, thus now having more in common with Nkomo than he would have imagined some forty years previously when Sithole wrote:

> *Following tactical differences with our leader, I led a splinter*

> *group, the Zimbabwe African National Union (Zanu) together with Leopold Takawira, Herbert Chitepo, Robert Mugabe, Enos Nkala, the Malianga brothers and others. Unfortunate as it was, it happened. We wanted more confrontational politics. Nkomo and others that remained with him were more cautious, a trait that in my observation remained constant throughout Nkomo's political career.*
>
> *After independence, particularly during Matebeleland conflict in the 1980s, he chose the pragmatic and cautious path when some among his supporters were calling for a more confrontational path. In the end, it is his pragmatism that triumphed* (*Zimbabwe Independent*, 9 July 1999).

Sithole added his voice to the restoration of the title Father Zimbabwe. In the same article he said:

> *Our government and the people of Zimbabwe must be praised for conferring on this man the highest honour, acclaim, and acknowledgement as 'Father Zimbabwe' at long last, for there is no one so deserving as Joshua Nkomo.*

There is no wonder, therefore, that the death of Nkomo was followed by long reflection on the political future of the country and inspired a re-imagination of the Zimbabwe nation in the 21st century. Official re-imagination of the Zimbabwean nation on the basis of Nkomo's political career and death saw Chen Chimutengwende, the then Minister of Information, Posts and Telecommunications, positing that the large multitudes that mourned Nkomo indicated that the spirit of African nationalism and patriotism was very much alive. He added that:

> *It shows Cde. Nkomo's seniority among our heroes. It also proves that the spirit of African nationalism will never die in Zimbabwe because it was the birth of our nationhood as a country. The numbers of young people who were born after independence and made it to the burial was unbelievably high. It proves that the picture, which is painted by the private and foreign-sponsored Press, is totally false and trash* (*The Herald*, 6 July 1999).

The editorial of *The Zimbabwe Mirror* of 5-9 July 1999 joined the process of re-imagining the nation in the context of the death of Nkomo. The editor wrote that:

> It was a national response as spontaneous as genuine grief itself, accompanied by the desire both to express gratitude for a life dedicated to selfless sacrifice for the people, and demonstrate a national consciousness so rare in this post-independence period. Those so accustomed to perceive the social process through a fragmented and shattered mirror would have been

shocked at such a cohesive and solid expression of Zimbabwean nationalism. Even political mischief makers and latter day 'tribalists' found themselves at the national shrine having to defer to a national expression that transcended age, ethnicity, and class, in the acknowledgement that all good nationalists belong to all the people.

It was estimated that a total of over 140,000 people attended Nkomo's burial at Heroes Acre. This unprecedented attendance obviously raised some questions in the minds of political analysts. The analysis had to do with the fate of the nation. The editor of *The Zimbabwe Mirror* asked rhetorical questions: 'what does all this mean? What lessons should be drawn from all this?' (ibid.). He drew the following answers: first, it meant that nationalism was still reposed in the hearts and minds of the old guard that was at the receiving end of a cruel and brutal colonialism. Second, that nationalism also pervades the young at heart provoked by the touching sacrifices and glorious contribution of such nationalists as Nkomo. Third, that perhaps the passing away of Nkomo rejuvenated national consciousness, at a time when the emergent political trend, particularly in the urban areas of Zimbabwe, has tended to demonstrate a shocking obliviousness to the values of both nationalism and the history of the struggle.

The death of Nkomo raised other issues including the future of the Unity Accord, the loyalty of the Ndebele people to the Zimbabwe nation, Matebeleland and Midlands violence of the 1980s, the power equation in the government structure itself, and above all the durability of the prevailing peace and stability in the country. It is no wonder therefore that Mugabe took advantage of the burial of Nkomo to regret the violence that happened in Matebeleland in the 1980s. For the first time Mugabe came nearer to apologising for the atrocities committed.

Conclusion

Mugabe is comfortable with the dead and he uses them in a necrophilic way to re-imagine the nation. This is not only predicated on the rewriting and writing of the roles played in the struggle for independence by the leading departed Zimbabwean nationalists, it also involves constant dialogue with and re-invention of that past. While using heroes in his present Third Chimurenga crusade, Mugabe has also maintained his streak of unforgetting and unforgiving as indicated by his selective veneration of heroes of the liberation struggle. For instance, such political figures as Ndabaningi Sithole were written out of the record of the nation. Mugabe is implicitly 'writing' his own story and his own legacy. He has become the 'author' of heroes and without his blessing no one can achieve hero status in Zimbabwe, while the definition of what makes a 'hero' is not intended for discussion.

With political mediocrity taking centre stage in Zimbabwe, Mugabe has taken it upon himself together with close Zezuru allies/relatives to reconstruct the nation into a family epic revolving around him and selected, usable heroes, while marginalising or excluding other fallen heroes from the national pantheon. Tongogara, the war-time commander of ZANLA and an eminent politician in his own right,[1] was excluded from the list of eminent heroes honoured in Zimbabwe's Silver Jubilee Awards of April 2005. Such open discrimination sounds a warning about the complexities of Zimbabwe's political history and how it is selectively harnessed by those manning the state for purposes of power consolidation and state reconfiguration. While it is true that history is not made by great men and women, an analysis of the individual heroes' histories juxtaposed with the official histories is a crucial window into the hidden past and highlights current distortions of the political evolution of the nation at large. At the top of the heroism pyramid is a living hero in the form of Robert Mugabe who is manning the state and presiding over the 'selection of hero process' and then narrating the distorted history of those who are selected as heroes for current political expediency at the National Heroes Acre.

Endnotes

1. He died mysteriously in a car accident immediately after the Lancaster House negotiations of 1979.

7

Mai Mujuru: Father of the nation?[1]

LENE BULL CHRISTIANSEN

Women have a great role to play in uniting the nation because they are the household builders, mothers of the future generations and wives to the rulers. The more women cooperate, the more prosperous will be our nation (Joyce Mujuru/ Teurai Ropa[2]).

Can 'Mother Mujuru' become the icon of power in Zimbabwe? Can she establish herself in the Zimbabwean political imaginary of power in a position above 'the boys' club' – as a new 'Father of the Nation'? And if so, will this in effect make her 'one of the boys' appearing on the political scene as 'a man', or can the imaginaries of power be negotiated? Are there slippages and fissures in the gendered language of power and authority in Zimbabwe, through which a woman president might emerge? And if so, will this be perceived as a victory for a Zimbabwean feminism? These questions come to mind when analysing the debates that surrounded the appointment of the well-known liberation war veteran, and former Minister of Women's Affairs, Joyce Mujuru aka Teurai Ropa[3] in 2004 as Vice-President of Zimbabwe. This debate[4] that took place in the few 'independent' newspapers and in internet-communities concerned her credentials as a politician and as a representative of 'Zimbabwean women'. The question around which they centred was: is she a woman (e.g. a feminist) – or is she a 'pawn' in the games of men?

The debates were framed by a vigorous infighting going on in the elite of ZANU-PF, the party which has been in power since Zimbabwe's liberation in 1980. As the ageing President seemed likely to be replaced in the foreseeable future, leading members of the party had begun positioning themselves in a bid for his succession. These power struggles within ZANU-PF cannot be said to have diminished since 2004 – their details the subject of a different study. Mujuru's appointment as Vice-President was, however, part of President Mugabe's immediate intervention in the struggles that surfaced in 2004. In addition he ostracised a faction of the party headed by the formerly powerful information minister, Jonathan Moyo, who was expelled from the party in the same move. The events that led to Mujuru's appointment have been depicted by Moyo as an ethnically based demonstration of power by the President and his 'old guard' in the Politburo, disguised as a promotion of the female agenda. '[I]n reality', he argues, the ZANU-PF Women's League had been 'hijacked' by the President and the First Lady so as to appoint Mujuru as their candidate (Moyo, 2006a, 2006b & 2006c). However events may have unfolded within ZANU-PF, the context gave rise to speculation about the background to Mujuru's appointment: critics of the regime considered her a conservative 'safe bet' for the President and his loyal party supporters, of whom Mujuru's husband is considered the leading figure.

At the ZANU-PF conference in 2004, President Mugabe presented Mujuru with the words: 'Don't be deceived by that body, she is a young woman' (BBC, 2004) apparently pointing to her stature which could be described as traditionally built. However, in the few comments made by Mujuru herself, she neither highlighted her age nor her gender. Rather, she made references to her liberation-war credentials, her long-standing loyalty to the nationalist cause and to party influence through the ZANU-PF Women's League. But, while President Mugabe defined Mujuru's appointment as a 'victory for women of Zimbabwe', a number of feminist critics as well as political opponents downplayed this so-called victory by ascribing her political ascendancy to the political power held by her husband, Solomon Mujuru,[5] a retired army general, and one of the original leaders of ZANU and ZANLA;[6] or to Mujuru's relative political pliability that would render her a 'safe bet' to the rest of the 'boys'. Speculation about the relationship between Mujuru and her husband developed into a regular discourse in the independent and foreign press, where the Zimbabwean Vice-President was curiously but repeatedly described as 'wife of powerful former army general Solomon Mujuru'.

Thus this chapter discusses how the power relations in the Zimbabwean political elite work through and iterate particular gendered imaginaries of power. It goes on to consider how these are both contested and maintained in certain feminist discourses, so that arguably the elite ZANU (PF) female politician remains in a liminal (or limbo) position, as her political gendered identity is called into question from different sides.

Analysts of gender and nationalism have generally agreed that national projects are gendered projects (Chadya, 2003: 153) and have described national projects as part and parcel of a 'global patriarchalism' (Walby, 2000: 523-30). This would correspond well with Horace Campbell's description of the political elite in Zimbabwe as a patriarchy that is haunted by what he calls 'patriarchal anxiety and masculinist confusion' (Campbell, 2003: 136). Campbell asserts that a patriarchal model of leadership is endemic in southern African countries like Zimbabwe that have experienced liberation struggles, because of the legacy of war politics

(Campbell, 2003: 268). In his description, nationalist politics and the development of a discourse of patriarchal power went hand in hand to ensure the leadership of the political elite after liberation (Campbell, 2003: 84). This was done through an invention of a traditionalist perception of gendered power relations in Africa as a deeply historically rooted form of 'traditional African leadership' (whatever that in particular instances would mean).

That historically rooted gender roles is something unique to Africa is questionable. Indeed, from a gender perspective it has been suggested that national politics generally provide a stage on which to play out perceptions of power as a masculine attribute (see: Nagel, 1998). Similarly, feminine attributes are articulated in contrasting terms, where women's ascribed roles in the national project are given a symbolic character. As in Zimbabwe important women have been hailed as 'mothers of the nation'[7] (Nagel, 1998: 254-58). Thus one can see how both men and women are positioned differently in the 'script of national politics', and how women's and men's roles, might not merely depend on a person's gender, but be constituted of a more complicated set of negotiations within the official 'cast'.

As such, on the Zimbabwean national political stage a discourse of kinship, of 'Fathers' and 'Mothers' of the nation has played a key role. The President represents himself as the 'Father of the Nation' in a classical paternalistic style, but also, as 'the head of the family' in an Africanist traditionalist sense, and as 'the husband of the nation' who is entitled to clamp down on any one who attempts to 'steal/rape' his wife; that is, the people. Likewise, departed leaders of the liberation struggle are also depicted in these terms, just as their wives are valorised as wives and as true icons of African mother – and womanhood (Chadya, 2003: 154). This metaphor of kinship can be seen as feeding on 'traditionalist' versions of pre-colonial social structures; a construction which had an impact in the early nationalist movement under colonial rule, and which is being 'recycled' in present-day politics as a 're-Africanisation' of Zimbabwean culture (Christiansen, 2005a & 2005b).[8]

Connected to these images is the image of the liberation war soldiers valorised as 'heroes of the nation'. In the liberation war, the political leaders had traded on traditional images in order to convey their own leadership in terms of masculine power, and a celebration of masculine virility as a source of community leadership and power (Lyons, 2004: 213-15; Campbell, 2003: 165). Thus, the hero status is ascribed a distinctly masculine quality. The soldier is depicted as the 'quintessential Zimbabwean masculine man' fighting for the liberation of his nation. Following this masculinised image of the hero, a rewriting of women's participation in the struggle for liberation ascribed women the role of 'mothers of the revolution', and depicts patriotic womanhood as motherhood (Lyons, 2004: 141-

42; Rooney, 1991: 57). As the President and his political elite represent themselves as the rightful leaders of the nation through their role as liberators of the nation, the attributes of the liberation-war soldiers are ascribed to the political leadership in a way that underlines the imagery of 'fathers and husbands of the nation'.

This could suggest that women, who participated in the struggle, are being 'written out' of the liberation war history altogether. However, a particular iconography of women fighters does exist. One of the most prominent of those women is Joyce Mujuru, who as a woman fighter has served to personify women's equality in the Zimbabwean nationalist movement (Lyons, 2004: 168). In this chapter, we argue that there is a discrepancy between the masculine ideals of the 'liberation war hero' and the 'official' role played by Joyce Mujuru before and after liberation. (Women's liberation personified through the 'woman warrior' does not sit easily with ZANU PF's idea of male hegemony.) These tensions are revealing in the debate to which this chapter refers.

A number of women hold positions within the ruling party, but it can well be argued that Joyce Mujuru, despite her relative youth, is the senior female politician in Zimbabwean politics. Mujuru began her political career at the age of eighteen when she joined the liberation forces. She quickly rose through the ranks of ZANLA to become one of the first female commanders, the youngest member of the Central Committee, and towards the end of the war, the head of the ZANU Department for Women's Affairs in Mozambique (Weiss, 1986: 20; Lyons, 2004: 110-111,137). Likewise, after independence, Mujuru proceeded to be the first female and youngest cabinet member, first holding the position of Minister of Youth, Sport and Recreation, but quickly moving to the newly created Ministry of Community Development and Women's Affairs, which aimed at transforming 'women's status so that they can assume their rightful role in society as participants alongside men on the basis of full equality' (Mujuru in Nhongo-Simbanegavi, 2000: 134). She has held a number of posts both in the government and in the party and has remained a loyal supporter of President Mugabe throughout this time (Mujuru in *New African*, 2005). Both during and after the liberation war, Mujuru was the leader of the ZANU Women's League. After 1980, and in alignment with the ZANU-PF Youth Brigade, the former continued the traditions of women's work maintained during the war, i.e. arranging social activities and education for women and youth. Restricting women's political action within ZANU to charities, education and social events generated disappointment within the Women's League. Indeed, a number of leading members, for example Julia Zvobgo[10] left the League to form other women's organisations in order to assert political pressure on the new government. Frustrated by this development, Mujuru belittled the new organisations, saying they were 'meddling in politics' (the task of the party leadership – their husbands), and pointed out that the new organisations were only to be tolerated if they kept to organising 'charities' (Nhongo-Simbanegavi, 2000: 135-37).

This general association of women with youth (and children) cast women and women's proper activities in the domestic sphere and subordinate to 'real politics', the business of the party leadership (the men). Joyce Mujuru, did not, however, play down the imagery of the 'woman fighter':

During the war. We were even much ahead of them [western oriented feminists] because to really see a woman holding a gun, going to face with the enemy when she is pregnant as well, is something else (Mujuru in Lyons, 2004: 168)[11].

Mujuru's general description of women in the liberation war holds true to the official image of Mujuru, which has been part of the official iconography of women warriors during that period. Both during and after the war Mujuru has been upheld as an icon of the 'African woman warrior' – a heroine, symbolically 'holding a baby in one arm and an AK47 in the other'. Tales of her exploits – she had famously fought a two-day battle while in the late stages of pregnancy and personally shot down an enemy helicopter with her semi-automatic rifle – became part of the official image of women's participation in, and feminist liberation during the war (Lyons, 2004: 111-112; Nhongo-Simbanegavi, 2000: 2-7). Mujuru, however, does not ignore the fact that her personal story was exceptional; and that the focus given to the women warriors during war was not so much an effort to construct a role model for Zimbabwean women, as it was to rally support from external donors to the struggle (Mujuru in Lyons, 2004: 167).

This image is, however, still an integral part of Mujuru's present self-representation. On the occasion of Zimbabwe's Independence Jubilee in 2005 the magazine *New African* devoted an issue to Zimbabwe's liberation struggle, featuring what the editors might have considered a broad selection of dignitaries from Zimbabwean society. Strikingly this amounted to a long list of ZANU-PF men and Mujuru. When interviewed, the latter highlighted her combat 'credentials' as laying the foundation for her advances in the liberation army and her following political career:

What I can tell you is that I am part of ZANU – I have always been since when I was 18 years of age, that was when I really got to know about this liberation movement whose armed wing was ZANLA.

[...] But the comrades saw it fit that I should go for further training. Perhaps they saw some potential in me. Their decision, in fact, came after I had been involved in a heavy contact with the enemy and I had shot down an enemy helicopter. That

happened on 7 February 1974, just before I turned 19 (Mujuru in *New African* 2005).

This modest self representation follows Mujuru's description of her decision to join the liberation forces, and especially her evaluation of the background that made her especially fitted for military service:

My father never treated me like a girl; he never did that because most of us in the family were girls and he couldn't spoil us anyway. Therefore, all the chores reserved for boys were done by us. So I managed to take advantage of that chance and learn to do certain extraordinary things that girls of my age didn't do at the time. Therefore, it was easy for me to take advantage, again, of the recruitment that was then taking place in my home area into the liberation army (Mujuru in *New African* 2005).

As she describes her father, so Mujuru also describes President Mugabe as someone who has never taken into account that she is a woman. When confronted with the charges laid against her, that her appointment was the product of her weakness as 'a soft lady out to look after the back of a retired president' (*New African*, 2005), Mujuru responded by describing her relationship with the President:

I can say that the president is part of what I have gained in my personal life. He has not treated me as a girl or woman at all. He has treated me as a person with the capability of doing certain things (Mujuru in *New African*, 2005).

However, she does think that being a woman played a role in her gaining the vice-presidency. In line with President Mugabe's congratulation to Zimbabwean women for a 'feminist victory', Mujuru ascribes the political negotiations that went on before her appointment as a pressure asserted on the leadership by 'the women's group'[12]:

[...] whatever I am doing now is not a personal wish as such. I go according to what my people want because even for this vice president, I didn't go all out to campaign for it. It was the women's group in the party that went to the presidium and spoke about it. [...] So when they [the party] held their congress again last year, they decided that the country should have a woman vice president [...] (Mujuru in *New African*, 2005).

Nonetheless she maintains a submissive attitude when it comes to political agency within the party and in the government. She states several times that she does not 'go after' posts, but accepts them as they are given to her by the party, the leadership or the President, always referring to those in the third person, thereby discursively separating herself from any personal political agency. She also maintains this distinction when she talks about the 'women's group' in the party, who had lobbied for women's equality within the party, and as part of this process put her forward as their candidate. That is, her being nominated as a woman (incidentally) is depicted as an act of trust on the part of the President, who, as she stated, did not as a general rule take into account her gender, but accepted her because she was the candidate advocated by the women's group in the party, now that the party (not she) had decided to push for women's emancipation.

This rather neatly wrapped representation can be said to serve at least three purposes for Mujuru. Firstly, it establishes her as loyal to the president, something that she emphasises throughout the interview. Secondly, Mujuru personifies the kind of feminism that argues that women in powerful positions act as role models for woman in general, thus becoming champions of women's equality by the mere fact that they are in a powerful position. In this way, her personal political agency as a feminist is diminished to a function of 'the women's group' in ZANU-PF, who had lobbied for her as an icon of women's equality (remembering her outstanding 'achievements' in the masculine line of action during the war and later in the political sphere). Thirdly, Mujuru establishes a 'non-gendered' discourse about her own political career. She has, she claims, never been treated like a woman, although she is an 'icon of Zimbabwean feminism' in official discourse. By her own account, however, this is not an important feature. Rather, she very carefully balances the image of the fighter (equal to the men) with a submissive position vis-à-vis the male dominated leadership of the party, which she does not challenge either on concrete issues or for the purpose of personal political advancement.

This type of female political involvement is, as elsewhere, also challenged in Zimbabwe. Scholars and political activists like Everjoice Win have continuously called into question women politicians who participate in politics on the 'side of the boys' (see for example: Win in Frank, 2002), just as other African feminists and gender scholars have drawn a connection between leadership problems and the issues of violence against women and problems of women's equality in society in general (Mama, 1997: 53-58; Niehaus, 2005: 65).

Representing the Movement for Democratic Change (MDC) position on the appointment of Mujuru as vice-president, two female MDC politicians Priscilla Misiharirabwi[13] and Grace Kwinjeh[14] sparked a debate regarding the role of women in Zimbabwean politics in two articles that appeared on the *New Zimbabwe* web-page[15] after Mujuru's appointment. These articles were followed up by others on the web-page and in other media; mainly in the independent newspapers.

In *The Financial Gazette* writers of 'The National Report' were cautiously optimistic about the prospects of a woman who might become the next president. While Mavis Makuni simply suggested that Mujuru should 'look east' to her Asian counterparts for inspiration on how to keep playing a key role in 'high stakes' politics (Makuni, 2004), Charles Rukuni stated that even if there were people within the party that doubted Mujuru's chances of survival in ZANU-PF, her 'anointment' by the President could ensure her the 'real' presidency. After weighing the 'pros and cons' he quoted an anonymous former supporter of ZANU-PF saying that:

> *Mujuru is Mugabe's trump card. She has all the right credentials. She is a former freedom fighter. She is a woman. She is fairly clean. But most of all, she can protect the family fortunes. [...] President Mugabe could not appoint anyone who could do a "Mwanawasa" on him, someone who would haul him before the courts like Mwanawasa is doing to his benefactor. [...] he is safe with Mujuru* (Rukuni, 2005).

While one might ponder on the curious term 'fairly clean', which might be taken to mean that the anonymous informant regards Mujuru as not as tarnished by corruption scandals as her male counterparts, or that this is a particularly female quality on her part, the argument was given a 'positive spin' by Rukuni, who entitled his piece 'Mujuru is here to stay'. The same positive attitude was not echoed in Grace Kwinjeh's first article entered on *New Zimbabwe* in December 2004, though it also asserted that Mujuru's appointment could largely be ascribed to Mugabe's wishes. However, her view was that: 'Mujuru sadly is a beneficiary of everything we have hated about Zanu PF – dictatorship, tribalism, sexism and lawlessness' (Kwinjeh, 2004), her argument being that the appointment was carried out through a patriarchal style 'top down' process within the party in order to divert public attention away from the party's failures:

> <u>Sexism</u> *because Zanu PF women then became mere pawns in a big political game. While Zanu PF would want us to believe that women acted out of their own volition, we know that is not true.*
> *Like the land issue, the women are now a weapon to hoodwink the general populace into believing that the party is reforming and cares for the welfare of women. Beset by a leadership crisis, coupled with a growing national unpopularity, Mujuru is a window-dresser. Zanu-PF hopes to use <u>him</u> to turn around that party's flagging fortunes (Kwinjeh 2004)* [my emphasis].

Kwinjeh's 'slip of the tongue'; in calling Mujuru 'him', fits well with her overall statement that Mujuru is utterly unfit as a champion of women's rights in Zimbabwe, because, as Everjoice Win puts it in Shona, 'Joyce Mujuru *murume pachake'* .... She is a real man, and she can stay as one of the boys' (Win, 2004b). The same discourse was put to me in a conversation with WOZA spokesperson Jenni Williams; 'she is a man'[16] was her reaction to a question about the possible usefulness to the women's movement in Zimbabwe of a female Vice-President. The logic of this discourse is that as part of the patriarchal system Mujuru's position disables rather than enables her with regard to feminist agency, and that this positioning makes her 'one of the boys': 'a man'. This way of depicting a woman in power as 'a man' could be interpreted as a 'return' to perceptions of gender and power that ascribed particular identities to women in power (particularly older women) so as to render them part of the male leadership (Amadiume, 1987). However, I would argue that in these feminist discourses of gender and power, there is no attempt at ascribing Mujuru's political position to a non-western or pre/post-colonial gender-power-identity matrix; on the contrary, depicting Mujuru as a man is ironically used to dismiss her claims to feminism in a derogatory way.

It is claimed that as a window-dresser Mujuru and official ZANU-PF feminism will always play second fiddle to President Mugabe's policies, because they have always done so. They claim, therefore, that Mujuru's version of feminism within the auspices of ZANU-PF in fact strengthens existing gendered power relations:

> *Yes, we are going to have the traditional women empowerment talk, sewing machines in this and that project, the usual ululations and dances. That is Mujuru's mandate to be mother, with Mugabe as the domineering father, and Solomon as the all powerful husband* (Kwinjeh, 2004).

In a second article Kwinjeh and Misihairabwi unfold their critique by stating that women's empowerment and rights are part of a general rights crisis in Zimbabwe. They see women's emancipation as part of a greater rights issue, and therefore question Mujuru's ability to be a feminist agent of change:

> *Putting Mujuru in the vice-presidency does not change the fact that ZANU-PF remains the same dictatorial regime with nothing to offer the people of Zimbabwe. It is still the source of our misery. <u>Women and children</u> form the majority of the 3 million people need food aid,. They are the <u>victims</u> of the collapsed education system [etc.].*
>
> *[...] Even those women who have been in parliament in the past 24 years, it is clear that they have operated within the framework defined by the men. Thus their failure to push the women's agenda at a broader national level* (Misihairabwi & Kwinjeh, 2005) [my emphasis].

These two critics lay a dual charge on women in politics, stating that they must not only act as agents for women's rights but also for social and political change in general: 'the issue of gender power relations cannot be separated from the whole fight for human rights and democracy' (Misihairabwi & Kwinjeh, 2005).

Other feminist activists follow this same line, when commenting on the then ongoing 'Operation Murambatsvina'.[17] In their view Mujuru has let down the feminist movement in Zimbabwe by supporting the government's policies; this because, as a feminist, they claim, Mujuru is supposed to work for what they call 'women's issues':

> *I have failed to understand why Mujuru, as a woman, mother and second most powerful person in the country has allowed such suffering for <u>her countrywomen and children</u>. How has she allowed Operation Restore Order – derisively known as the Zimbabwean tsunami – to continue?* (Thomas, 2005) [my emphasis]

By grouping in women with children, and pointing out that they together form the largest group of victims of the failed policies of the government, both Thomas, Misihairabwi, and Kwinjeh (inadvertently?) construct women as a group, and not only as victims of failed social policies. Indeed, it can be argued that this conventional pairing of 'women and children', is reminiscent of the classical ZANU-PF division of labour (described above), and implies a subtle contemporary construction of women as 'the weaker sex'.

In response to these articles a debate-forum was opened on the *New Zimbabwe* web-page. Here readers who identified themselves as living both in Zimbabwe and in the 'Diaspora' gave their views on the appointment and commented on the two articles by Misihairabwi and Kwinjeh (*New Zimbabwe*, 2005). There was a general support for their arguments. However, some commentators, especially those who claimed to be living in Zimbabwe, were critical towards Mujuru, Misihairabwi, and Kwinjeh alike because they are all politicians. This mistrust of politicians in general amounted to a critique of the MDC along the same lines of ZANU-PF i.e. for not being genuine about ensuring women's equal participation in the political leadership of their parties.

One of the commentators, identified as 'Galakatshane UK'[18] took a classical 'first things first' approach when claiming that:

> *I would like to say the struggle for emancipation has not reached that stage. A stage where we seek to emancipate key groups in our society. We are still at a stage where every Zimbabwean must be freed from this totalitarian regime [...] Therefore, I think we need to start right at the beginning. Emancipate all Zimbabweans, whites, blacks, Indians, Coloureds, <u>women and children</u> (New Zimbabwe* 2005) [my emphasis].

While dismissing feminist claims in Africa by using the age-old argument that general social evils must be taken care of before feminist claims on equality can be attended to (Holst Petersen, 1995), Galakatshane's position shares two features with Thomas, Misihairabwi, and Kwinjeh's critique of Mujuru. Firstly, Galakatshane also groups 'women and children' together; and secondly, he claims that women's emancipation cannot be separated from emancipation from the totalitarian regime.

Within Misihairabwi and Kwinjeh's approach to the problem of the 'totalitarian regime' it is held that any feminist alignment with the repressive patriarchal system is a sign of weakness:

It must be understood that Mujuru is only acceptable to Mugabe as his Vice President because she does not threaten his hold on power, either nationally or within the ruling party. She has been propelled to the party's top most position precisely because she poses no threat to any of the distinct factions [...] and of course the Mujuru faction led by her husband Solomon.
(Misihairabwi & Kwinjeh 2005).

The two activists hold it that even within the faction of the party that bears her name, Mujuru is considered the weaker part, and thus, it is implied, is still in a submissive position vis-à-vis not only the President, but also her husband, who hold the 'real' power. So, while disagreeing with Misihairabwi and Kwinjeh about the role of Mujuru's husband in her appointment as Vice-President, Win nevertheless finds Mujuru's elevation highly regrettable:

One can't help but be angry with little text and email messages congratulating me/women for Joyce Mujuru's election as Zimbabwe's new Vice President. There are female persons. Then there are women's women. The only thing Mujuru [...] shares with other women is biology (Win, 2004b).

Win, unlike Misihairabwi and Kwinjeh who are direct political opponents to Mujuru, argues that the latter does have overwhelming political credentials in her own right, has not been tarnished by scandals of corruption, and cannot be dismissed as a mere puppet of her husband's powers. However, Win maintains the dual claim on women politicians that was stated by Misihairabwi and Kwinjeh, namely that 'What we need are women who will use their leadership positions to liberate themselves, and other women. Trading on their biology alone is not good enough' (Win, 2004b). She ascribes the political agency that has 'elevated' Mujuru through the ranks of the otherwise highly patriarchal ZANU-PF elite not to Mujuru herself but to 'Mugabe and his men', who are said to use Mujuru as a scapegoat for their own shortcomings: 'Once again we see women being brought [in] when things are so bad that she ends up getting the blame should nothing change for the better' (Win, 2004b).

At least two conflicting ideals of what a woman in Zimbabwean politics should be emerge from these debates. Mujuru is (and has always been) a 'poster child' for the kind of feminist emancipation that 'beats the boys at their own game', thus elevating herself to a position of power alongside 'the boys'. Here this woman can become a role model for other women in their struggle to emancipate themselves. In opposition to this image, Mujuru's critics put forward an ideal of 'genuine feminist leadership', which should derive from a democratic mandate from 'the women' who look upon their leader as a tool for change of the patriarchal power relations – not someone who works within them. As such, both Mujuru and her critics maintain that they are the champions of feminist action, because they believe that they uphold the standards set before them. Mujuru finds her personal political career 'in a man's world' the epitomising proof that female emancipation in Zimbabwe was made possible during the liberation war, because she was able to break the constraints of the female role under which she understood other women to be living. For Mujuru, the price of such liberation has been absolute loyalty to the party that facilitated her freedom. This feature is, however, in the eyes of her critics, the principal proof of her weak status as a feminist politician. That is, to see Mujuru as a female politician, who has been elevated rather than having elevated herself is an analysis that is shared by both Mujuru and her feminist critics. The former perceives not 'campaigning' for her own political appointment as a virtue, and firmly believes in being handed assignments, which she accepts as her duty and will faithfully implement. However, this loyalty towards the party and the leadership is perceived by her critics as her greatest weakness. Thus, when Charles Rukuni hinted that her male counterparts in the bid for the presidency do not regard her particular kind of loyalty as a personal virtue, though it has served her well in her appointment; and the feminist critics measure her successes in terms of her ability to 'push feminist issues'.

While these representations are seemingly contradictory, it will be argued that they serve to position Mujuru securely within the boundaries of the nationalist imagery of power. By claiming her long-held nationalist convictions and faithfulness to the liberation struggle and the party leadership, she affirms her rightful place within the party elite. She also skilfully negotiates the masculinised imagery of power, by simultaneously referring to her 'power attributes' in terms of her liberation war 'credentials', and in the same move, placing them securely in the past, having left her army affiliation to her husband after the war. Likewise, her critics and others, who ascribe her political advancement to her husband's political powers and/or to a relative weakness on her part – while attempting to undermine her credibility in relation to their own feminist ideals – coincidentally serve to underline Mujuru's own image as a loyal party soldier. Ironically, in addition, they ascribe her feminine 'virtues' such as subordination and passivity, which serve to 'naturalize' her seemingly unnatural elevated status vis-à-vis her husband. As such, Mujuru as a female politician in a powerful position is – with the unwilling help of her critics – able to negotiate a role for herself in the masculinised imagery on the stage of Zimbabwean nationalist politics; a role that secures her a naturalised position in the political elite without seeming to pose a threat to the gendered power relations. Having successfully negotiated these seemingly contradictory images into a role that seems to fit her, the leap towards appearing as the 'Father of the Nation' seems not so steep; after all she is already by some considered 'a man'.

ENDNOTES

1. 'Mai Mujuru': Shona for 'Mother Mujuru' is Joyce Mujuru's much used honorific/praise name.
2. Teurai Ropa quoted in Lyons (2004: 213).
3. Upon joining the liberation forces many recruits changed their names in order to protect their family in Zimbabwe from prosecution in the event that they were caught by the Rhodesians. Teurai Ropa means 'spilled blood' and was Joyce Mujuru's assumed name during the liberation war.
4. For the purpose of this article I have limited myself to analysing the immediate debates surrounding her appointment; those that took place in 2004-05. It should, however, be noted that some of the material that is used as 'background' has appeared at a later date, most notably Jonathan Moyo's depictions of the so-called 'Tsholotsho Saga'.
5. Like his wife, Solomon Mujuru assumed a different name, Rex Nhongo, during the liberation war.
6. Rex Nhongo had joined ZANU in 1971 after defecting from ZAPU (the Zimbabwe African People's Union). Here he very quickly rose in the ranks of ZANLA (Zimbabwe African National Liberation Army), which was the armed wing of ZANU (White 2003: 17). After independence ZANU incorporated the 'PF' (Patriotic Front) in its name. Patriotic Front was the name under which ZANU and ZANLA and their counterparts ZIPRA (Zimbabwe People's Revolutionary Army), which was the armed wing of ZAPU, had jointly negotiated during the Lancaster House Conference that ended the liberation war.
7. This should not, however, be confused with the work of (most notably) Irene Staunton (1990) and Zimbabwe Women Writers (2000), who have contributed to the writing of Zimbabwean women's dedication, sacrifices and efforts in the liberation war.
8. The further descriptions of Zimbabwean nationalism below are, if not otherwise cited, also based on this work.
9. It should, however, be noted that apart from recently published, and much needed scholarship on the issue of the role of women in the Liberation War such

as Nhongo-Simbanegavi (2000) and Lyons (2004), to which this article owes much, descriptions of women warriors have mainly focused on the few icons of the struggle such as Mujuru herself.

10. Julia Zvobgo, together with Teurai Ropa and Sally Mugabe, had led the ZANU Department of Women's Affairs during the liberation war. This had from the very beginning, however, been viewed as a 'club for the commanders' wives' – Teurai Ropa was the wife of the ZANLA's Operations Commander, Sally Mugabe was the wife of the President of ZANU and Julia Zvobgo was the wife of the party's Publicity Secretary Edson Zvobgo (Nhongo-Simbanegavi, 2000: 51).

11. Extract from an interview conducted by Tanya Lyons in Harare in March 1997 in relation to her research for her book Guns and Guerilla Girls (2004).

12. I assume that Mujuru refers to the aforementioned ZANU-PF Women's League.

13. Priscilla Misihairabwi-Mushonga was at the time MDC's Shadow Minister for foreign affairs.

14. Grace Kwinjeh was at the time MDC's representative to the European Union.

15. Like a number of other web-communities, the *New Zimbabwe* web-page offers Zimbabweans in 'the Diaspora' as well as those living in Zimbabwe, who have internet access, a forum for exchange of news and political debate, forming an emerging 'public sphere' for a larger 'imagined Zimbabwean community' that is not limited geographically and therefore avoids the present government's control of the media. Judging by the number of participants participating in online debate forums on the web-page, it appears to be widely used. However, precise statistics on users and usage was not available at the time of writing. It is also possible that the usage of this particular web-page may have changed somewhat after 2004.

16. The conversation with Jenni Williams took place in Copenhagen at the conference 'Civil Society, Activism and Human Rights' organised by Amnesty International and the Danish Zimbabwe committee 6 October 2005.

17. Murambatsvina: 'Restore Order'/'Drive out the trash' is the banner under which the government has carried out demolitions of so-called 'illegal settlements' and persecuted informal traders etc.

18. This would indicate that this person lives in the diaspora, and is not immediately involved in debates within Zimbabwe. However, as it is only an internet pseudonym, it is not necessarily possible to read much into this 'fact', it could also indicate the person's chosen 'position from which to speak' or an attempt to disguise his or her identity.

8

Masculinities, race and violence in the making of Zimbabwe

JANE L. PARPART

Violence breeds violence and the victims of violence become violent themselves.... The methods of violence developed during the War of Liberation have spread through our society. It has become part of our social and political language (Kaulemu, 2004: 81).

The Youth Camps set up to 'educate' Zimbabwean youth in patriotic history deny any place in Zimbabwe's history to whites or to those blacks who oppose or criticize the ZANU-PF ruling party (Chiumbu, 2004). Systematic rape of young women in the camps is widespread along with widespread use of drugs and alcohol (WeNews: 5 Sept. 2003). Not surprisingly, attacks and rapes of women seen as opponents of the ruling party have increased dramatically (and the majority go unreported) (www.peacewomen.org, 12/2003).

Introduction

After decades of bloody conflict, most Zimbabweans were reassured by President Robert Mugabe's conciliatory opening speech at independence in 1980,[1] when he spoke of friendship – and even love – between former enemies, promising that 'the wrongs of the past must now stand forgiven and forgotten' (Weiss, 1994: 5). The new government's rhetoric was particularly progressive in regard to gender. Reflecting its exposure to Marxist-Leninist ideologies, the new state promised a future where men and women would share power and responsibility in the home, workplace and political arena. A ministry of women's affairs was established, with powerful support from Mugabe, and progressive legislation was passed giving women new legal rights. A new world seemed to be dawning in Zimbabwe, with new men and women at the helm.

Yet, today the ruling party encourages young party activists to rape women who belong to the political opposition or refuse to chant slogans of support for the ruling party, ZANU-PF. The President brags openly of having 'degrees in violence', and threatens to bring his opponents to their knees. A narrow race-based nationalism has emerged, where whites and those blacks who oppose the ruling party, are condemned as 'sell-outs' and enemies of the state. Mugabe has positioned himself as the 'father' who will protect his people and Zimbabwean culture from the imperialist West. However, the ruling party's struggle to retain power has often been played out on women's bodies. Indeed, policing the bodies of women who do not ascribe to or submit to male authority has become one of the prime goals of the Green Bombers, as the youth camp 'graduates' are known. These youth have become a symbol of the ruling party's dominance, its warrior masculinity and its clear message that women who 'belong' and submit will be protected – those who do not may suffer the humiliation of rape and even death.

Thus, gender roles and relations are at the heart of current power struggles in ways that seemed unlikely in 1980 when the new government was basking in world approval. Yet this should not be surprising. The legacy of racism and violence in Zimbabwe has long roots: reaching back to pre-colonial conflicts over land and power; complicated and intensified by colonial and settler rule; and exacerbated by a long, brutal struggle for majority rule. This legacy has shaped the way men and women have understood their place in an often violent and unpredictable world. It has pitted competing notions of manhood and womanhood together in a complicated and often unforgiving history.

The chapter explores this gendered process and its contribution to Zimbabwe's violent past, present and possible futures. It deliberately includes all racial groups, on the assumption that Zimbabwe cannot be understood without addressing the experiences, beliefs and behaviour of all participants. The chapter draws on memoirs, literature, and scholarly articles. Many are openly biased, some are silenced – particularly blacks, Coloureds and Asians in the Rhodesian forces – but the aim is not to discover a 'truth', but rather to explore the many ways men and women have understood and experienced Zimbabwe's gendered and violent past (and present).

Masculinities and violence

While violence and conflict is shaped by economic, political or cultural contexts, it is also deeply gendered. As Cynthia Enloe argues, people are not inherently violent – indeed, men (and women) have to learn to accept certain kinds of violence as normal. 'No person, no community, no national movement can be militarised without changing the ways in which femininity and masculinity are brought to bear on daily life' (1993: 20, 120). 'Militarizing gender before the first shot is fired is necessary for governments preparing for war. Men have to be socialised from boyhood to see their masculine identities tied to protecting women while tolerating violence' (Enloe, 1993: 63). Thus masculine values become tied to the ability of men to protect 'their' women and children, and men who cannot do so are often ridiculed as failed, feminine men. Attacking enemy women both emasculates the enemy (male) and reinforces the masculinity of the perpetrator. The rape and murder of women and children are an act of war, often applauded by women as well as the perpetrators (Cockburn, 2004).

Assumptions about masculinity/ies, as well as gender roles and relations, often change during periods of struggle/war, leaving a destructive legacy with a long shelf-life. As Enloe reminds us, a declaration of peace does little to undo the militarised masculinities required to carry out violent acts (1993: 3). Moreover, nationalist movements have all too often proven more committed to patriarchal power than gender equality, whatever their official 'ideology' on the matter, particularly once power has been won and structures of authority put in place. Indeed, much evidence supports Enloe's concern with 'how nationalist ideologies, strategies and structures have served to up-date and perpetuate the privileging of masculinity' (1995: 14). Clearly in the Zimbabwean case all of the various nationalist parties[2] (including the settler regime) were deeply patriarchal, despite their rhetoric about gender equality. Control over women's bodies was paramount – whether over one's 'own' women or enemy women (Barnes, 1999; Nhongo-Simbanegavi, 2000; Ranchod-Nilsson, 2006). Thus, the period leading up to, during and after independence needs to be examined through a gender lens if we are to understand how ideas about and practices of being men and women mutated to underwrite and perpetuate violent conflict.

Pre-colonial and colonial gender practices

In 1850, Zimbabwe was dominated by two ethnic groups – the Shona, long-term inhabitants in the region and the Ndebele, a splinter of the militant South African Zulu/Ngoni peoples, who conquered the south-west region after 1840. Women in both societies had some power and influence, particularly in domestic and spiritual arenas, but senior men, particularly 'big men' with many followers, were seen as the natural leaders of society. Control over women, as well as junior males and children, thus was a necessary condition for male success and was regarded as a crucial element of true manliness (Schmidt, 1992; West, 2002). However, tensions between the two groups festered, often cast in masculine terms, with the Ndebele belittling Shona military skills, and the Shona reacting with resentment and sometimes appropriation of the Ndebele language (SiNdebele) and warrior mythology/past. 'SiNdebele signified the epitome of a very physical masculinity: an ability to use the knobkerrie and the myths of the Zulu fighters like Shaka' (Shire, 1994: 149).

The consolidation of colonial rule was characterised by the emasculation of many African men, through a wide range of small but hurtful and harmful actions by settlers – such as having to step off the pavement when a European passed by, not being allowed to speak English to officials, ridiculing and undermining traditional cultural practices, being called 'boy' no matter one's age and doing 'women's work' as household servants in European homes (Vambe, 1976). Of course, some Africans benefited from the colonial system, obtaining education and employment that offered respect and leadership positions in the African community. Some managed to create households with many dependents, thus establishing an alternative to the African 'big man' model (Holland, 2005; Ranger, 1995; Summers, 2002; West, 2002). The British preferred martial societies (Streets 2004) – an 1886 settler diary, for example, described the Mashona as 'a dirty cowardly lot' while praising the Matabele [Ndebele] as 'bloodthirsty devils but a fine type' – which may have offered some Ndebele respite from emasculating colonial practices (Ranger, 1979: 3)[3] While all colond men and women were constrained by the realities of European colonial power, these gendered myths of martial abilities (and incapacities) caused deep resentments and continue to haunt Zimbabwe today.

For Europeans, this period was characterised by a widespread identification with frontier versions of muscular masculinity, with particular emphasis on the link between prowess at sport, physical toughness and ability to deal with the challenges thrown up by the harsh African environment. There was a lot of 'hard living and drinking' as well as a sense of community developed through shared hardships (Tredgold, 1968: 21; Jacobs, 1995). This masculinised imaginary was reinforced by memories of the African uprisings in the 1890s (the First Chimurenga),[4] and the settler heroes who crushed them (Lovett, 1977). Indeed, militarism was 'woven deep into the constructions of settler masculinity' (Morrell, 2001: 139), no doubt reinforcing tendencies towards a militant masculinity that celebrated white male sexuality, toughness and racial superiority (Vambe, 1976; McCulloch, 2000).

During the Federal period (1953-64), however, promises of multiracial partnerships and genuine efforts in that direction by a small section of the white community encouraged some aspiring black Africans, Coloureds and Asians to dream of a future where men (and occasionally women) of all racial and cultural backgrounds would have an opportunity to participate in the life of the Federation. The Capricorn Society and a few other liberal organisations became places where multiracial elites met and sought ways to make partnership a reality (Hancock, 1984; Hughes, 2003; Muzondidya,

2005; Tredgold, 1968). These organisations called for a world where all educated and 'civilised' men could meet and work together (Tosh, 1999). This ideology attracted many black, Coloured and Asian elites who thought they had a chance to 'make it' under these conditions. Formal education (particularly mission education), Western dress and food, and access to a modern/Western lifestyle were the 'keys to the kingdoms' and became a preoccupation of aspiring and established elites. Women joined this quest, supporting their husbands' struggle for respectability by running modern households with 'properly' dressed children who studied hard and behaved like model citizens for a multiracial future (Muzondidya, 2005; Ranger, 1995; Weiss, 1994; West, 2002).

Those who saw little chance for themselves within this elite world tended to be more sceptical, and to remain wedded to local notions of masculinity, gender relations and respectability. Indeed, the privileges of patriarchal authority, particularly for senior men, must have been an attractive alternative to the rewards of Western 'civilization'. However, as urbanisation and education penetrated the countryside fewer people were able to wall themselves off from Western influences. Young people increasingly spent time in the cities. City folk returned, bringing new ideas and goods. Debates over how to balance local traditions, particularly gender regimes that reinforced male authority and respect for elders, with the need for 'progress' and 'modernity', thus continued to concern both urban and rural communities (Thompson, 2006). Indeed, African patriarchy often worked hand in hand with Western patriarchy to control black women, through legislation, social pressure and overt threats such as the rape of working women during the bus boycott in 1956 (Barnes, 1999; Raftopolous, 1999; Scarnecchia, 1999).

However, as the Federation foundered and prospects for genuine multiracial partnership declined, the attraction of Victorian ideas of progressive manhood came under fire. While some Africans (mostly elites, but not entirely) continued to believe in the possibility of a multiracial democratic future, ironically militant, muscular images of masculinity became increasingly attractive to many, both whites and blacks, as the right-wing Rhodesian Front triumphed in the polls and set about creating the white-dominated state of Rhodesia and the nationalists called for authentic African manhood to rise up and challenge the settler state (Caute, 1983; Sithole, 1977).

The UDI period: masculinities, race and the struggle for power

The Rhodesian Front's claim to power was based on assertions of white technical and martial superiority, and the self-proclaimed duty to protect both European-style 'civilization' and progress and their dependent women and children. The Rhodesian Front's determination to defy British opinion and to set up a white-dominated state, in the face of both internal and external opposition, fostered a militantly masculinist discourse. The new government and media urged white men to devote themselves to protecting white privilege and 'civilized' living standards. A militant, martial mentality was encouraged (Hancock, 1984; Moore-King, 1988). Whites who remained wedded to multiracial solutions were ridiculed as weak, feminine and impractical (Ellert, 1995: 89-91).

At the same time, the Rhodesian state, with its small white minority, could not survive without loyal supporters from all races in the country. Consequently the discourse of militant white male triumphalism had to be moderated to attract black, Coloured and Asian supporters. To that end, the Rhodesian regime insisted that white rule would bring development and progress to loyal citizens from all races and backgrounds, while the nationalists would ruin the economy and return the nation to the Stone Age. Those benefiting from the system were inclined to believe these arguments, even more so because many blacks, Coloureds and Asians were put off by the aggressive behaviour of young nationalists, who threatened people who could not produce their party cards, and harassed 'sell-outs', such as the beating of a female teacher in Harare and raping of teenage girls in the townships (Ellert, 1989: 1-2; Muzondidya, 2005: 100-01; Skimin, 1977: 97). Moreover, Rhodesian support for chiefs reinforced the 'big-man' mythology underpinning rural and much urban male power and all supporters of the government were repeatedly congratulated for siding with 'modernity' and 'progress', rather than the 'evils' of communism, terrorism and African nationalism (Bull, 1967: 141).

However, by the late 1960s, the limits of advancement for loyal blacks, Coloureds and Asians became increasingly apparent as opportunities for jobs and land failed to develop and white privilege was entrenched in legislation and institutional life. Widespread disenchantment with the lack of agricultural opportunities fuelled peasant discontent, providing a rural base for nationalist opposition. Nationalist agitation, even when cast in moderate language and practice, met with ferocious opposition, including lengthy jail sentences and banishment. The regime refused to face its growing unpopularity among Africans, blaming attacks on the few communist extremists (Tredgold,1968: 244-46). Moreover, the failures of nationalists' early military challenges encouraged a cocky belief in the superiority of white military prowess. Indeed the Army Chief of Staff dismissed the attacks as the work of 'garden boys' (Fuller, 2004), reflecting the widespread assumption that blacks had neither the stomach nor the skills needed to successfully prosecute a war. For the security forces, the conflict was 'a jolly good war', providing opportunities to brag of one's exploits at popular watering holes like the Makuti Motel while vehicles with dead guerrillas waited outside (Ellert, 1989: 13). This behaviour, along with the daily insults endured by blacks and other colonial subjects, fuelled opposition to the regime and undermined moderate Africans. White men who openly ridiculed black men in order to impress girls and prove their manly 'courage' were particularly resented (Raeburn, 1978: 66-68). Increasingly, a military solution was seen as the only path to majority rule (Sithole, 1977).

In the early 1970s, the nationalist attacks intensified, assisted by support from bases in Zambia and Tanzania. However, the campaigns were neither particularly successful nor well organised, leading to disputes between the various nationalist groups over tactics. ZAPU remaining wedded to more formal Soviet style warfare, reinforced by 'proper' military discipline and Russian assistance, while ZANU forces adopted Maoist guerrilla tactics, and even sent some cadres to China for training (Raeburn, 1978: 97). These disputes spawned assassinations, rebellions and conflicts, made worse by their frequent alignments with ethnic, racial and class divisions (Kriger, 1992; White, 2003).

Thus, as the war intensified in 1973 the question of loyalty and commitment became central to those who aspired to power within the nationalist movements.[5] And the issue of loyalty was often framed in masculinist terms. Blacks who worked for the regime or believed in gradual, multiracial change were branded as 'sell-outs', as loyal lapdogs to the white settler regime, incapable or unwilling to act like men and protect their culture, their families and their societies. To identify and kill 'sell-outs' thus became a mark of loyalty to the nationalist movement and a sign that one was truly a nationalist warrior, unafraid and willing to kill even close kin for the cause. Indeed, *chimurenga* battle songs urged people to crack the heads of 'sell-outs' and whites (Pongweni, 1982). The label 'sell-out' thus became a means for disciplining one's own group, for legitimating violence and all too often, for grabbing property and getting rid of personal enemies – particularly attractive to poor young men (and women) bent on challenging senior males (Kaarsholm, 2005; Kriger, 1992; Maxwell, 1999; Staunton, 1990; Werbner, 1991; see novels by Chinodya, 1989; Kanengoni, 1997; Vera, 2002).

While many women actively supported the struggle, the war was primarily seen as a struggle between men, over leadership, resources and loyal followers. The war was largely framed as an opportunity for 'real men' to end white/male domination and to complete the work of the First Chimurenga. While socialist slogans abounded, race, land and male power were central tropes of nationalist discourse. A large, attentive audience burst into applause when John Moyo declared that 'We, the Sons of the Soil, have become foreigners in our own country', because of 'our unwillingness to fight like men'. 'It is high time,' he urged, 'that we acted like men to retrieve our stolen land' (Sithole, 1977: 2). When tensions erupted along ethnic lines, disputes were often cast in masculine terms. One young nationalist complained that ZAPU leaders were belittling the Shona as 'natural cowards' while trumpeting Ndebele bravery. Those who dared to challenge allegedly authoritarian and anti-intellectual commanders were branded as 'sell-outs' and often met a brutal end (Tshabangu, 1977: 12-13, 17; Raeburn, 1978; White, 2003). Only loyal followers were 'real men'.

Nationalist documents often called for women's liberation and democracy for all (including women), however, this rhetoric was largely for foreign consumption. The old notions of men as protectors and women as the protected largely shaped the roles of women (and men) during the war. While some women gained authority and combat experience, most were relegated to domestic roles, often raped or seduced and then banished to camps for unwed mothers if pregnant. Indeed, as the war grew more violent, women were pulled out of the front – which was seen as 'a situation for real men' (Nhongo-Simbanegavi, 2000: 34, 82). Moreover, guerrillas frequently forced local girls to sleep with them, ignoring frustrated parents and leading to many unwanted pregnancies (Staunton, 1990: 49-50; Werbner, 1991).

Ironically, as the war began to heat up after 1973, the Rhodesian regime also struggled to differentiate friends from enemies. The regime realised that Africans who seemed friendly during the day were often assisting guerrilla fighters at night. Intelligence about the 'terrorists' became almost impossible to obtain, except in the cities (Lovett, 1978). This uncertainty undermined relations between (and within) the Rhodesian forces (white and black) and the local populations, aggravating tensions and suspicions. In an effort to garner support, the regime drew on the language of masculinity and manliness. The war propaganda of the Rhodesian state not only vilified the nationalists as dangerous, Godless communists, bent on destroying civilisation, but also characterised them as failed men, who cared nothing about protecting innocent women and children. The young Rhodesians sent to fight were told that the war 'was a glorious adventure, an easy test of manhood, a war that was right and always honourable, a war where the good were white and the evil were black, a war as simple as that' (Moore-King, 1988: 3, 51, 77).

Indeed, the war was represented as the quintessential place for turning boys into men. The men in the armed forces were compared to the heroes of the 1890s uprisings. Most men felt the war was a test of their manhood – 'this kind of thing makes a man of you' (Weiss, 1994: 52). Regiment recruiters trumpeted the slogan: 'It's a man's job to protect God's own country' (Bond, 1977: 124). When soldiers went to town, they would harass civilians, telling young men 'Get a fucking haircut, you civvies. When are you going to join the army, you wanker?' (Cocks, 1988: 23). Men who refused to join the war were ridiculed as failures. Women joined the chorus (Cocks, 1988: 15). Thus the discourses of war reinforced both the manliness of those who fought and the lack of manly qualities among men who refused.

Among soldiers, moreover, sexualised, masculinised language continued to be a central discourse differentiating those who knew how to fight, had been hardened by war and those who had not. New recruits were accused of being 'a little cunt' or 'fucking fairies.' Inexperienced soldiers in the field were razzed by the experienced fighters, who asked them 'What are you fuckin' fresh puss doing here – eh?' The experienced soldiers compared themselves with the newcomers by reminding them that 'This prick's fucked more chicks than you *okes* have had hot breakfasts!'(Cocks, 1988: 9, 23, 36). This is just a small sample of the sexualised language used in the war, but it reminds us how gendered and sexualised the performance of war can be.

The trauma of war, the deaths and the killing of the 'enemy', was also framed in antiseptic and masculinist terms. Soldiers described the war as 'a fine punch up'. Fighting was a 'contact' and killing was sanitised as 'scribbling', 'culling', 'slotting', 'drilling', 'wasting', 'snuffing', etc.. Those killed were dismissed as 'munts', 'gooks', 'Affs' or 'terrs', all fighting for Godless communism (Fuller, 2004: 59-60). Killing became a numbers game – the more 'terrs' killed, the greater the celebration (Lovett, 1977). Moral scruples were for women and weak men, not the fighting men of Rhodesia. As one former soldier said, 'We were all mad in that war. That's why we were so fucking good' (Fuller, 2004: 66).

Intense bonding also developed. As one soldier wrote, 'It is easy to feel forgotten in the bush, not only for the chap who has no family or girlfriend. All of us at times ... feel alone and scared'. Letters from home and parcels from the Loyal Women's Guild helped (MacBruce, 1983: 37), but the daily camaraderie at base and during combat was a crucial survival strategy (Lotter, 1984). Many of the units even developed their own language. Most partied hard. The Rhodesian Light Infantry (RLI) had regular parties which did not end till every officer's stiff-front shirt had been torn off (Bond, 1977: 90). The nature of guerrilla warfare no doubt intensified bonding. Long periods of sitting around, waiting and worrying, were broken up with sporadic, deadly encounters with the enemy. Soldiers dreamt of home, but the daily reality facing most Rhodesian forces (and the increasing number of reservists on rotation duty), was framed by an intense, almost homoerotic environment which inspired life-long friendships and emotional ties (Cowderey and Nesbit, 1987: 161). Indeed, as Cocks reminisced, 'comradeship took the place of everything outside the RLI ... even families and lovers ... and would save the lives of many of us later on' (1988: 22).

Ironically, while racial hierarchy defined much of the armed forces and remained a central trope legitimating the war, the realities of war increasingly undermined racial divisions and hierarchies. Except for the entirely white RLI and the Special Air Service, Rhodesian security forces depended on black and Coloured recruits for their very survival. While the superiority of white officers remained largely unquestioned, the idea that whites could win the war on their own evaporated, and recognition for black and Asian soldiers increased, albeit unequally (Lovett, 1977). The counter-insurgency units, particularly the Selous Scouts, fought in small multi-racial groups with white Scouts blacked up for weeks at a time. They sang *chimurenga* songs, learned the language, habits and codes of the guerrillas and sought in every way to pass as the enemy. Captured guerrillas were often 'turned' or 'tamed' and integrated into the scouts. While 'tamed' suggests femininisation, these men were often particularly effective and ferocious fighters and were acknowledged as such. Moreover, openly racist behaviour was not tolerated, and at base, 'white and black soldiers intermingled, held evening braiis, drank and sang *chimurenga* songs' (Ellert, 1989: 95; Reid-Daly, 1982). This embodied transgression of supposedly fixed racial, cultural and ideological divides, suggests the possibility that long held 'certainties' about race, manliness and courage were being disturbed by the struggle, at least in certain quarters (White, 2005).

After 1976, the war grew more deadly, and more ambiguous as the internal settlement[6] unsettled racial tropes. The war was no longer blacks against whites, but a struggle over power and legitimacy. The Rhodesian forces became increasingly multiracial. Most Coloureds had fought on the Rhodesian side, but by 1978, five-sixths of the SS were black, with black officers playing an increasingly important role (Reid-Daly, 1982: 66). The Muzorewa government condemned ZAPU and ZANU forces as 'terrorists'. Dirty tricks increased – including poisoning water and clothes, killing accomplices and scorched earth tactics wherever 'terrorists' were found (Ellert, 1989: 108-09; Caute, 1983). To make matters worse, the paramilitary forces set up to protect civilians, 'included the dregs of society – both black and white – who largely used their position to steal, rape and pillage' (Ellert, 1989: 26,181). 'These attacks were seen as motivated by greed, jealousy, revenge and a desire for status' (Alexander and McGregor, 2005: 79). The nationalist forces were little better. They continued to torture and kill 'sell-outs' and suspected sorcerers/witches (Alexander, 1996; Staunton, 1990: 127-28; Werbner, 1991: 150-51), attack missionaries, shoot down two civilian planes and to abduct school children (Lovett, 1977). Both sides adopted a shoot first and ask questions later approach, with devastating consequences for civilians (Cowderoy and Nesbit, 1987; Fuller, 2004).

The violence often had a sexualised, masculinist character. Women were often victims, attacked by both sides. Young women in the nationalist armies had to fend off sexual advances from fellow soldiers, often leading to rape. The comrades frequently raped and tortured 'enemy' women (Nhongo-Simbanegavi, 2000; Werbner, 1991). Women teachers at the Elim Pentecostal Mission were raped and killed by guerrilla forces (Ellert, 1989: 117-18). The Rhodesian forces routinely stripped naked, raped and threatened to drown African women suspected of collaboration. Sometimes, hot porridge or sharp objects were inserted into their vaginas, often with deadly effects (Fuller, 2004: 62-63; MacBruce, 1983: 99). Some of Muzorewa's forces brought back from Uganda soon took to burning huts and raping rural women (Ellert, 1989: 142). Even the protected village guards routinely demanded sexual favours (Nhongo-Simbanegavi, 2000: 6). The rapes were often public performances, on both sides, asserting the masculinity of the rapists and the inability, i.e. emasculation of their men.

The heightened violence in the last few years of the struggle left deep scars on civilians and soldiers. Violence and death had become a daily occurrence, always possible, always unpredictable, always at close quarters. While many soldiers and civilians had recoiled in horror – one pilot recalled the intimacy of killing as 'particularly horrifying ... [I] have never quite got over it' (Cowderoy and Nesbit, 1987: 46-47) – for many, violence had become a way of life. An RLI soldier who started not wanting to enjoy killing, admitted that he wound up 'speaking of killing "gooks" as "fantastic" and "terrific"' (Weiss, 1994: 49). Many guerrillas became inured to violence as well. As one woman recalled, some became 'very fearful people. They had been in the bush for such a long time and some of them were almost like animals. ...They were not as warm as ordinary people' (Staunton, 1990: 130). As another noted, 'People with guns are made mad by them' (Werbner, 1991: 158). Many former fighters, on both sides, could not adjust to 'peace'. Some killed themselves, many frightened their families and communities, others tried to hide their past and fear of reprisals silenced open discussion of past injustices and hampered the possibility of reconciliation (Cocks, 1988: 9; Kriger, 1992: 41-42; Reeler, 2004; Werbner, 1991: 157-58).

Not surprisingly, violence continued after independence. 'sell-outs' continued to be killed, leading many to flee the country or deny their past (Kriger, 1995; MacBruce, 1983). Internal nationalist struggles, largely along ethnic lines, led to a violent civil war against the Ndebele 'dissidents'. The Korean-trained Fifth Brigade perpetrated brutal atrocities against the 'dissidents' that are still remembered by many as worse than anything done by the Rhodesian forces. The wanton brutality of the conflict inflamed ethnic tensions and has left a sense of betrayal and suspicion that continues to haunt the region (Alexander and McGregor, 2005; Chan, 2005; Werbner, 1991). And despite official support for gender equality, much gender violence had reached epidemic proportions after the war (Jacobs, 1995: 258), particularly in Matabeleland (Vera, 2002), and up to today. Campaigns against prostitutes (often equated with single women) in the 1980s (Ranchod-Nilsson, 2006), attacks on homosexuals and the criminalisation of homosexuality, sexual assaults on women belonging to the opposition party (Itano, 2003) and the ridiculing of opposition politicians as 'tea-drinking lackeys of Blair-Bush imperialism' (Moore: 2005 157; Reeler, 2004) remind us that the gendered legacy of war and violence does indeed have a long and destructive shelf-life.

Conclusion

As we have seen, the violence of both government and nationalist forces in Rhodesia spawned insecurity, atrocities and suspicion, and a population inured to violence in everyday life. The evidence suggests that the hyper-masculine, warrior imagery used to fuel the struggle on both sides fostered a vision of masculinity that prized physical toughness, ability to commit violence and loyalty to a cause and to one's fellow warriors above all other characteristics. Enemies were feminised while success in war and the ability to kill became the litmus test of successful manhood, often vociferously supported by women as well.

The transformation of so many men, and women, into killing machines, inured to solving problems with violence, and accustomed to valuing martial masculinity above all other approaches to life, has, I believe, ingrained deeply held attitudes and practices that have had a tragic legacy. The violence in post-independence Zimbabwe resonates with Enloe's warning that gender roles and relations are transformed by violence and that this transformation has long-term consequences for the way people think and behave. Indeed, when one looks at post-independence atrocities, it is apparent that patriarchal hyper-masculine practices have continued to shape key institutions of power, particularly the government and the army. Gains for some young men and women during the liberation struggle have largely disappeared (Barnes, 1995), while the privileged have come to believe that those who challenge their dominance deserve abuse, torture and even death. A celebratory narrative of the liberation struggle continues to legitimate atrocities against Zimbabwean citizens. As Stephen Chan points out, the bloodshed of both wars has 'never been requited by apology and the disavowal of violence'. Only reconciliation, for both public and private traumas, 'can take the nation forward, can allow the state sound citizens, and can allow citizens to be sound individuals' (2005: 380). Moreover, as much of the violence in Zimbabwe has been deeply gendered, moving forward will require a much more nuanced understanding of the way masculinity/ies, gender and race have shaped, and been shaped, by Zimbabwe's violent history.

ENDNOTES

1. Zimbabwe was colonised by the British in 1890, the British South Africa Company ruled till 1923, responsible government of Southern Rhodesia (SR) was established in 1923, SR joined Northern Rhodesia and Nyasaland in the Federation of Central Africa (1953-64) and the settler regime declared Rhodesia an independent state (1964-80).
2. The nationalist opposition began with the SR African National Congress in 1957. Despite bannings, two major parties emerged: the Zimbabwe African People's Union (ZAPU) headed by Joshua Nkomo in 1961 and Zimbabwean National Union (ZANU) in 1963, initially headed by Ndabaningi Sithole, later by Robert Mugabe. ZAPU was predominantly Ndebele while ZANU was Shona, thus often reinforcing ethnic rivalries. Abel Muzorewa led the African National Congress (ANC) that participated in an internal settlement with the Rhodesian regime in 1977, but lost power to ZANU-PF in 1980 (Ndlovu-Gatsheni 2005).
3. While Asians were often regarded as effeminate by British colonialists, very little has been written on the masculinity and gender practices of the small Coloured (mixed-race) and Asian communities in Zimbabwe (Muzondidya 2005; Streets 2004).
4. *Chimurenga* means to struggle or cry out in Shona and has been associated with African struggles for independence since 1896, the Second Chimurenga being the independence war. Mugabe is using the same language to legitimise the recent land restructuring and attacks on members of the opposition party.
5. For debates over the level of commitment of civilians to nationalist forces, see Alexander 1996.
6. Muzorewa's ANC, Sithole's ZANU (Sithole) (also known as the African National Council) and Chief Chirau agreed to an internal settlement and Musorewa was elected in 1978. Smith retained considerable power and protection for whites. The 'solution' received little international support (Ndlovu-Gatsheni, 2006)

9

It couldn't be anything innocent: Negotiating gender in patriarchal-racial spaces

ANE M. ØRBØ KIRKEGAARD

The Rhodesian settler project depended on the co-operation with black men, *and* on the Othering of them. Masculinity was a vital part of this double movement of practical proximity and narrative distance; cross-racial co-operation between men concerning the control of women, and the sexualisation of the 'African'. The racialised discourse on 'African' masculinity contributes to the preservation of distance between the African Other and the European Self. The latter generally evades being objectified and studied, as it is itself the master of objectification of others. Consequently, scientific curiosity has mostly been directed towards those who are constructed as different and exotic (McFadden, 2000), rather than towards those who construe themselves as Norm. Research on white Zimbabweans is lacking. In this chapter we examine the performance, reproduction and contestation of masculinity among white Zimbabweans. Those white Zimbabweans whose voices are represented below belong to a rapidly shrinking category of Zimbabweans. They are Eurasian second generation commercial farmers. The voices are Peter, Beatrice, John, Louisa and Patricia's. The interviews were conducted in September and October 2000, on what were then their farms in eastern and northern Zimbabwe.[1]

Contested terrains
Colonial masculinity developed both in the drawing rooms and scientific and explorers clubs in European capital cities. It also developed at the various colonial frontiers in the Americas, Africa and Asia. In other words it was constructed in the reflexivity between the scientific work by 'softies' and armchair anthropologists, who never left their comfortable European upper- and middle class homes, and by the tough men's men. According to colonial myths, the latter discovered new territories, peoples and natural phenomena, which fed European fantasies, wallets, corporations and civil society. Even though there are no frontiers left in Southern Africa, the ideal of frontier manliness – colonial masculinity – lives on in private as well as public relations. It manifests itself in the continually successful claim to power and authority by men.

A gendered continuum links Zimbabwe under black majority rule to colonial Rhodesia. Most significant about this continuum is the patriarchal grip on power, despite the inherent contradictions in the androcentric social structures. Ian Smith's expressed passion for the traditional patriarchal married family, signified by male dominance and female subordination, was contradicted by high divorce rates, illegal abortions and domestic violence (Smith 1997; Godwin and Hancock, 1995). This split between ideal and reality still exists and is expressed in different ways by all the interviewees. Peter, middle-aged son of a dominant white patriarch legitimates the patriarchal system he grew up with, while also downplaying its significance, when he claims that 'we tend to be chauvinists. We try to keep our maleness although we fail. I mean we fail. We try and pretend that we are sort of a rough bunch, we are all male and we are the boys, but really, when you get home it's a different story.' He goes on to explain that the jokes men tell about women are 'chauvinist jokes, male slanted jokes' but that these jokes do not 'draw a comparison on what it's really like'. His argument is that 'most men are respectable towards women and are decent. In Zimbabwe anyway.' Respect and decency is however conditional, and dependent on women's conformity with social norms of decency – heterosexual and monogamist house wife-ing and mothering.

Having personal experience of non-conformity Patricia explains that 'if a woman is strong and capable and questioning and has an opinion, she would definitely be threatening their male ego. So they are not comfortable with women in that way'. At one point she exclaims that 'the men are the greatest problem' in marriages. Her experiences of being at odds with the ideals unmask the reality behind the rough bunch mentality repudiated by Peter. Her marriage nearly broke down because she insisted on working full-time outside the home, something her husband found very difficult to accept. His argument was that his income was more than enough to support the family. To her, working outside the home was however not a matter of economics, but of pursuing her own interests. She explains the opposition towards women's pursuit of non-marital and non-mothering interests with Zimbabwean men's inability to:

cope with a wife being independent, having an opinion of her own, a life of her own, perhaps her own income. Wives must rather downplay their role quite significantly and be there for them. To sort of serve them, make sure the meals are right and be around the house and that sort of thing.

Reasoning around the issue of manliness, chauvinism and masculinity Peter exposes the contradiction of his own argument. His mother performed her home-oriented wife-ing duties as expected, fulfilling the functionalist female roles displayed in masculinist-sexist jokes. He juxtaposes his upbringing with a sexist joke: 'I was raised in my parents' shadow of a subservient wife that will wash, iron-- - -you know what WIFE stands for, you have heard that one? Washing, Ironing, F-ing [fucking], etc.' However, while the dominant image of male-female relations in the home is that of the authoritative husband and the subservient wife, social and political tension is building up as the colonial ideals of a frontier manliness are challenged by women, who contest male authority in their daily lives, as Patricia does.

Even so, the differences between women and men are generally experienced and explained as being natural, as unchangeable givens with their roots in our foggy historical past. Butler has critically noted that 'it is precisely through the infinite deferral of authority to an irrevocable past that authority itself is constituted' (Butler, 1993: 108). In accordance with this observation gender difference is perceived as an inherent part of our bodily and emotional set-up, and as the reason for relational problems between women and men. Beatrice, in the interview, claims that 'men are different to us, they can go off there and sleep with that one and that one and it can mean absolutely nothing to them, whereas we don't work the same way, it means more than that to us.' She claims that sex 'means more' to women because women, in contrast to men are reproductively oriented while men are focused on pleasurable sex with no strings attached; they want free lunches. To her, 'more' contains the central qualities of femininity: reproductive love, responsibility and continuous care spanning a whole lifetime. The contradictions between women's and men's sexuality creates marital problems as men, according to Beatrice, are more sexually oriented than women. This is expressed either in men's perceived excessive demand on sexual services at home, or their search for extra-marital substitutes to cover their needs. As a logical consequence of Beatrice's reasoning women naturally build safe heteronormative married nests in which to bring up children, while men need to be firmly bound to family responsibilities through the marriage contract. The female urge to create safe nests 'for children to grow up in' is, however, costly in terms of time and energy. Hence, men need to 'go out there' and bring in the bread and the butter. Beatrice has completely embraced the social and economic organisation of the Zimbabwean state and society, which is based on the construction of gender differences as biological and nature-given. She is unaware of the historical place and space in which the gendered narrative she lives by was slowly constructed – nineteenth century upper- and middle class England (Weeks 1989; Handwerker, 1990).

Beatrice is seriously interested in issues of gender differences, and is preoccupied with building bridges between the two sexes. She has taken her husband to courses on gender communication, and has read what she clearly finds to be authoritative books – *Men are from Mars* and *Why men don't listen and women can't read maps* – on the subject. The courses and the books confirmed her preconceived perceptions and explanations of biology as the grounds for gender differences. Hence in her private quest for understanding what she experiences as biological differences between men and women Beatrice reproduces bio/logical gender discourses. This bio/logic also explains her and other women's experience of male authority and female subordination as historically natural rather than cultural. It implicates her (and other women and men) in a process of continuous confirmation of the correctness of feminine subordination under masculine authority.

However, even though behavioural difference may generally be perceived as nature-given, this does not mean that everyone accepts such difference as purely biological, and hence unchangeable. Patricia links what she calls masculinist 'attitudes' to 'the fact that men were always the elevated partner in everything in this country. They were the ones who you never questioned. A wife never questioned her husband.' In her private life she has challenged the socio-economic structures, which have been constructed with the support of the infinite deferral of authority to the irrevocable past. She has not however challenged the socio-sexual structures, which force women (and men) into hetero-normative marriages so as to be accepted as social beings:

I couldn't see a future for myself as a single woman in this country. I knew if I was going to carry on here I had to get married because, once you have a certain age in this country there is no social life for you. If you're not a couple – forget it! You then must be a woman out on the lookout, sort of thing.

Women going out on their own to enjoy themselves, she concludes, are perceived by men as free to prey on for a one-night stand.

Controlled spaces

Women and men tend to socialise separately. As John describes dinners, whether at home or out on town, 'the men always are together, standing around the pub and the girls will *always* be sitting together. That's how the evening always starts. We don't mix very easily initially.' Even though 'everybody is mixed' in the end, he says that 'men do a lot together, as men. I don't know whether that is a forming trait or what but I think generally the men in this country are criticized for it, in that we tend to prefer male company.' Pondering, he repeats that 'men in this country enjoy male company. I don't know what it is, I really don't know why. Men tend to gravitate together.' This very marked social division of women and men is often explained, and also in the end by John, by the fact that women and men talk about very different things. Women discuss matters concerning children and home-making, while the men will talk about work, sports and politics. It is assumed that men do not enjoy talking about home and children, so called 'women's matters', and that women take no interest in work, sports and politics.

However, reasons for particular social arrangements, which keep women and men separate may also be found in deep-seated conflicts over power and control among men and between women and men. In cases where women and men do find common interests and begin to socialise outside socially acceptable norms, the consequences may be severe. Louisa's experience of this is explicative. Some years back a young man, who was new to the area, approached her house, 'he wanted to build a house and he wanted some help. And him and I became quite good friends.' She describes it almost as meeting a soul mate; 'I mean, immediately there was like ... rapport. It was really great.' Socially nothing much happens in her home-town 'and there's so little opportunity for friendship and interaction with people of different backgrounds.' However, her in-laws felt very unsettled by her making friends with the man who, apart from being ten years younger than her 'was a very good-looking guy.' A brother-in-law approached the man, threatened him 'and said: "Listen, you don't go near her again! You keep away!" And I was flummoxed because I couldn't believe it.' Louisa's analysis is clear: 'I mean the fact that he was male. If it had been a woman it would have been different. They couldn't see that it could be anything innocent. I mean, you could not be friends with a male. You *must* be having something going with it.' Louisa lost a friend, in her own understanding due to the socio-sexual structures of Zimbabwean society; as a woman you cannot be just be friends with a man. Her brother-in-law took it upon himself to rectify the probable mistake (or blunder) committed by his sister-in-law by making up with the young man *as a man* through verbal threats of retaliation if he did not pull out.

The uneasiness with which female-male friendships are perceived also has its background in Zimbabwe's colonial history. Zimbabwe was not just a colony but a settler colony. Settler colonies are dependent on a steady influx of both women and men, and upon the continuous reproduction within their borders of new generations of settlers, or righteous citizens, as many settlers would argue them to be (Stasiulis & Yuval-Davis, 1995; Jacobs, 1995; Lowry, 1997; Kirkegaard, 2004). However, women were not colonisers and settlers on an equal footing with men; they were brought in or accepted as companions because they were necessary for the imperial settler project to succeed, and they were subjected to rigorous social measures of control both in private and in public. In Zimbabwe, male colonisers and colonised found common ground in at least one particular issue of major importance to the development of contemporary Zimbabwean gender structures, i.e. the racialised control of women's sexuality and reproduction (Schmidt, 1987; Kirkegaard, 2004). The organisation of the colonial state around the socio-sexual control of women was, in the everyday lives of individual Zimbabweans, translated into men's management of women's space, and social and sexual relations. Simultaneously, settler men guaranteed themselves rights of access to women of all backgrounds, except the married women belonging to the white community (Kirkegaard, 2004). To uphold the social structures on which both politics and economy rested and still rests it was, and is essential, to continuously reproduce discourses and practices which keep women in place at home with the children, or at least on a tight leash from that particular reproductive space. Consequently, the general expectation in contemporary Zimbabwe, as well as in colonial Rhodesia, is that women, whether black or white, should not work for wages outside their homes, and they should not want to do so either. The social and economic order rests on male breadwinners and female care-takers. But it is an order which is slowly being eroded: 'In my father's time, my parents' time, you became a housewife. There was no such thing as seeking a job,' which according to Peter has changed as a growing number of women enter the working force, even as managers. Of course women always have worked outside the home, particularly women from low-income groups (Godwin, 1996; Godwin and Hancock 1999 ; Barnes, 1999), but their need or wish to work is circumscribed by norms, which herald home-making and discredit wage-working mothers. Beatrice sums up these expectations and their consequences, much like Patricia also does: 'I think Zimbabwean men are chauvinistic. They expect a lot from their women folk: [I] "want my coffee like this and my tea like this, my bed made like this, my clothes like this" and they don't have to do any of that and their women organize somebody else to do it for them. The traditional Zimbabwean men don't cook or anything.' In other words the socio-economic structures of colonial Rhodesia formed a family organisation, which had and continues to have outward effects, and consequently influence not only private economies and arrangements, but also formal and informal sectors in society.

Going fishing with the boys: catching the qualities of masculinity

The masculine ideal is one of individualist and rough toughness, clear-cut messages and rational decision-making, legitimated by references to the harshness of nature, the unruliness of women or the Other, and the difficult political climate. Yet, in a situation where men are dependent on each other, in a hierarchical structure, such ideals may be difficult to live by. Norms are altered to accommodate the dominant and authoritative male, a process in which men are feminised in their internal relations. Peter shares his working days with his father and two brothers. The working relationship between them is marked by a classical patriarchal hierarchical structure; father at the top and sons falling in under his authority. Peter explains how this relationship works: 'We understand each other and know how to speak political speak, politically correct speak. You don't call a spade a spade here, it's a grey spade, not black or white. We know how to speak around things, we know how to avoid conflict.' To call a spade a spade is usually a sign of maleness. However in this particular context it is used to describe his wife who is different: 'She likes to get things over and done with, out, the air cleared. We don't clear the air, we just avoid it, we sort of forgive and forget and carry on.' She behaves like a man; she is the manager of a local firm; her social status is wife and mother. Roles clash in her as they do in her husband who is feminised in relation to his father. This makes her difficult for others to place in clear cut categories, as she continually moves between spaces, which are generally held separate between the sexes. He however remains safe within the markers of masculinity, living up to the demands placed on men. He is married with children, keeps his own house and staff, and successfully displays his fatherhood publicly but his feminisation is concealed in the family and accepted as norm among men.

The rough bunch, individualistic and punitive masculinity developed in the colonial context, where men were legally the sole rulers within the family, fostered a femininity characterised by secondary-ness. As Patricia describes it, women consequently 'put all their trust in their husband, and he's the provider, and they'll be taking the backseat their whole life.' Her reflections on Zimbabwean masculinity lead her to ask how male and female attitudes, behaviours and expectations 'are linked.' She concludes: 'I don't think that the one can be there without the other.' In other words, she suggests that masculinity and its practical consequences for her in her own life is directly linked to femininity. Through her lived experiences of being a bearer of femininity in a society heavily marked by androcentrism she has arrived at the same conclusion as gender researchers, i.e. that masculinity can exist only in contrast with femininity (e.g. Butler, 1993; Connell, 1999).

Masculinity can only be described by the lacking properties in its feminine opposite and through the erasure of the feminine. In other words, describing what a Zimbabwean 'man's man' is, or by what Zimbabwean masculinity is signified, necessarily ought to involve describing what its opposite – femininity – is not. This is exactly what John does, as he struggles to explain what he himself dubs 'Zimbabwean masculinity'. The pauses are long. His arm resting on the dinner table and his eyes wandering out through the windows as if he hopes the right formulations will pass by and help him in his endeavour to explain the essence of masculinity:

This friend of ours, the mother and father of all these, as I said

> they've got three girls, now he's a very ... ehm ... very much a man's-man ... ehm ... you know, he's a ... you know what I mean by a man's-man? He is not at all effeminate or you know he, he would much prefer male company. He loves to go on boys fishing trips. And ... I think a lot of us Zimbabweans are like that.

Again, he returns to men's orientation towards male company: 'We, we tend to be very male orientated.' He comes no further than repeating that going fishing with the boys is what masculinity is about. However, when describing their neighbour's daughter the words start coming to him, and he finally manages to explain what the properties of masculinity are: 'His daughter, the one daughter, actually worked with him on the farm as a farm manager at one stage, 'cause she was very rugged and *manly*, and of course he loved that. You know, she rounded up the cattle, and she worked with him every day on the cattle, and he just loved having her around and she was very rugged.' He goes on to explain that she was 'rugged' already as a little girl:

> When they were little kids in the district and we would have a crowd here and all the kids would be playing rugby on the lawn and that sort of thing, Heather was very much as tough and rugged as any of the boys were, and they often seemed ... if they could choose anybody for their rugby team they'd rather have Heather than some of the boys there to play rugby.

In describing the qualities of what it means to be a man, he has however robbed Heather of her feminine properties. Realising this, he hastens to confirm her femininity through her heteronormative, monogamous and married reproductive sexuality: 'But she's a very effeminate person, and she's married, got her own kids and she, she's still a lady. She's not, she's not in any way wrong or different, she's a lady.' Not only is her lost-and-found femininity used to establish the contours of the masculine, but the stability of masculinity is also articulated in Heather's transformation from rugged tomboy to feminine wife and mother.

As suggested by the realities of Peter and his brother's working relationship with their father, masculinity should not be understood as a behavioural blueprint guiding every man's behaviour. Masculinity and femininity 'point beyond categorical sex difference to the ways men differ among themselves and women differ among themselves, in matters of gender' (Connell, 1999: 69). Peter's work and income are tightly bound to his conspicuous demonstration of appropriate respect for the authoritative father. In other words, men are not just men among men. They are differently positioned in relation to each other, depending on a number of hierarchical structures, including sexual orientation, age, class and racial definitions.

This contrasts with Beatrice's perception of gender difference as tied firmly in men's bodies and brains, and consequently behaviours. In her view men are by definition less sensitive in sexual matters than women, they are less committed to family life, and they are unable to manage a home, because they are differently constructed from women genetically. In contrast to women, they are literally unable to see what is wrong in having sex without being in love, they have to be legally bound by marriage to care for their offspring, and they are dependent on women to create respectable and well-functioning homes. This contrasts with the conclusions reached by Patricia, who claims that the major obstacle for women is not the genetic differences between women and men, but the social and economic structures, which privilege men, and allow them the space and authority required to be 'the elevated partner in everything'.

Similarities: the construction of patriarchal-racial spaces

Masculinity is not expressed in a homogenous body of tradition and custom, but is continuously reproduced and challenged by external and internal contradictions and the political struggles over power. The particular historical circumstances under which Zimbabwe evolved, continue to inform local perceptions of what it means to be a man. A question to be asked with this in mind is whether the expressions of masculinity represented above are vastly different from masculinity as expressed among other groups of the Zimbabwean population, for instance the black majority.

Discussing that question necessitates an understanding of homosociality, the social segregation of women and men, as central to the construction and reproduction of male ideals in a patriarchal society. Institutionalised and informal male homosocial interactions function to exclude women, and subordinate masculinities (e.g. homosexual men) from central spheres of power. This segregation strengthens masculinity, because women and men constantly re-enforce discourses and practices which sustain the social institutions constructed on its basis. When John describes how men tend to 'gravitate together' he is unable to explain why this happens, while Peter accepts without questioning the male orientation on the farm, where he shares his working days with his father and brothers. In both contexts, socialising with friends and income generation, men spend their time with other men in spaces into which women are never or seldom accepted or invited. Within these spaces men not only bond and network, they are also de-masculinised in informal and formal hierarchies of power. The humiliation of men's feminisation among men is a threat to masculinity, as it firmly places men, and not only women, in un-authoritative positions. When Peter and his brothers 'forgive and forget and carry on' in their work on the farm, they are implicated in the reproduction of masculinity in a male homosocial space in which they are *expected* to behave like a woman; they 'take the back seat' to quote Patricia, in relation to the authoritative male, in this case the father. In other words not only women, but also men are inferior to the relatively few privileged males endowed with legitimate authority in the family, in the community and on the level of the state. The separate social and economic spheres, which women and men live in, result both in a separation of interests between them, and in distance and detachment. Consequently, John explains men's preference for male company by their shared interests, while Peter illustrates the distance and detachment from women through the explication of the abbreviation WIFE. The person with whom a man is expected to share his sexual desires, and with whom he shares home and parenting responsibilities is stereotyped as an impersonalised service station, and as someone whose interests are apolitical and economically unproductive, focused on reproduction and care.

This corresponds with Beatrice's understanding of women as 'natural' carers, whether legitimately married, at home with the children, or out on the town where they pose as 'that one and that one' whom men have sex with when they are not at home. Louisa's experience of making friends with a man breaches the unwritten rules of homosociality, constructed around fe/male difference and distance. Making cross-gender friendships implies that the difference and distance is fictional or that one of those implicated is sexually deviant. It might however also be read as a cover for illegitimate sexual intimacy. The two former interpretations threaten the stability of masculine power. The latter, however, strengthens it as men make up between themselves without female interference. Hence, the friendship was intercepted by Louisa's brother-in-law and accepted as ended by her new friend, who thereby contributed in confirming her in-law's sexual-reproductive rights in her. The interference is explained as protection against predatory male sexuality, and is based on the male decency which Peter refers to. Married women are off market; single women are accessible.

A society in which women and men are treated 'as bearers of polarized character types' (Connell, 1999: 68) may be defined as having the modern concept of masculinity. Men are privileged over women in political and economic spheres while they let a few individual women through the net, moving upwards, and a few men, moving downwards. This exclusion is rooted in the naturalisation of the polarised character types masculine and feminine. These are perceived as mutually exclusive characters. In other words, the one is what the other is not. This naturalisation of mutually exclusive characters is reproduced and secured through a homosocial organisation of society.

Connell argues that this particular concept of masculinity is linked to the creation of the modern state through the religious and civil wars in sixteenth and seventeenth century Europe (Connell, 1999, see also Laqueur, 1995). The formation of the modern state formed both modern sciences and the imperial quest for power and wealth: 'With masculinity defined as a character structure marked by rationality, and Western civilization defined as the bearer of reason to a benighted world, a cultural link between the legitimation of patriarchy and the legitimation of empire was forged' (Connell, 1999: 187). However, because he focuses on the West, Connell fails to see that those who were defined as living in this 'benighted' world and thence were subjected to Western masculine reason successively became a creative and oppositional part of that very civilisation.

The inclusion of the Other into various European imperial projects was based on practices of exclusion. These exclusionary practices were based in a scientific concept of culture, constructing non-European traditions and customs as deviant, while defining the European ditto as the modern norm. Hence, the construction of *an* African tradition became that which defined the contours of modernity. In other words, it is deeply modern to be 'traditionally African', irrespective of the historical-geographical origin of that which is constructed as African. Consequently, maleness in contemporary Zimbabwean discourse on the authentic African man includes the modern concept of masculinity. In this discourse women and 'sissies' (Aarmo, 1999) are secondary to 'men's men' not only politically and economically, but also socially. Predatory and violent (hetero-) sexual prowess is considered a basic signifier of maleness.

Conclusion

The voices represented above have been extracted from research material which also included black Zimbabweans. I have however chosen to focus on the construction of masculinity among whites, not because their constructions of masculinity are different from blacks' but because there are so many similarities. The question raised above, whether white Zimbabwean masculinity is vastly different from black masculinity, brings us back to the basic issue of culture and power relations. Yuval-Davis claims that 'identities – individual and collective – are specific forms of cultural narratives which constitute commonalities and differences between selves and others' (Yuval-Davis, 2002: 43). When such narratives are constructed at a violent colonial intersection, the differences between Self and Other are magnified at the expense of similarities. Successively, the similarities between coloniser and colonised paves the way for the definition of common interests and politics. The consistent adoption of sexist and racialised politics and economic structures not only draws up lines of serious societal conflict, but also tends in time to erase alternative perceptions of social organisation, leading to the amalgamation of similarities in the 'cultural stuff' (Yuval-Davis, 2002: 43) of both coloniser and colonised, particularly in areas of common interest. Studying masculinity not only among black Zimbabweans but also among whites unmasks subtle social positionings, which cut across Zimbabwean society in unsuspected ways. What it means to be a man in contemporary Zimbabwe is socially and politically constructed as differing depending on racial belonging.

However, I argue that the differences are found in racialised *discourses* on masculinity, whereas *in practice* they are firmly rooted in gender rather than in 'race'. When talking about the qualities of manliness, both women and men relate to and negotiate the imperially rationalised patriarchal framing of manhood in remarkably similar ways across the racial barrier. The masculine and the feminine are constructed and understood as polarised character types in which sexual potency, superiority and dominance are associated with men (Kirkegaard, 2004). The differences that were once between white and black patriarchal ideals of manliness were erased through the interaction of different hierarchies – e.g. patriarchal, racial, class, sexual. Manifest in socio-economic and socio-sexual relations based on homosocial patterns of interaction in private as well as in public, it has become an integrated part of Zimbabwean tradition and custom.

ENDNOTES

1. The interviews form part of a larger research material, including both white and black farmers.

10

'Boys': Performing manhood in Zimbabwean drama

Praise Zenenga

This chapter examines the supremacy of masculine power and authority in Zimbabwean drama. I argue that masculinity, like imperialism, is a phallocentric, supremacist ideology that subjugates and dominates its subalterns (both male and female). Although the terms masculinity and manhood are not synonymous, their meanings are closely related in so far as they refer to 'the assemblage of qualities regarded as characteristic of men; maleness, manliness' (*Oxford English Dictionary* [OED] online). Within the Zimbabwean context, masculinity like manhood is also a social construction and it means different things at different times to different people (Kimmel, 2006: 5). As such, I will use masculinity and manhood interchangeably because my analysis adopts a wide range of meanings for both terms. In this chapter, the meanings of masculinity and manhood are not only limited to men's social duties, values and collective qualities perceived as pre-eminently belonging to or characterising a man but are also broadened to include the manifestation of an inner essence related to being a man rather than a woman, being an adult male as opposed to a child (OED). According to Connell's observation, both terms do not exist except in contrast to femininity or womanhood (Connell, 1995: 68).

Manhood and masculinity are 'defined by the drive for power, for domination, [and] control' (Kimmel, 2006: 6). Similarly, power, authority, rank and action are central in defining other terms like subaltern and hegemony which are also central terms in my analysis. The concept of hegemony deriving from Italian Marxist, Antonio Gramsci's analysis of class relations refers to the cultural dynamic by which a group claims and sustains a leading position and supremacy over others in social life. Zimbabwean history shows that 'at any given time, one form of masculinity rather than others is culturally exalted' (Connell, 1995: 68). The similarities and differences between the Rhodie man and the new Zimbabwean man are worth exploring. Although both possess macho qualities described above, there are certain socio-cultural and economic factors that shape their manliness.[1]

Constitutional and Christian values do not allow the Rhodie man to be polygamous while the new Zimbabwean evokes cultural arguments to marry many wives. However certain cultural norms, values, taboos and intricate extended family networks still govern the ways in which new Zimbabwean men treat and relate to women. For example, it is a serious taboo to beat or insult one's own mother. Certain Shona rituals and ceremonies also allow women to perform male roles or duties and vice versa thus challenging the rigidity of male-female binaries. In the context of my discussion, hegemonic masculinities refer to the ways in which men attain and maintain dominance (supremacy) (Gramsci, 1996: 57) over other gender categories. On the other hand, Spivak's (1988) article, 'Can the Subaltern Speak?' and the rise of post-colonial studies sparked renewed interest in the term subaltern. While Spivak frames the subaltern as female (Spivak, 1988: 308), my analysis treats it as an inclusive term which refers to inferior or subordinate gender categories.

While contending that both male and female identities are not only biological but also historical and social constructions (Connell, 2000: 29), I am primarily interested in exploring parallels between sexual and political oppression and their impact on identity formation as reflected in the two plays I have chosen to analyse. The notion of dominant masculinities implies the existence of subaltern femininities. Since theatre as a literary genre thrives mostly on conflict, these polarised gender categories provide a perennial source of drama for Zimbabwean playwrights. As such, the performance of masculine hegemony becomes the central focus in my analysis of Gonzo H. Msengezi's *The Honourable MP* (1984) and Tsitsi Dangarembga's *She No Longer Weeps* (1987). The central question I explore in these two plays is: What does it mean to be a man at a particular period in post-independence Zimbabwe? Kimmel contends that the answer to this question 'depends heavily on one's class, race, ethnicity, age, [and] sexuality' (Kimmel, 2006: 5). Theatre is an ideal site for unmasking Zimbabwean masculinities in a localised context. Two of the country's popular theatre companies Amakhosi Theatre and Rooftop Promotions serve as examples of how the male body is culturally inscribed within discourses of masculinities (Louie, 2002: 7). The fact that both theatre companies have male proprietors reflects traditional patriarchal attitudes towards women. Zimbabwean society still frowns upon women who work in or with theatre. Chitauro, Dube and Gunner have argued that while actors are seen as heroic figures, actresses are often considered potentially loose women (see Chitauro, Dube and Gunner, 1994).

Amakhosi Theatre began as 'The Dragons' karate club based at Stanley Community Hall in the high-density suburb of Makokoba in Bulawayo in 1980 and was the brainchild of Cont Mhlanga, a working-class factory worker. Since Amakhosi's inspiration derived from various karate and kung fu action movies, starring Bruce Lee and Jackie Chan, screened in most community halls throughout the country, it led to a reinforcement of a hegemonic model of masculinity. Hollywood kung fu films, and Amakhosi's early stage productions, perpetrated images of a 'macho man', whose power is made manifest in brute physical strength and unerring silence (Louie, 2002: 8). With an initial predominantly male cast, Amakhosi emphasised masculine attributes associated with executing revenge, vanquishing opponents of all colours and sizes, and attaining victory against all odds (Louie, 2002: 145-46) as depicted in the movies the actors saw and presumably what they thought the audience wanted. In this way, they decided the content for their female viewers.

Instead of pedalling the negative male figures, Mhlanga and members of Amakhosi focused more on the positive attributes that karate offers. Amakhosi went through an interesting transition in which they started using the same art form to subvert the macho image and create the something other as reflected in the new identity formations that its members embodied. Karate, a traditional Japanese form of unarmed combat, is steeped in a doctrine of self-defence that emphasises high levels of self-discipline, self-respect, and good behaviour through intense meditation, as opposed to aggressive and criminal behaviour. Part of the training requires those committed to the sport to quit drinking, smoking, and taking drugs. Instead of fomenting violent behaviour among Amakhosi artists, the karate cult not only promoted physical and mental fitness but also produced sober, disciplined and respectful men. Amakhosi's transition from sports to theatre 'did not mean an end of the karate club [...] [because] even today martial arts are still a part of the company's physical training' (Rohmer, 1999: 145). Although Amakhosi started with a male cast, it later began to incorporate women thus making a bold statement about female equality. Amakhosi women took up karate not only for self-defence and self-discipline but also to achieve the mental and physical fitness necessary in theatre.

In this chapter, I have deliberately chosen to focus on a male playwright and a female playwright respectively, in order to compare and contrast their gendered perspectives. Such an approach also helps to compare and contrast Dangarembga and Msengezi's depictions of how masculine hegemony, obtained during the early years of political independence in Zimbabwe, helped to shape male identities in relation to the general historical conceptualisations. According to Howson (2006), 'gender at any particular historical moment can only represent the configurations of practice emergent from the milieu of social relations that incorporate and organise power' (Howson, 2006: 57). My analysis acknowledges the historical specificities in which both the playwrights and their characters are operating and further contends that Zimbabwean men are not a homogenous category because there are inevitable differences in ethnicity, skin colour, economic status and circumstance. With such a 'growing recognition of the interplay between gender, race and class, it has become common to recognise multiple masculinities: Black as well as White, working-class as well as middle-class' (Connell, 1995: 76). Historicising the experiences of black Zimbabwean masculinities not only helps to avoid over-simplification but also helps us to understand the evolution of unique masculine identities. This approach also unpacks the milieu of class and race while scrutinising the gender relations operating within them (Connell 1995: 76).

Although Msengezi and Dangarembga predominantly focus on middle and upper-class male characters, the issue of diversity among Zimbabwean masculinities should not be obscured (Hunter and Davis, 1992: 466). Msengezi's play *The Honourable MP*, provides readers/audiences with a wider range of social classes. They include thugs, university students, middle-class professionals, domestic servants, peasants, farm workers, teachers, pastors, and the ruling class. Reference is also made to the white colonial male figures. As in other societies, masculinities in Zimbabwe are fluid. Robert Morrell argues that masculinities:

Should not be considered as belonging in a fixed way to any one group of men. They are socially and historically constructed in a process which involves contestation between rival understandings of what being a man should involve (Morrell, 2001: 7).

In *The Honourable MP*, for example, different characters have different notions of what it means to be a man in Zimbabwe. While Pfende thinks that being a man means acquiring many houses, cars, farms, electronic gadgets, and having multiple sexual partners; peasants and workers in his constituency think that being a man means becoming politically articulate and serving one's community. While this resonates with the definition of manliness that would be given within a white community, it does differ qualitatively from the idea of service provided by the traditional chief or headman. Although they too were expected to serve the community in a traditional sense, it is the post-independence concept of *chef* that provides the idea that the community is beholden to the man who is their representative and therefore entitled.

The two playwrights present readers/audiences with a multiplicity of manhood as opposed to their singularity (Howson, 2006: 58). Middle-class characters like Freddy and representatives of the ruling elite like Shakespeare Pfende constitute the hegemonic gender in the two plays. To a larger extent, both Dangarembga and Msengezi identify manhood as a multi-faceted construct. This means that both playwrights define what it means to be a man not only in terms of individual characters but also in terms of the characters' responsibilities to their families and the world at large (Hunter and Davis, 1992: 471). In analysing hegemonic masculine interests and identities, it is important to examine how gender roles, styles and stereotypes themselves underwent significant changes in Zimbabwean history.

Black manhood under colonialism

To a large extent, the material and historical specificities of Zimbabwean masculinities lie in the 'subalterneity' of black masculinity under colonialism (Sinha, 1995: 7). Although manhood in pre-colonial Zimbabwean societies was not undifferentiated, colonialism played a significant role in constructing the hierarchical patriarchal system that has shaped present-day masculine identities depicted in the plays under discussion. I further contend that both the traditional Zimbabwean patriarchal culture of subjugating the female and a colonial culture of subjugating the black race have contributed to the constructions of contemporary male identities. Such an intrinsic and extrinsic context in the constructions of male identity creates paradoxical masculinities in Zimbabwe and other post-colonial societies. They are a hegemonic class born out of a hegemonic social reality. The fluidity of masculine identities in history illustrates that the coloniser and the colonised dichotomies were themselves historically constructed categories and as Sinha (1995) argues, 'the relations between the two were neither fixed nor given for all time' (Sinha, 1995: 1).

With the exception of teachers, church-men, chiefs, headmen, translators and policemen, the majority of colonised males were often regarded as 'boys' not men. In addition, the use of the term did depend to some degree on the education, class and political persuasion of the white colonist. The social construction of black manhood in colonial Zimbabwean culture is rooted in the idea of 'Black as Boy' thus conjuring the image of a perpetually immature, deficient and child-like adult who needed the constant control, and paternal guidance of the white race. Also at the core of the 'boy' image is an allusion to the limited capacity of mind (Hunter and Davis, 1992: 466) and the absence of maturity that makes one an adult. Labelling black men as a 'boys' was a performance of power also meant to assert the white's superior status within the colonial context thus reinforcing the idea that the boy was a junior.

Black males could perform their manhood only within the microcosmic world of their children, wives and communities. The colonial political economy even stripped black males of these small worlds because it compelled them to leave their rural communities and migrate to find employment in cities. As a result of the migrant labour system, black males lost both public honour and private mastery. The black male's colonial identity as an eternal boy and servant resulted in the adaptation of the term 'boy' into the indigenous Shona and Ndebele languages as 'boyi'. The term assumed a wide range of meanings such as, 'a male child,' 'a servant/employee' or just 'the African race'. The term lost its demeaning and emasculating connotations and assumed a new meaning as a race marker. With the rise of nationalism, the term 'boy/s' came to denote a positive black/African masculine identity.

Black manhood and the liberation struggle

Although apartheid was not official policy in colonial Zimbabwe, it was the *de facto* reality. The colonial milieu's unbearable weight of racism and economic marginality gave birth to new and exciting black masculinities. The collective disillusionment and anger over the denial of manhood, identity and peoplehood (Hunter and Davis, 1992: 467) led to a brutal armed struggle that became not only an expression of manhood but also a quest for self-determination as expressed in the traditional and liberation war mobilisation song, *'Zirume rinogaro virimira vamwe'* (the man who constantly denigrates/violates others) and the chorus goes *'Tondobayana!'* (We will fight each other). In sharp contrast to the negative stereotypes of black manhood depicted as deficient, illiterate, slow-witted and distorted, the period of the liberation struggle gave a positive twist to the notion of 'boys'. The colonised Zimbabweans appropriated the term 'boys' and positively transformed it to mean the black freedom fighters. The liberation fighters in turn referred to each other in masculine terms as brothers and comrades in arms though there is ample evidence that women also played an active role and contributed significantly.[2] This goes to show that within the public political sphere, nationalism as an ideology that guided the liberation struggle was constructed from a masculine perspective. Nationalism emphasised racial unity namely black and white but ironically this was not enough to stop the ethnic divisions. Additionally, it also failed to take cognisance of obvious gender and class disparities that continued to widen after independence.

The liberation struggle in Zimbabwe continued to reinforce traditional pre-colonial and colonial masculine attributes. Violence, resilience, toughness, valour, sacrifice and martyrdom were considered the preserve of men during the struggle. In this way, warfare consolidated masculine prestige (Dudink et al., 2004: 27-28). National heroism sidelined women and applied only to male fighters. Though the legendary Mbuya Nehanda who led the first wave of the liberation struggle in the 1890s known as the First Chimurenga was a woman, women were relegated to mere subjects during the Second Chimurenga that brought political independence. In spite of women's active participation in the liberation struggle, masculine hegemony created discourses intended to write out the women's contribution. For example, the colonised space was oftentimes equated to the vulnerable female body. While this imagery emphasised the fertile and productive nature of body and place as well as the power to yield crop, it obscured their agency to also destroy what was yielded. The actual liberation war experience proved that the woman's body like its masculine counterpart is also capable of ruthlessness, violence and valour if forced. However, Martha's reaction in *She No Longer Weeps* is rather extreme and the violent conclusion can be attributed to Dangarebga's own spirited feminism.

Black manhood and the transition to independence

The Honourable MP and *She No Longer Weeps* are set during the first decade of independence, and depict new notions of masculinity that came into being with the new nation. The first wave of black masculinism in a politically independent Zimbabwe follows a different pattern. Although the colonial dispensation created political and economic impediments to black male role-performance, the period following the attainment of independence began to produce blacks who could assert the manhood that racist colonial institutions and economic deprivation had denied them for almost a century. However, it is ironic that while Freddy in *She No Longer Weeps* tries to assert and perform like a man as much as he is able, he fails to make a clean break with the mother figure as shown by his preference to marry a conforming, and domesticated woman comparable to his own mother. It can also be argued that the sentimental attachment real men often had to their mothers is actually a part of their male role as protector and head of the family. In essence, real men want submissive domesticated women or pretty subservient dolly birds. Explaining why she opted out of her relationship with Freddy, Martha turns the whole idea of manhood on its head and argues that the head of the family expects the smallest chores to be done for him, as if he were a child. 'Our society expects men to remain children for too long and I, in the end, I rebelled' (49). The colonial stereotype of the black male as a 'boy' seems to be dogging the new middle-class.

The emerging black masculinities inherited African traditions in the form of pre-colonial patriarchy in order to legitimise and guarantee the dominant position of men and the subordination of women within the new nation state. This process of continued gender control is seen to operate within the complex milieu at various levels, such as the collective and institutional, as well as personal face to face and in sexual contexts (Connell, 2000: 29). After attaining political independence, Zimbabwean black males took over key institutional domains such as the statehouse, boardroom, academy and pulpit (Carnes and Griffen, 1990: 1) formerly occupied by their colonial predecessors. Characters like the Honourable Shakespeare Pfende in *The Honourable MP*, as well as Freddy and Martha's Father in

She No Longer Weeps, illustrate how post-independence Zimbabwean patriarchy managed to legitimate its domination through political, educational and religious institutions. Msengezi and Dangarembga depict forms of gender subjugation and segregation prevalent in political, educational and religious spheres within the new nation. Immaculate's name for example, suggests that the Catholic Church is being satirised for its repression of women or rather for maintaining them in a position of virginal subservience. Women such as Immaculate, Martha's mother and sister are portrayed as complicit actors within the dominant patriarchy.

Today middle-class black male Zimbabweans have legitimised images of typical violent, despotic, polygamous, hustling, patronising fathers as their preferred identity. This becomes such a seductive stereotype that a number of young black males yearn to embrace it (Reese, 2004: 3). State-controlled media from the colonial times to the present have reinforced these stereotypes. In his conversation with rural based teacher Choto, Shakespeare Pfende thinks that masculine attributes like violence, controlled and directed aggression, a competitive spirit and a desire and ability to achieve are highly desirable and must be emulated. He boasts, 'Chadoka and I cannot drive the same type of car. What is a chief in the eyes of an MP? A local director of several, foreign-owned multi-national corporations' (Msengezi, 1984: 12). For Pfende and his class, this becomes a way of legitimising their masculine hegemony. Through similar hegemonic processes, abusive, violent, lecherous, childish, and irresponsible characters like Freddy in *She No Longer Weeps* enact such culturally accepted masculine identities so long as they commit themselves to paying bride-price in line with established traditional customs. It is therefore not surprising that society seems to endorse Pfende and Freddy's male licence for sexual aggressiveness. They are allowed to go unpunished until the victims decide to take their destinies into their own hands.

During the early years of independence, nationalist politics and education worked together to promote the development of a more diverse construction of manhood. While education and politics are critical to the freed people's ability to negotiate the public arena of the market economy, they are also crucial factors in enabling a once colonised male to actually assert his identity as a free man. Connell noted how notions of manhood in changing societies are reshaped to fit the emergent economies (Connell, 1995: 84). In *The Honourable MP,* Isabella's childhood sweetheart, Victor, represents how education elevates one's social status. As a university student, he refuses to bear responsibility for Isabella's pregnancy because she is a poor, working-class woman:

> *After some time I started to feel dizzy and started vomiting each morning. I was pregnant. I went to the university and told*

> Victor my case but he laughed at me. He said, 'How can a young university student, in his final year, reading History honours impregnate an illiterate toilet cleaner like you?' Many other students laughed at me and told me to go back to the ghetto. I later aborted and was ill for six months. I started roaming the city looking for a job (Msengezi, 36).

University education allows Victor to climb the social ladder and he now aspires to join Pfende and Freddy's class; Isabella rightly asks, 'Isn't Victor a member of this clan of hungry wolves?' (Msengezi: 36).

Pfende embodies the manly ethos of the post-independence black middle- and ruling-class elites. Besides fulfilling normal dominant gender role expectations like success, enterprise, resourcefulness, competition, aggression, post-independence Zimbabwean masculinities came to be identifiable with the three Cs: car, cash and cell-phone. Additionally, they have to have a 'small house' (euphemism for a mistress) as a show of affluence. They justify having a series of girlfriends as a practice inherent 'in our culture' as we were and still are polygamous. Nascent traits of such masculinities are decipherable in Shakespeare Pfende's character. Though born out of colonial degradation and despair, Pfende's kind of masculine hegemony is doomed to what I call 'failed masculinities'. In both the public/political and private spheres Pfende and Freddy's behaviour as men culminates in self-destructive policies. Similarly, present-day Zimbabwean business and ruling-class men have come to be identified with excessive corruption, greed, bad governance, lawlessness, the spread of HIV/AIDS and an unprecedented economic melt-down. Such tragic hypermasculinities are in sharp contrast to earlier constructions of denied manhood. Zinyemba observes how Choto's manhood contrasts with Pfende's. 'Unlike Pfende, Teacher Choto is level-headed, practical and morally upright. He is meant to contrast [with] the MP in a way which, as the play progresses, becomes aggressively obvious' (Zinyemba, 1986: 91). In other words, Choto the teacher represents a more progressive and positive alternative masculinity.

In order to sustain masculine hegemony, the dominant social group also leads by aligning itself ideologically to the broader community of interest and identities (Howson, 2006: 60). Although Mrs. Matsika and Mrs. Chiwara represent the Women's Association for the Protection of the Illegitimate Mother (WAPIM) in *She No Longer Weeps*, they participate in subjugating other women as seen in their scathing attack on Martha's independence and struggles against male dominance.

> Martha:... *(Telephone rings.) Excuse me. (Martha exits to the bedroom.)*
> Mrs Matsika: *Heh! She's worse than they say.*
> Mrs Chiwara: *She's like a stone. I wonder how any man could*

have found her warm enough to lie with. (Martha returns.) (Dangarembga, 1987: 50) Similarly, women like Martha's sister Mercy not only demonstrate total complicity with patriarchal hegemony but have also internalised the dominant male ideology that they act against their own gender. When Martha falls pregnant while in college, Mercy considers her an outcast and throws her out:

> *'There are some things' she told me ...and I swear she looked just like my father ... 'There are some things,' she said, 'that simply aren't done. Decent girls don't sleep around or at the very least they don't get pregnant. You have done both. You will have to suffer the consequences. I wish I could help you,' she said, 'but I can't keep you here. Our father and my husband both say you must go'* (Dangarembga, 1987: 11).

This scene shows that other than in certain traditional rituals, women can also perform masculinities in their everyday lives in ways that aid the subjugation of other women.

In *The Honourable MP*, the performance of manhood by female characters assumes a new dynamic. By virtue of her class and status as wife of a ruling class elite, Pfende's wife, Immaculate behaves exactly like her predecessor the white woman in that she is not only subservient to her husband but is also confined to home and to a role of mother, cook, and carer. Because of her frustration and lack of recognition for herself outside a clearly defined subservient female role, she exercises her limited power over someone more vulnerable. Immaculate takes pleasure in harassing Spencer, her male employee. Spencer suffers not only because he is a poor domestic servant but also because he belongs to the looked-down-upon ethnicity. He is one of the poor Malawian migrant labourers who took up menial jobs as domestic servants and farm workers. Although Pfende has a good working relationship with Spencer, Immaculate rudely commands him to run around like a child and denies him the right to take time off his work. Spencer resists and complains saying: 'African oppress African now. This independence – ah ya' (Msengezi, 1984: 26). Such examples underscore the fact that manhood is only a social construction and both men and women can perform masculinities in different contexts.

The two plays also serve to show that contemporary black masculinities in Zimbabwe have their own unique traits. Even though these identities emphasise certain masculine identities common in open market economies such as hyperaggressiveness, hypersexuality, excessive show of wealth, their specific historical experiences have produced some unique characteristics related to traditional notions of the real men (*madoda sibili*). These are personified by what Kimmel calls the 'warrior' archetype (the traditional *mushavi*: a 'hunter/farmer' archetype in other Zimbabwean cultures) referring to the male soul that thrives on challenges, the wild and individuated qualities (Kimmel, 1995: 178). It is therefore important to analyse how the masculine model once grounded largely in the experience of the dominant colonial culture navigates and negotiates the changing experience under self-rule within the context of a burgeoning market culture of the post-cold-war dispensation. I also argue that education, political power and material wealth play a significant role in constructing post-independence male identities in Zimbabwe. Pfende and Freddy behave licentiously and assume that their post-independence masculinity allows them a licence associated with the freedom to do whatever they like including sexual aggression. Pfende's primitive accumulation of wealth (cars, houses, farms and electronic gadgets) gives him the feeling that he can conquer any woman no matter what her education or social standing might be.

Dangarembga and Msengezi's plays illustrate that in spite of their education and excessive westernisation, middle- and upper-class Zimbabwean men like Freddy and Pfende are not interested in completely divesting their identities of certain traditional patriarchal practices and codes of behaviour such as violence and polygamy or multiple sexual partners that serve to consolidate masculine hegemony and privilege. Unlike the traditional performance of manhood shown through bravery, physical fitness, group cohesion, resourcefulness, and the capacity to protect and support women, contemporary black middle- and upper-class masculinities in Zimbabwe seem to emphasise individualism, cunning, abuse of women and cut-throat competition where tough guys like MP Pfende and Freddy are players of women. In Msengezi and Dangarembga's plays, additional competition is reflected in enterprising or career women like Martha and to an extent Immaculate. These characters break with traditional stereotypes of the stay-at-home mum and are constantly fending for their families in such a way that their resourcefulness surpasses or equals their male counterparts.

Challenging black hegemonic masculinities

Hegemonic black males in post-independence Zimbabwe not only face challenges from femininities but also from subordinate and marginalised forms of manhood that developed within and through other social relations, such as those structured around the concepts of race, class and ethnicity (Howson, 2006: 63). Not all masculinities are hegemonic. Complicit and marginalised masculinities constitute what Morrell terms 'non-hegemonic categories' (Morrell, 2001: 7). Msengezi amply demonstrates that although men as a group enjoy institutional privileges at the expense of women as a group, they share very unequally in the advantages these privileges provide (Howson, 2006: 63). Shakespeare Pfende abuses his elected position as an elected legislature when he indulges in corrupt activities like smuggling, adultery and property accumulation at the expense of the male members of his electorate.

In contemporary Zimbabwe, the marginalisation of black working-class men in the current situation resulted not only from the development of an open market economy, the IMF/World Bank induced Economic Structural Adjustment Program (ESAP) but also from the ascendancy of black male figures into political office. Such changes gave rise to middle-class and professional masculinities, which in turn emphasised career, status, intellectual ability, ambition, fatherhood and breadwinning, as well as a new emphasis on fashion, grooming and appearance (Howson, 2006: 63, Wernick, 1994: 51). Although these middle- and upper-class males represent mainstream masculinities, it does not follow that men of low income fail to endeavour to perform according to the dominant male ideology. In both plays, subaltern men like the thugs in *She No Longer Weeps* (1987) and the peasants, and workers in *The Honourable MP*, (1984) achieve an alliance with subaltern femininities to bring about the downfall of hegemonic masculinities and their complicit femininities.

The two playwrights depict the romance of socialism prevalent in the eighties. In line with the socialist ethos of the time, Msengezi exposes the vulnerability of black hegemonic male figures whose power base is built on quicksand and easily collapses when challenged. However, it is ironic that in reality, the socialist dream has not yet been realised, twenty years later. The identification of a cluster of hegemonic attributes such as sexual promiscuity and an excessive show of wealth, does not mean that all men will conform to these values in practice. It is only a measure of male hegemony that those who fail to provide for their families like the 'middle-aged man in tattered white overalls' (Msengezi, 1987: 30) 'do not count as a "men".' (Dudink, Hagemann and Tosh, 2004: 47). Instead of aspiring towards the (negative) symbols associated with hegemonic black males, subordinate and marginalised men assume a more positive identity especially in *The Honourable MP*. Msengezi shows how their power as men lies not in money, property or high political office but in uniting subaltern men and women against profligate male hegemony. A contrived ending which emphasises the unity among subaltern genders and classes (peasants and workers) in Pfende's constituency gives *The Honourable MP* a socialist resonance.

Martha, the main character in *She No Longer Weeps* is perceived as a threat to masculinity because she can sustain herself and is free to choose her own sexual partner. In one instance, she challenges Lovemore, her boyfriend saying, '... I don't want you thinking that just because I let you sleep in my bed, you can come here and tell me how to live my life' (Dangarembga, 1987: 44). On numerous occasions, Martha assumes patriarchal authority, including over her excessively religious father, whom she tackles head on. She sees herself battling masculine hegemony on several fronts: 'To the extent that I am a woman and have my personal battles to fight with the taxman, my employers and lecherers in the street, I am fighting for all women' (Dangarembga, 1987: 50).

In contemporary Zimbabwean culture, professional women, like Martha, who run households, buy properties and have public lives, are not only seen as a threat to men but are negatively labelled. In Shona for example, the saying, *'Mukadzi uyu murume pachake,'* directly translates as 'this woman is her own man'. It is important to note that within the Zimbabwean social context, some women who have appropriated patriarchal power and dividends also use this language. Everything about Martha (her education, discourse, style of dressing, salary) is a threat to Freddy's masculinity.

> *You are a bitch, Martha. Never forget that. No man will ever want you. Even if I hadn't spoilt you. You wear trousers like a man, you drink like a man, you argue and challenge men as though you were not a woman yourself. What you don't know is that that education of yours is good for only one thing ... it lets you earn money. That's the only reason why men like women like you, otherwise you are useless. But even that education of yours is gone now ... pregnant. You are finished. Women like you have no place in Zimbabwe* (Dangarembga, 1987: 9).

Ascribing masculine identities to struggling or independent women like Martha is meant to embarrass them and make them feel like outcasts if they don't conform to patriarchal hegemony. These masculine femininities are only seen as positive when they act in alliance with hegemonic males.

Black masculinities and violence

Msengezi and Dangarembga depict a wide range of masculine violence which 'includes not only physical and sexual violence, its threat, or both but also emotional abuse, economic violence, and institutional violence' (Bowker, 1998: 56). In *The Honourable MP*, Immaculate is threatened with physical violence when she asks her husband Shakespeare Pfende whether he has given her car to one of his mistresses. In response Pfende threatens other males subordinate to him with violence in one of his rants:

> MP: *(Angry) Woman, woman, you are now going out of bounds. I will smash your skull if you are not careful. (Pointing her in the face) If you continue sticking your tongue out and shouting abuse at me, I shall beat you. Datsun, Datsun, Datsun. What is a Datsun 120Y to me, the Honourable MP*

> *Pfende? I shit into men's faces and they smile at me, and what of you, a woman? If you don't want to lose your teeth, shut up, okay?* (Msengezi, 1984: 23)

Pfende is not only threatening his wife into submitting to male authority but is also sending a warning to any of his male subordinates who might dare to challenge him. As such, he constructs a myth of invincibility around the masculine identity he has chosen to represent. Pfende's character represents what Morrell calls a 'post-colonial masculinity' which seeks not only to affirm Zimbabwean nationalism but also to silence competing forms of manhood which are emerging amongst less affluent and economically secure African men who are critical of the classed nature of the *status quo* (Morrell: 2001: 24). The teacher, workers and peasants in Msengezi's play represent masculinities that challenge Pfende's class.

Although masculine violence was a feature of traditional Zimbabwean patriarchy, colonialism also played a part in reinforcing and perpetuating it. As a violent system, colonialism triggered off the Fanonian cycle of 'violence and counter violence' or 'circle of hate' (Fanon, 1963: 70) which continued into the post-independence dispensation. Fanon argues that post-colonial violence is a necessary feature of the reconstruction process and asserts that, 'Violence used in specific ways at the moment of the struggle for freedom does not magically disappear after the ceremony of trooping the national colours' (Fanon, 1963: 70). As a result of subjection to colonial violence and the demeaning 'boy' stereotype within the Zimbabwean context, the colonised black man embarks on a quest to prove his masculinity to the black woman resulting in acts of both physical and psychological violence.

All varieties of male violence against women depicted in the two plays 'are a form of men's power over women in either asserting or maintaining dominance' (Edwards, 2006: 56). This means that violence is used to sustain black male dominance in post-independence Zimbabwe. Within the larger social context sexual violence and transgressions by men like Pfende, Freddy, Victor, and the Headmaster are legitimised in that they are depicted as inevitable and, therefore, forgivable. In both plays, physical violence, in particular, is predominantly more socially acceptable as a practice for men or boys rather than for women or girls. Conversely, men or boys are often acutely embarrassed if they become victims of violence and particularly if that violence is inflicted by girls or women (Edwards, 2006: 45). In *She No Longer Weeps*, the masculine hegemony which Freddy represents faces its ultimate humiliation and death when Martha physically grabs a knife and chops off Freddy's manhood.

For both Dangarembga and Msengezi violence is not necessarily masculine but can be cyclical in the sense that violent male hegemony breeds violent femininities as shown in Martha's actions when she physically castrates Freddy while hired bouncers pin him down. In *The Honourable MP*, it is Pfende who first threatens peasants and workers with violence when he pulls out a pistol at a political rally. Ironically Pfende ends up on the receiving end when the teacher wrests the gun from him and points it at him. The teacher, peasants and workers quickly effect a citizen's arrest and charge Shakespeare Pfende with corruption, smuggling, looting and sexually abusing Isabella who worked as his secretary. As a man, Pfende is in dereliction of his political duties as one of the peasants spells out in the charges laid against him:

> *Know how to talk young man. We sent you to the city to be our eye and our ear as you say, to speak to them in Parliament, to argue, to talk like a man with something between his legs. What did you do? [...] he went on to build himself a big European house like the one in Bharamani's farm over there and bought himself many cars* (Msengezi, 1984: 42-43).

Ironically this speech reinforces the male hegemony that it purports to be standing against because it adopts the discourse of manhood which is premised on virility and aggressiveness. The play's socialist resolution is founded on phallocentricism, which does not have room for women. Such a resolution reinforces the myth of the father as the ruler and it becomes obvious that Pfende will be replaced by another man.

Conclusion

To an extent, these two plays constitute a set of narratives about the various ways in which masculine hegemony is performed in the context of identity formations in a constantly changing geo-political terrain. Patriarchal representatives like Pfende and Freddy continuously perform and play out their manhood on women, their wives and mistresses as well as other men of a lower social classes. The women who dare challenge this patriarchal domination are often silenced, become neurotic, exiled or imprisoned, tamed and re-domesticated, like Martha. From the denouement of the two plays, Msengezi and Dangarembga seem to be suggesting that femininities can only attain victory if they act in alliance with other subjugated masculinities.

Endnotes

1. See also Ane Kirkegaard and Jane Parpart's chapters in this volume. Research still needs to be done on cultural and moral differences among black and white elites in their relation, for example, to the value or status given to conspicuous consumption or to the work ethic.
2. See *None But Ourselves* and *Mothers of the Revolution* and the docu-drama film *Flame* which highlight women's role in Zimbabwe's liberation struggle.

11

'A man can try'[1]: Negotiating manhoods in colonial urban spaces in Dambudzo Marechera's *The House of Hunger* and Yvonne Vera's *Butterfly Burning*[2]

GRACE A. MUSILA

This chapter suggests that the male subject in the colonial urban space often occupied an ambivalent position on the margins, in his relationship with both the women, and the colonial urban economy. Through a reading of Dambudzo Marechera's *The House of Hunger* (1978) and Yvonne Vera's *Butterfly Burning* (1998), we submit that the urban space both offered men certain freedoms – found in the gendered colonial economy – while simultaneously destabilising and redefining their identities. This had varied results as men struggled to retrieve, construct, and evolve various senses of manhood in the continually shifting social terrain of the urban space, and its fluid topographies of gendered relations.

In many respects, *The House of Hunger* and *Butterfly Burning* focus on the microscopic detail of men and women's encounters in the colonial urban space, and offer rich insights into the ways in which the city unveiled both the creativity and vulnerabilities of men and women as it disrupted conventional gender roles. In *Butterfly Burning*, Vera expressly attempts a reconstruction of colonial Bulawayo, thus providing interesting insights into gender(ed) relations;[3] while *The House of Hunger* offers an unflinching gaze at the colonial black urban experience. Thus we see the two texts as complementary and engaging in a conversation on the unstable terrain of manhood within an urban perspective.

Mapping colonial urban spaces

Miescher and Lindsay (2003: 10) observe that in colonial Africa, the advent of urban economies, opportunities for education and wage labour, challenged the political power and dominant masculinity of older males, and even undermined local political hierarchies.[4] They suggest that while colonial racism denigrated black men, it 'did not prevent the assertion of powerful masculinities outside its gaze'; a fact that complicates the popular theses of the emasculation of the black man (ibid: 21). Similarly, studies suggest that African men were innovative in negotiating between local and western ideals of manhood, and often succeeded in meeting the normative expectations of both societies, by finding ways of reconciling the two.[5]

That this was possible was because traditional patriarchy largely coincided with the highly gendered colonial administrative structure, which for different reasons, had a similar interest in keeping women in the domestic and men in the public domain. In Rhodesia, like many British colonies across the continent, boys were educated at the mission schools, in preparation for entry into the European-dominated, mainly urban, economy, while women's education centered on issues related to the general management of the domestic sphere (Schmidt in Hansen, 1992; Veit-Wild, 1992). This was with a view to influencing modern African families to espouse the Christian vision of the 'proper' family.

Apart from formal education, African men enjoyed various other privileges, chief among these being legal access to urban space as the economy found use for male migrant labour. Exempt from pass laws in a system where such documentation legitimised an individual's existence and assured access to waged labour, women had no visibility[6] in the official urban space. They could not, for instance, own property without a man's name being attached to them (ibid.)[7]. This minority status 'bestowed formal control of all African women on the African men as women had no direct recourse to the law in their own right' (ibid; 6), extending legal affirmation to traditional patriarchy. On the other hand, such invisibility afforded women a range of opportunities for the subversion of the system; opportunities that men could not enjoy since as Terri Barnes (1999) notes, the pass laws rendered any 'invisible' man a criminal, subject to disciplinary action. Thus, despite enjoying a range of privileges accruing from the patriarchal colonial system, these remained within the confines of a racial hierarchy, in which the black man succeeded the white man and the white woman. Carolyn Brown's essay title 'A "man" in the village is a "boy" in the workplace'[8] captures this situation, where, while affirming black masculinity in the black sociosphere, the system concomitantly infantilised black men in relation to white society.

Within the new economic and socio-cultural order of the city, male subjects found themselves having to construct alternative manhoods. However, they did or attempted to do so within a context where traditional masculinity's core values of dominance over women and wage-earning were increasingly contested. The colonial city was thus a very ambivalent space in which the combination of racial epistemologies, traditional patriarchy, and the gendered colonial economy with its numerous fault lines, significantly destabilised gender identities and roles. A similar ambivalence emerges in the two novels' treatment of manhood, as they debate the conventional grammars of masculinity — including assumptions of dominance, and gendered nationalist histories – and articulate possible alternative manhoods.

Furthering the nation

Ideas of infantilisation and emasculation form part of the semantic repertoire of gendered nationalism in Africa. Indeed, with time, they have calcified into a normative shorthand of speaking about the nation. The emasculation thesis has its roots in heteronormative constructions of manhood in African societies along lines of dominance, control, and provision or responsibility for the 'weaker' members of the society, chiefly women and children. The two novels treat the question of gendered nationalism in different ways, with the male characters occasionally exploring alternatives outside the gendered script of the masculinised nationalist histories.

In *Butterfly Burning*, Fumbatha carries the burden of the nation and its liberation; a perspective that remains muted throughout the novel, as the main narrative shifts focus from the grand nationalism and heroism of the hanged 'rebels' to the personal lives of ordinary people in an ordinary township. Fumbatha's father was hanged on the banks of the Umguza River for opposing the white settlers in 1896, the same year Fumbatha was born. His mother sees his birth as the reincarnation of his father's spirit of resistance. In Fumbatha is seen the masculinisation of nationalist history, a process his mother mediates when she whispers into the child's palm:

> *Fumbatha, his small hand open and spread on the lap of his mother. She delivers words that are arrows ... Trapped in his fingers are the words his mother has given him. A single seed gives birth to seventeen more, to a thousand more* (10).

The novel however disrupts this process, as Fumbatha remains a closed fist around the potent message, which does not convert into revolutionary energy. The clenched fist is a conventional symbol of power, but in Fumbatha's case, it is static power that does not translate to active agency. The *chimurenga* spirit which we would expect to have been born in him remains a still-birth; instead, Fumbatha builds the colonial city brick by brick, working within the system instead of actively opposing it.

In retaining the revolutionary message as a latent power whose potential is never realised, it is possible to see both Fumbatha and Vera as rejecting gendered nationalist histories, and charting new ones. At a time when current official history in Zimbabwe vests a lot of mythical and political power on those who claim a stake in the country's struggle history, Fumbatha's rejection of this history makes a radical statement. He, instead, chooses to define himself in relation to the city. Having held the bricks that have built it in his hands, Fumbatha inscribes himself in the cityscape. Despite the mobility of urban migrant labour – black laborers being seen as temporary visitors within a white city – Fumbatha claims his roots in the city and its buildings. What is important then is that Fumbatha creates a new space, an alternative history, even though he does not really write a new narrative of being a man in the city. Despite transcending the limits of gendered nationalist narratives, he still subscribes to normative ideas of masculinity, which script men as workers and breadwinners and women as nurturers.

In defining manhood, many studies highlight the centrality of heterosexual activity and the breadwinner's role as a popular definitive feature of what it means to be a man in many societies (Cleaver, 2002: 9). In his relationship with Phephelaphi, Fumbatha nurses a traditional view: for him, she should be the mother of his children, the homemaker who nurtures his exhausted spirit when he returns from long periods at work, while his role is to meet the family's needs. He also sees himself in the role of father, a potential made more urgent by his fast-approaching old-age.

Both Fumbatha and Phephelaphi are, ironically, victims of colonial capitalism. Fumbatha's desire for a child and a family unit is in direct conflict with Phephelaphi's dreams for herself, and the gender and racially exclusionary structures that lie in her path. Inadvertently, the economy foments a crisis in Fumbatha's relationship, by affording black women a chance to enter formal employment, while simultaneously rendering their female reproductive capacity an obstacle to their aspirations. This is a classic case of the tension that existed between traditional patriarchy and colonial capitalism. In rejecting married and pregnant women, it was hoped that this would discourage disruptions to the traditional African family, which provided the stable foundation to the requirements of colonial labour. However, this system depended on submission to its rules, something that Phephelaphi was unable to do. She yearned for more than domesticity, more than motherhood, and thus her pregnancy prompted a crisis in her relationship with Fumbatha.

> *She wanted the sense of belonging before that kind of belonging which rested on another's wondrous claim... before he reached out his strong arm and did all that for her and made her feel empty and waited upon* (69).

She does not realise that Fumbatha knows no other way of being a man; he cannot fathom her need for an identity beyond him. The conflict between Fumbatha and Phephelaphi is rooted in a battle of control over her body. Fumbatha's response to Phephelaphi's decision to abort their child is framed within notions of manhood and parenting, through which he feels Phephelaphi has denied him the opportunity of fatherhood. Part of his desperation to become a father, and to keep a hold of Phephelaphi, lies in the sense of rootlessness that attends the urban experience of Makokoba.

The House of Hunger expresses a similarly deep-seated suspicion of both pre-colonial African history and nationalism as a response to colonialism (Taitz, 1996). In the novel, Zimbabwean pre-colonial history is portrayed as equally marked by violence and betrayal, suggested by the allusion to Lobengula and the Shona-Ndebele conflicts in pre-colonial Rhodesia (43). While acknowledging that colonialism negated black identity, as in the allusion to the 'heart of darkness' – to which the students in the narrator's class are believed to belong, the novel registers disillusionment with African nationalism as a hollow mythologisation of an imagined African (Taitz, 1996). Stephen, the self-declared Afrocentrist, aligns himself with a hotchpotch of intellectuals including Nkrumah, Kaunda, Che, Castro, Stalin, Mao, Kennedy, Nyerere, as well as the Heinemann African Writers Series (63), which, as Gagiano observes (2000) only serves to underline the superficiality of his identity. The skepticism about nationalism is emphasised by the narrator's doomed search for black heroes and the portrayal of Stephen as a hollow character. Yet even this critique falls short of engaging with gendered nationalism; indeed, it appears to endorse the masculinisation of nationalist histories. But it is in its treatment of violent masculinities that the novel offers its most suggestive critique of the colonial urban space and men's responses to its changing dynamics.

Muscling it out in *The House of Hunger*

In *The House of Hunger*, Marechera narrates colonial urban life as one shot through with different forms of violence. Chief among these is poverty which leads to the complete degradation and negation of the black people's humanity. Social institutions such as the church, schools and the home also become sites of intense violence, some of which directly result from poverty: e.g. the violation of privacy that a single room means for the narrator's family, where the children become privy to the most intimate interactions between their parents; the educational system results in dual consciousness as the narrator finds it difficult to reconcile the Eurocentric educational experience with his own background. It is in light of these disorienting conditions that the novel uses the symbol of the house of hunger, a metaphoric reference to the dysfunctional and schizophrenic nature of the narrator's mind, his family, the township and the nation at large (Gurnah, 1998).

These forms of violence breed various psychoses in the men, as they attempt to achieve some degree of dignity in their dehumanising circumstances. A case in point is Harry. Here is a classic case of the native whom Frantz Fanon (1967) describes thus:

> *The look that the native turns on the settler's town is a look of lust, a look of envy; it expresses his dreams of possession – all manner of possession: to sit at the settler's table, to sleep in the settler's bed, with*

his wife if possible. The colonized man is an envious man (30).

Harry embraces western modernity wholesale and tries to fashion out an identity for himself as a 'civilised man' (*The House of Hunger*: 11). He finances this lifestyle by becoming a Special Branch spy in the student organisations. To complete this civilised identity, Harry exclusively dates white women, since 'they've got everything nigger girls don't have' (13). For Harry, 'nigger girls are just meat. And I don't like my meat raw' (13). Through Harry, the novel explores one response to the racialised colonial dynamics, in the form of self-hatred and an unquestioning aspiration towards whiteness.

But Harry is not alone in this. *The House of Hunger* also chronicles instances of how illusions become a mode of transgressing the narrowness of options open to people. One such is photography, a mode that allows urban dwellers to explore alternative identities aligned with symbols of modernity, affluence and sophistication, otherwise mostly beyond their reach. The narrator observes that

> Solomon is now a rich man. His studio is papered from floor to ceiling with photographs of Africans in European wigs, Africans in mini-skirts. The background of each photo is the same: waves breaking upon a virgin beach and a lone eagle swiveling like glass fracturing light towards the potent spaces of the universe. <u>A cruel yearning can only be realised in crude photography. The squalor of reality was obliterated in an explosion of flashbulbs and afterwards one could say 'that's me, man – me! In the city.'</u> (11). [my emphasis]

Beyond the escape into this paper-thin world of glossy illusion, the characters in the novel often find themselves responding to violence with violence. Indeed, one of the definitive features of urban male identity in *The House of Hunger* is violence. The novel is held together by a chain of violent experiences linking the various characters. The novel opens with a description of the narrator's brother, Peter's violent disposition. The latter returns from jail raging about the 'bloody whites' which 'seemed to be roasting his mind and he got into fights which terrified everyone so much' (2); but at the same time, people see him spoiling for a fight and they like him for that. In this incident, Peter, unable to hit back at the colonial system, feels the need to reclaim his sense of power and sense of a coherent, dignified, autonomous self, through violent expression. In this essentially dehumanising environment, Peter becomes further destabilised when faced with Immaculate's beauty, innocence and faith in humanity. He is unable to handle such an affirmation within an environment that seems bent on erasing such positive values; hence his determination to destroy the idea which so unnerves him. In the novel various men beat women to a stain, a symbol earlier used in reference to the train that smashes the narrator's father to the same. The train can be seen to allude to modernity, industrialisation and the colonial economy as a whole together with their emasculating effect on local manhood.

The House of Hunger explicitly embraces this thesis, as a way of explaining instances of violence: i.e. an act of displaced frustration and anger with the impregnable colonial system made on the weaker members of the society, notably women and weaker men. In a different context, Tina Sideris (2000) offers an alternative interpretation of these violent masculinities, suggesting that dominant gender discourses often fail to provide men with alternative symbols of masculinity other than superiority and the necessity of control. In circumstances which threaten these aspects of identity, extremely violent forms of sexual control are enacted, in attempts to lay claim to the elusive dominant identity of power. These men appear to borrow from the grammar of colonial control to reclaim their threatened manhood. Faced with the oppressive system, they fail to imagine alternative ways of being men, and most importantly, of remaining human, in dehumanising circumstances. They fail to relate to themselves in a self-affirming manner, and instead, seek that affirmation by imposing their control on weaker members of their environment.

Violent masculinities occupy a hegemonic position in the novel; they seem to boast of the community's approval. In the novel, 'the people saw Peter's longing for a fight and liked him for it' (2). Similarly, the community assembles and watches as a man beats up his wife, then rapes her. This voyeuristic audience serves to affirm such masculinities which later filter down to the younger generation, as when Harry and Edmond settle their argument with a grisly fight at school. In both instances, the spectators, themselves victims of all sorts of violence, are drawn to the spectacle enacted by one of their own.

Perhaps the prevalence of violent masculinities has to do with the inaccessibility of other modes of relating to the self and others. Within a hostile and rough urban environment, with limited avenues for responding to institutionalised violence, the body remains one of the few – if not the only – object over which the individual retains ownership; and even then, only partially, as they remain subjects of the state. Pain and pleasure become important vistas in constructing relationships with the self, and with the Other; while physical power – in the ubiquity of political, social and economic powerlessness – is jealously guarded and celebrated, as the last breath of life, in an almost literal sense.

Such masculinities thus become hegemonic: the only viable option within the circumstances. Moodie and Campbell's[9] observations about male migrant labourers seem to apply, as the harsh urban conditions reflected in the novel combine to catalyse the production and performance of aggressive modes of being human and male, in conditions that seem to negate the former, while not offering suggestions about the latter. As Wood and Jewkes (2001) suggest, there are 'links between violence, a sense of powerlessness and multiple structural factors – e.g. poverty, race, traditional patriarchy – which produce varying forms of vulnerability outside the immediate arena of gender'; vulnerabilities which, one might add, often impact on gender identities and enactments of gender roles. Segal affirms this view, arguing that feelings of insecurity make men prone to over-compensation for what they perceive to be weaknesses by enacting excessive and aggressive posturings (Segal, 1990: 131).

While acknowledging the legitimacy of these theories for understanding male violence in *The House of Hunger*, what seems to emerge is that women were better able to anchor themselves in the turbulent city environment, and find ways of coping with their circumstances. In effect, the male characters would seem to lack a certain versatility, the key ingredient in adapting to changing power dynamics. People in positions of perceived privilege (in this case, the traditional man) find it difficult to adapt to any threat – temporary or otherwise – to their position of dominance, as they are illiterate in the grammars of perceived subordinancy. Yet, as the following section reveals, the urban space was above all dynamic in its disruption of the master scripts of conventional gender roles and identities.

Shifting economies, shifting roles: sampling twilight pleasures

As noted, the colonial economy in Rhodesia was highly gendered, in its attempt to 'construct a system in which young African men served as migrant wage labourers in the European economy, African women engaged in agricultural production in the reserves and older African men maintained law and order at household and village levels' (Schmidt, 1992: 6).

Despite this, women found their way into the urban space and created their own micro-economies. These complemented the official colonial economy, and thrived on its margins, often feeding off its gaps and cracks. In *Butterfly Burning*, the women offer commercial sex, illegal local brews, and shebeens, which together provide the men with much needed diversions from the pressures of urban life; the chief among these being, ironically, the official exclusion of migrant labourers' families from the city. In the novel, Zandile, Gertrude and Deliwe are prostitutes who manage to live off their sexuality, on the fringes of Bulawayo's economy. Similarly, in *The House of Hunger*, prostitution forms the economic backbone of women's lives, with women like Nestar managing to live in opulence off their sexuality.

Beyond the socio-economic space these women's activities occupied –

the very movement of women into the urban spaces was an act of subversion of both African patriarchy and colonial capital; the commercial economy of sex created radical shifts in sexual relations between men and women in the city. Men found themselves revising their assumptions about sexual transactions, women, and female sexuality; traditional morality and monogamy for women become redundant.[10] This gave women the power to negotiate sexual relations as a financial transaction, a totally new experience for both parties: men traditionally subscribed to ideas of sexual entitlement and female sexual availability[11] as part of what Connell (2005) terms the patriarchal dividend.

These sexual transactions, however, are presented differently in the two novels, thus revealing subtle complexities. In the light of the urban colonial pressures facing both men and women in *Butterfly Burning*, sexual transactions often create emotional bonds between the women and their clients; a certain intimate space in which they clasp at the warmth of each other's bodies and claim some humanity and intimacy. Hence we see Zandile's different responses to her white and black clients (33-34): with her black clients she lingers over the whiplash marks across a man's breast, 'ribbon of seared skin', 'deep tooth marks buried behind the legs' and 'flesh newly cut' (34). In these moments, she connects with these men at a level that extends the boundaries of a commercial transaction between two strangers. After taking white clients however, Zandile

> *picks some loose change from the mantelshelf and spits into the fire, black saliva hissing as it hits hot coal. Then she steals a cigar from an embossed gold case, clamps the lid carelessly down and replaces this fine property on the bedside table. As soon as she can, she throws the stolen cigar away. Her disdain is complete* (33-34).

Interestingly, colonial control of native populations was underpinned by a range of gendered anxieties towards both their male and female subjects. These manifested themselves in the need to control African sexuality; a need that, though rarely given official acknowledgement, nonetheless had a great deal to do with the gendered approach to the native populations in most colonies. Long before actual colonial conquest, a range of myths about Africa(ns) were in circulation in Western societies.[12] Among these, inflated myths of black sexuality – both the black man and woman – formed the centerpiece of colonial mythology on Africa. With colonial occupation, these myths translated to various ambivalent anxieties about black sexuality, which lay in the grey areas between desire and repulsion, acceptance and resistance. These anxieties took the shape of racialised panics, in the form of the black, yellow and white perils; with the first two being concerned about the (assumed) threat of black men to white femininity, and the accompanying terror of miscegenation; while the white peril was the black men's fear of the possibility of the abuse of black women by white men.[13]

Yet, as suggested above, white men were not averse to black women; indeed, some went to extremes to assert their ownership of black women, as suggested by Gertrude's white boyfriend in *Butterfly Burning* who shoots her dead when he 'found her talking to another man at her door, when he called on her after midnight' (122).

It is in *The House of Hunger* however, that white mythologisation of black sexuality, and particularly the bipolar attraction-repulsion ambivalence emerges. In the novel, Nestar cashes in on the white male fascination with black sexuality and gets catapulted to wealth. As she tells us 'white men have a thing about black women' (51). Nestar's extensive catalogue of sexual experiences with her white clients gestures at the white mythology of an exotic black sexuality, as the men indulge their sexual fantasies and make Nestar perform a range of sexual activities that grant them sexual pleasure (51-52). But curiously, while the white men in the novel seem to have no reservations about sampling black sexual delights, they display a violent resentment of black men's sexual relations with white women, as indicated by the violent beating the narrator and Patricia receive when the white boys in the college discover that they are sexually involved (72-73).

In *Butterfly Burning*, Boyidi finds himself seduced and taken away from his wife, to become Zandile's live-in 'houseband'. In this arrangement, Zandile subverts the conventional marital arrangement by being the one who not only persuades Boyidi to live with her, but also becomes the chief breadwinner in the family, literally providing for her man. The urban environment, with its many pressures and problems – chiefly poverty and oppression – loosens the hold of social convention and legitimises such arrangements: the traditional values, where men are the dominant partners and breadwinners within heterosexual relationships, become difficult to maintain.

However, beyond these socio-economic pressures, Boyidi is said to stay with Zandile 'only to save his own life' (122). She 'destroys anything that Boyidi looks at and admires' (122), and scalds his former wife with hot oil, when she comes after him. In this arrangement, Zandile controls Boyidi's sexuality, effectively allowing her to play the traditional husband's role, where the wife is expected to be monogamous. While he appears to enjoy their sexual relationship, Boyidi foregoes the traditional male privilege of multiple relationships with other women. Zandile reinforces this loyalty through violence, a conventionally male prerogative. In the highly volatile urban environment, violence is not the exclusive preserve of men, as with Zandile, who has been known to inflict physical violence on both men and women, when she deems them to threaten her perceived happiness. Nestar, similarly, recourses to violence in *The House of Hunger*, when the narrator's friend, Phillip, goes to her house after beating up her son Leslie, for assaulting his sister.

In *The House of Hunger*, men find release from the frustrations of their everyday life through sex and alcohol. Sexual activity is rife throughout the novel, yet it remains a desperate attempt to reclaim some power, or provide a means of self-expression through conquest. Virility as a defining feature of manhood permeates the novel as the popular mythology. The narrator contracts a venereal disease from his first sexual encounter but his brother, Peter, is joyous about the sexual adventures and reminds the narrator 'You aren't a man until you've gone through it' (3), effectively ascribing both the sexual act and the disease as a rite of passage into manhood. The sexual act is such a prominent marker of manhood that when the narrator's brother turns eighteen, he is given a VD set as a gift by his father: the inference being that manhood is synonymous with sexual activity. More importantly, this affirmation implies the ability to take risks and manoeuvre oneself safely around them.

Similarly, Peter celebrates his biological maturity as a man 'capable of making a girl pregnant' (48), by inviting the younger boys in the township to a 'demonstration' one evening. The narrator reports:

> *Peter stripped. He had bathed and oiled himself all over. He was lean and strong and handsome. The size of his organ astonished us. It was stiff and huge and its mouth was tense. He casually cradled it in his right hand fingers and began to masturbate* (49).

Peter's attainment of manhood is achieved upon, and illustrated through his attainment of physical maturity, which allows him to become sexually active. For the young boys, as for Peter, virility symbolises manhood and maturity. Indeed its achievement becomes a serious pastime for the boys who are initiated into heterosexuality through peep-shows when they follow prostitutes – who have nowhere else to take their clients – into the bushes to observe their intercourse. The narrator's mother also views heterosexual activity as a marker of 'growing up' to manhood. She reprimands the narrator for his delayed entry into heterosexual activity, and his continued masturbation that stains her bed sheets.

In presenting Zandile as the breadwinner in *Butterfly Burning*, and the narrator's mother as the one who socialises the narrator into sexual maturity in *The House of Hunger*, the two novels would seem to be reinforcing conventional structures of masculinity. Hence, by implication, the two women appear to be masculinised. Yet, in neither novel is this so: rather the two women fill the gaps left by the male failure to perform their traditional roles; thus further exemplifying women's versatility in adapting to new gender roles in the city.

Conclusion

Despite its vested interest in promoting African patriarchy in Rhodesia, both colonial capitalism and the state subscribed to the racialised hierarchy: white man at the apex, followed by the white woman, then the black man and the black woman at the bottom. In essence, while the black men enjoyed certain gendered privileges, which increased what Connell terms the patriarchal dividend; access to this dividend was a complicated affair in the colonial urban economy. The latter, while creating alternatives to the often exclusionary traditional patriarchy, simultaneously lowered the patriarchal dividend, with women increasingly charting out independent lives that undermined male dominance. Similarly, the oppressive colonial order marked by institutional violence – both physical and structural – left little space for the construction of positive or affirming masculinities. Consequently, the enactment of a range of violent masculinities formed a desperate attempt to lay claim to some forms of recognised selfhood.

Segal (1990) observes that masculinity is essentially unstable as suggested by its dependence upon the steady confirmation of power 'from what can prove unstable social institutions' along with its 'hierarchically understood difference from what can prove insubordinate "others", a category which often includes women and men seen to be subordinate on the basis of any range of factors' (123). It is these constructions of masculinity, which require an assertion of hierarchical difference, that make it difficult for men to construct alternative masculinities that depart from the need for dominance over what are considered subordinate groups. These constructions of gender identity inscribe hierarchies and reinforce dangerous binaries that, in turn, narrow the space for negotiating alternative identities.

Under these circumstances, the men in both novels find themselves having to adapt to new gender dynamics. Ultimately, the men react differently, with varying degrees of success in terms of the social viability of their chosen responses. What emerges from these novels are complex manhoods, enacted in the attempt to retrieve threatened identities, and to compensate for destabilised gender identities: brave attempts to keep up with the complexities of new power dynamics, in the belief that whatever the circumstances, a man can – and indeed must – try to be a man.

Endnotes

1. This phrase is borrowed from Durosimi Jones' short story 'A man can try' (De Grandsaigne, 1985). The story chronicles a British colonial administrator's last days in Sierra Leone before he travels to Britain to marry his white fiancée. He leaves behind an African woman, Maria, with whom he has lived for eight years,

and their young son. This story gestures at colonial anxieties about, and attraction to, the highly mythologised black female sexuality, along with the fear of miscegenation, often referred to as the 'yellow peril'. I am using the title partly to allude to these anxieties, but also in reference to the black man's attempt to cope with the new urban dynamics in much the same way: Trevor in Jones's story persuades himself that despite the major differences between his fiancé and Maria, 'a man can try' to survive the change.

2. I am grateful to Robert Muponde, Ashleigh Harris and Kizito Muchemwa for sharing their rich insights on certain aspects of this chapter.

3. In an interview with Jane Bryce, Vera once said that *Butterfly Burning* 'celebrates some of the elements of urbanization which came with colonization and the creativity which it unleashed for people to survive these things. I'm writing about my city, Bulawayo, and I'm celebrating it' (Muponde and Taruvinga, 2002: 224).

4. In the African canon, Ngugi wa Thiong'o's *The River Between* is a case in point, where formal education opens up new arenas of power and social capital which create alternative masculinities and access to patriarchal power. In an ageist and culturally hierarchical Kikuyu community, Waiyaki's exposure to formal education and his teacher status affords him power, which actually seems to threaten the senior masculinity of the Kiama elders.

5. See Holland's 'Troubled masculinities in Dangarembga's *Nervous Conditions*' (Ouzgane and Morrell, 2005).

6. This official invisibility is one of the ironies of the state, both colonial and postcolonial. Brian Chikwava's award winning story 'Seventh Street Alchemy' (in Staunton, 2003) explores this official invisibility in post-colonial Zimbabwe. In the story the state attempts to charge a prostitute with disturbing public peace, in the course of trying to get a passport. However, the state is unable to charge her, because to do so, it needs to establish her identity, and without her passport, she officially does not exist, and therefore cannot be charged with any crime.

7. This had been the case in England too, until 1870. It is worth noting that these laws were an anachronistic continuum of Victorian values. See Francoise Basch's Relative Creatures (1974).

8. Brown, in Lindsay and Miescher (2003).

9. Cited in Morrell's 'The Times of Change: Men and Masculinity in South Africa' in Morrell, ed. (2000).

10. In her research among commercial sex workers in Nairobi, Nikki Nelson talks about the way in which the women 'cleared sex-work of all immoral connotations. It was referred to as 'selling from one's kiosk' a reference to owning a small shop. They were defining sex-work as a commercialization of the reproductive role of women' Quoted in Newell (ed.) 2001.

11. See for instance Wood and Jewkes' (2001) essay, 'Violence, Rape and Sexual Coercion: Everyday Love in a South African Township', which explores assumptions of the sexual entitlement of men to their girlfriends' bodies, and the accompanying assumptions of sexual availability of these girls, for their boyfriends' sexual pleasure (134–136).

12. See Said (1995) and McClintock (1995).

13. These concerns continue to exercise both the black and white imagination, as recently as 2005, as suggested by the film *The Constant Gardener*'s portrayal of Dr.Arnold Bluhm, a black character whose sole function in the film seems to be a receptacle of the white male anxiety about black sexuality. The black peril is further explored in J.M.Coetzee's celebrated novel, *Disgrace*, in which it occupies pride of place as the moment of rupture in the narrative, while Zakes Mda's *The Madonna of Excelsior* examines the yellow peril in apartheid South Africa. The white peril has received greater expression in Afro-American literature than African literature, perhaps based on the prevalence of the abuse of black women in the history of slavery. Toni Morrison's *Beloved* provides a sensitive depiction of black women's fear of the white peril, based on an actual historical experience.

12

The nature of fatherhood and manhood in Zimbabwean texts of pre-colonial and colonial settings

MICKIAS MUSIYIWA AND MEMORY CHIRERE

Introduction

This chapter interrogates the notion of ideal fatherhood and manhood during pre-colonial and colonial Zimbabwe in novels written in Shona, Ndebele and English. However, it must be stressed from the outset that it is difficult to analyse fatherhood independently of motherhood since the two are mutually inclusive. Good fatherhood is normally attainable through being complemented by good motherhood. In Zimbabwean society whose both indigenous and European (mainly English) cultures are patriarchal, with fathers being heads of families and public institutions and with the socio-economic marginalisation of women often attributed to men, the endeavour to search for the idea of a good father in Zimbabwean literature is therefore justifiably paramount. In all socio-historical contexts fatherhood is defined by conjugal and family responsibilities (concepts of which are constructs of a particular culture), and these are relative to socio-economic changes obtaining in that particular society. A man's ability to accomplish such responsibilities earns him good fatherhood from his wife and children and also the community at large. Zimbabwean texts set in the pre-European era project ideal fatherhood thriving in the context of the agro-pastoral economy and supported by patriarchal values. In the same period national fatherhood is thematised to show leaders' abilities to execute their responsibilities of governance vis-à-vis the interests of their subjects. The colonial period which saw the imposition of an exclusive capitalist economy, informed by Europhone paternalistic values, precipitated the transmutation of African manhood and fatherhood. Through sustained and systematic impoverishment and subtle physical and mental manipulation, the powerful explosion of the colonialist package and its principal fragments of land dispossession, monetarisation of the economy, colonial labour and education, inter alia, deprived African men of normal manhood and fatherhood. This gave rise to alienated fatherhood, in the form of feminised fatherhood and nomadic fathering and their attendant socially deleterious consequences. In a word Zimbabwean literature depicts manhood and fatherhood during the colonial period as social tragedy.

Definitions of key concepts

The meanings of the terms 'fatherhood' and 'manhood'[1] so central to the articulation of the chapter's discourse, should be defined from the outset. Fatherhood is the condition of being a father, including the character, authority and responsibilities expected of a father. On the other hand, manhood is the state of being an adult man, normally as distinguished from childhood and womanhood. In further distinguishing the terms, it can be noted that while fatherhood is largely limited to a married man and normally with children, manhood is common to all adult men irrespective of marital status. In practice the terms signify the social roles a man in one or both of the social conditions is expected to execute in his interaction with others in his family and community at large. The practice of fatherhood and manhood are normally cultural constructs relative to a given society's cultural beliefs and economic system. Consequently, as is stressed in this chapter, the manifestation of these social conditions changes once there is an alteration in the cultural and economic life of a particular society.

Fatherhood in Zimbabwean texts of a pre-colonial setting

In Shona and Ndebele pre-colonial social settings the desire to create a family, seen as the most appropriate institution for the socio-economic survival, prosperity and security of a human being, necessitated fatherhood. Under clan ideology every man had a moral obligation to marry and to contribute towards the material well-being and social reproduction of his kingship group (Weinrich, 1982: 39). Thus fatherhood and its attendant responsibilities were sanctioned by a man's clan/family. As head of family a man had heavy responsibilities thrust upon his shoulders. The socio-economic failure of the family was always blamed on him. Okot P'Bitek (1986: 19) contends that because of such roles as fatherhood, in Africa man is not born free because he 'has a bundle of duties which are expected from him by society...' Generally Zimbabwean literature shows that the attributes of a good father include the ability to lead the family's life in every respect. Besides executing his conjugal responsibilities to the satisfaction of his wife/wives, he must care for and love his children and above all ensure family continuity upon his death by leaving his family with an estate. Good fatherhood also extended beyond a man's family to the clan and the entire community. In a sense chiefs, kings and village heads, also acted as fathers.

Nyamombe and Mjaji in Solomon Mutswairo and Geshom P. Khiyaza's respective novels, *Feso* (1956) and *Ukuthunjwa KukaSukuzukuduma* [The Abduction of Sukuzukuduma] (1978) are portrayed as fathers of their people concerned with the welfare of all their subjects. In Shona and Ndebele kingdoms, leaders were not only fathers of their immediate families but of their entire kingdoms. They earned good fatherhood through governing according to tradition and to the satisfaction of the people. This entailed maintaining and sustaining the freedom, welfare and integrity of their states. The name Nyamombe, which means 'owner of many cattle', signifies Nyamombe's resourcefulness. He keeps cattle on behalf of his people. So appreciative are his subjects to his good governance that they feel obliged to reciprocate their leader's generosity by finding him a wife. Likewise Mjaji also ensures the welfare of all his subjects as well as that of his immediate family. In Ndebele culture the role of a king as father is expressed by the fact that all his subjects were referred to as *abantu benkosi* (the king's subjects).

A convincing appreciation of good fatherhood also requires us to examine those fathers who failed in their responsibilities. The satirisation of irresponsible national fathers is a pre-occupation of Nobert Mutasa's *Misodzi, Dikita neRopa* [A Reign of Tears, Sweat and Blood] (1991); Patrick Chakaipa's *Pfumo reRopa* [Spear of Blood] (1961) and Solomon Mutswairo's *Feso*. Despotism punctuates the governance of Chirisamhuru in *Misodzi, Dikita neRopa*, Ndyire in *Pfumo reRopa* and Pfumojena in *Feso*. Invariably their people are in profound despair as they endure daily the tyranny and unpredictability of their leaders. Ndyire, whose name implies 'trickster' or 'exploiter' uses his power and authority to move around the chiefdom proposing love to other men's wives, levels false accusations against the men and sentences them to death. He believes every woman in his chiefdom is his. While courting Shizha's wife he boasts saying:

> *Pane munhu ane munda kana gombo zvaro zvisiri zvangu muno munyika here? Ndiani ane simba rokundirambidza kurima pandinenge ndichida? Gombo iri ndarida ndinoririma chete ndione chinouya* (1).

(Is there a person who has a wife or unmarried woman who is not mine in this chiefdom? Who has the power to stop me from taking any woman I want? I love you so much and I have to marry you and see what will happen).

In *Feso*, Pfumojena, like Ndyire, is a despot. 'Pfumojena' literally means 'White spear' and in Shona culture, *pfumo* (spear) symbolises war, suffering and death. His ruthlessness is shown through his regular witch-hunting exercises against perceived enemies whom he summarily executes. In contrast to the harmony enjoyed by Mjaji and Nyamombe's people, Pfumojena's people are in constant fear. As an allegory to African oppression under colonial domination in Zimbabwe, *Feso* projects the view that as an extension of a colonising culture, colonialism's imposition and assumption of fatherhood over Africans in the name of civilisation was nothing but outright oppression. The colonialist ideology and Europeans' paternalistic tendencies were exerting both subtle and overt brutality similar to what Pfumojena does. In Mutasa's historical novel based on the governance of the last Rozvi ruler, Chirisamhuru, we discover that there are some leaders who initially exhibit a high awareness of their mandate and respect of the wishes of their people. However, after some time they transmute into dictatorial and brutal fathers, trampling upon their people's wishes. Chirisamhuru fights and defeats the tyrannical usurper, Dyembeu, and tumultuously ascends the throne with unwavering support from the masses and the powerful religious authorities of the Mwari[2] oracle in Mabweadziva[3]. His name which literally means 'a calf herdsman', suggests he had numerous cattle. Figuratively it also suggests that he protected the vulnerable in society as a herdsman does to calves. Indeed David N. Beach (1980: 246) states that Rozvi rulers had large herds of cattle. Dyembeu means 'one who eats planting seed'. It therefore implies that Dyembeu was not a good leader; he would deprive his people of agricultural produce. Hence he was rejected not only by the rank and file of the kingdom, but by his own sons who teamed up with Chirisamhuru to oust him from power (Beach, 1980: 239). However, after consolidating himself in power, Chirisamhuru channels his energy and authority towards self-aggrandisement at the expense of the people. He shuns the spiritual advice from Mwabweadziva, refuses to adhere to the political traditions of the land and forces people to participate in projects aimed at projecting only his personal image. The people are whipped into line and the whole nation becomes exhausted while many die in the perilous projects and others killed for protesting against oppression. The title of the book, which translates to 'Tears, Sweat and Blood', aptly summarises the brutal nature Chirisamhuru's leadership suddenly turns into. Mutasa says:

... *Mambo wave munhu weshungu nehasha pose paari nokuda kokusabudirira kwebasa iri. ... ogara achibaya vanhu nepfumo rake Tipitipi* (74).

(... the King is now always of a violent temper because of the failure of his projects. ... every time he stabs people to death with his spear called Tipitipi).

As the importance of fatherhood at the family level lies in it being the basis of family development, so is fatherhood to the community. Similarly, while an irresponsible father is an impediment to his family's prosperity so is the same leader to his people. Pfumojena, Chirisamhuru and Ndyire all precipitate a tragic end to their lives, the suffering of their people and indeed the destruction of their kingdoms through dodging their responsibilities.

Bernard D. Ndlovu's historical Ndebele novel, *Laphuma Elinye*

Lingakatshoni [When mystery dawns] (1999) shows how the absence of the king as father can lead to the disintegration of the nation. In the novel, the Ndebele are migrating from Transvaal into Zimbabwe in two groups. The first comprising King Mzilikazi and the army and the second consisting of chiefs, women, children and livestock is led by Gundwane. The second group enters Matebeleland and stays for nearly two years without any news about the whereabouts of the king. A great division arises over whether they should install a new king now that Mzilikazi is rumoured to be dead. A new king should be found especially because critical ceremonies which are supposed to be presided only by the king, like *iNxwala*[4] are now due. While Gundwane's faction is in support of choosing a new king, Gwabalanda's is in opposition, insisting on waiting until their king's fate is ascertained. Although Gundwane's group goes ahead and installs Mzilikazi's son, Nkulumane, as the new king, Mzilikazi is eventually found to be alive. He comes to reassert himself as king, killing the leaders of the pro-new king group. The unity of the Ndebele people is greatly weakened by this event and the people are terrified.

Another instance where Ndebele and Shona writers discuss fatherhood is in the context of polygamous families. They tend to find them devoid of happiness and consequently an indication of the failure of fatherhood. However, some writers show that some men were able to lead and organise such big families into sustainable family happiness. In *Pfumo reRopa* Nhindiri is a polygamist but he leads his family well. In contrast, Ignatius Zvarevashe's *Kurauone* [Wait-till-you-mature] (1976) portrays the polygamous and ever-inebriated Gararirimo as having lost grip of the complex fabric of his big family. It is now reduced to intense hatred and jealousy among his children and wives. Violence and bloody family feuds punctuates Gararirimo's family life. Gararirimo has completely lost the image of a good father to both his family and community. The bloody conflicts in the family do not only destroy his family but his life as well. He resembles Unoka in Chinua Achebe's classic, *Things Fall Apart* (1958) in so far as he indulges in drinking at the expense of family welfare. A combination of laziness and addiction to palm wine leads to the embarrassingly bad reputation of his fatherhood. It is for this reason that Okonkwo fights hard to avoid the infamous stigma left by his father. Chinua Achebe (1958: 10) writes that 'during the planting season Okonkwo worked daily on his farms from cockcrow until the chickens went to roost'. Such men who fail to take firm control of family affairs are always condemned in *ngano/inganekwane*[5] (folktales). For instance, the *ngano*, '*Murume Akanga Akaparika*' (A Polygamous Man), a man is condemned for failing to discipline his second wife, who through hatred and jealousy intends to kill the senior wife's son but in the end mistakenly kills her own children (Fortune, 1980: 5-6).

Geoffrey Ndhala's *Jikinya* (1979) gives us a rare fatherhood whereby a Shona community agrees to foster a white baby whose parents had been killed by Shona warriors during the First Chimurenga. The novel demonstrates the fact fatherhood was, by and large, initiated and regulated by one's clan/family. When Chedu picks up a white baby, he had to bring it before the elders to decide on whether they would approve his intention to adopt it. It is paradoxical that Ngara elders allow Chedu and his wife to adopt the child despite its 'strangeness'; it is white and the writer says the Ngara people had not seen white people before. However, Ndhala's depiction of the Ngara and Changara people as not having seen white people before is not consistent with Zimbabwean history. As early as the twelfth century, the Shona had been trading with the Swahili Arabs and with the Portuguese from the sixteenth century (Beach, 1980). In spite of this historical anomaly, what Ndhlala attempts to foreground concerning the adoption of a white baby are the challenges indigenous people encountered in an attempt to conceptualise the new, sudden and complex reality of European encroachment as it threatened to forcibly ransack their cultures and worldview. Their attempt to conceptualise the rapidly and violently encroaching reality only results in the fragmentation of the Shona world outlook. Thus Chedu's adoption of Jikinya is realised out of the Ngara elders' fear of the spirits of the land's reaction if killing the baby was not the right procedure. Hence when a drought devastates the land, the neighbouring Changara people are quick to blame the Ngaras for their adoption of a 'strange' baby. In spite of this, Chedu is indeed a good father to Jikinya. He raises and gives her all the fatherly love, tenderness and care expected in Shona culture. Torn apart by the dilemma of cultural identity, Jikinya's death in the midst of a battle pitting colonial forces and the combined army of Ngara and Changara warriors also signifies the dilemma of the fatherhood which nurtured her. Though undesirable, her tragic death seems the author's only solution to terminate the strange and conflictual fatherhood which emerged out of the antagonistic Anglo-Shona cultural interface.

The adoption of foreign children was much more of a tradition in Ndebele than Shona society. Raiding was an economic branch in Ndebele society which did not only target grain and livestock but also women and children. Captured women were distributed to Ndebele men who assumed fatherhood over the children. As in Shona culture, this practice indicates that a man is not necessarily required to be the biological father of a child in order to assume fatherhood over it. This fatherhood was part and parcel of a national assimilation policy designed to enhance the security of the kingdom through increasing its human resources. Ndabaningi Sithole's *Umvukela wamaNdebele* [Ndebele Uprising] (1956) and Bernard D. Ndlovu's *Laphuma Elinye Lingakatshoni* show that all citizens of the

Ndebele kingdom coming from as varied ethnic groups as Sotho, Tswana, Kalanga and Shona were children of the king. In the latter novel, people address Mzilikazi as father and he in turn address them as children. Mkhithika who went in search of the king when Gundwane's group was preparing to install a new king, addresses Mzilikazi saying:

Yithi abantwa bakho, Ngwenyama. Sihambe sithungatha iganga lonke sidinga lapho ubaba owangena khona. Abantwana ekhaya bazinkendama ezingelamelusi (42).
('It's us your children, the Great Lion. We sojourned in the bushes searching for you, our father. The children back home are now sheep without a shephered.')

Fatherhood in Zimbabwean literature of a colonial setting

We should hasten to emphasise that the colonial factors impinging on fatherhood are closely inter-linked and that the misalignment of African fatherhood is the result of the oppositional and frictional interplay between Zimbabwean indigenous and Anglophile cultures. Rosamund Billington, et.al (1991: 68) state that 'colonial political, religious, economic and educational systems were all intended to supplant indigenous ones which were seen at best, as inefficient, at worst as primitive and barbaric'. Urbanisation, the monetisation of the economy, physical mobility and the embracement of western cultural sensibilities through education and Christianity were all concomitants of the same colonial system which affected Africans in varied ways. The so-called modern urban lifestyle of alcohol and sex for pleasure, which many African men and women fell into, were critical in the disorientation of African fatherhood. The alteration in the economic system which saw the movement of money to the centre of the people's lives had a direct impact on the social processes of life. The general endemic poverty which struck the majority of African families in the context of the dying subsistence agro-pastoral economy and the rise of the white minority-controlled colonial economy greatly diminished the capacity of many men to hold a respectable fatherhood status. With the traditionally big African family, the reserves with their mostly barren soils could not enable them to produce enough and therefore successfully execute their fatherhood roles. In spite of the fundamental alteration in the economic and social systems of the country, the same normative standards of a good father we saw in the pre-colonial setting were still expected. A father has to be responsible for the family's material, emotional and leadership needs. African manhood and fatherhood were therefore caught between the traditional conservative clan values and the so-called modernising but untested Europhilic ones.

In the texts under study, the tension between African and western cultures is often represented through the rural-is-good and urban-is-bad stereotypes where the former represents the beauty of traditional values and stability of life; and the latter, western values and their harmful impact on African culture. The physical separation of spouses was indeed an assault to matrimony. We discern from Zimbabwean texts that away from home, most men indulged in extra-marital sex, normally with prostitutes. The texts also show that some wives also did the same during the prolonged absence of their husbands. Either way, fatherhood (and also motherhood) is adversely affected. These scenarios are depicted in James Kawara's *Ruchiva* [Covetousness] (1982) and Tumai J. Machimbira's *Gondoharishari* [Habitual Womaniser] (1975). In *Ruchiva* although Tobias is a responsible father, providing more than adequately the material needs of his family, his wife who lives in the rural areas is not contented. Rudo decides to have an affair with Paul, a teacher at a local school. Ironically, unlike many of his colleagues Tobias is faithful to his wife. Though Rudo acknowledges her husband's ability to support the family materially, she cannot sexually endure the long periods her husband is away in Harare. Hence she invites Paul to sleep with her in the very matrimonial house her husband had built. She justifies her infidelity on the basis of human nature.

'Semurume wangu mari anotumira zvake yekuti ndinoidya ndichitosiya imwe. Asika ... kana musvondo chaimo muparidzi akasimuka achiti, 'mumhu haararami nesadza roga' (5-6).

(As a responsible husband, every time my husband sends me a lot of money which is more than enough for my spending. But ... even in the church the preacher stood up and said, 'a person cannot survive on sadza alone' (implying a person cannot live without sex).

Tsitsi in *Gondoharishari* finds the two-year period her husband, Goremucheche, is in Gweru seeking employment unbearably too long to wait. Unlike Rudo who still loves her husband but only desires sexual gratification, Tsitsi decides to jilt her husband and marry Gondoharishari regardless of the fact that Goremucheche had formally married and paid bridewealth for her. These episodes clearly indicate that the increased mobility in search of money which separated spouses was inimical to the institution of marriage. The fact that in the absence of their legitimate husbands Rudo and Tsitsi end up with surrogate husbands is indicative of how husbands were prevented by new circumstances from fulfilling their sexual responsibilities resulting in the sexual starvation of their wives.

While Rudo and Tsitsi's betrayal of their husbands can be explained against the increased physical mobility, Patricia's case in Barbara Makhalisa's *Impilo Yinkinga* [Life is a mystery] (1983) is different. Here we come across feminised fatherhood, whereby a man is uncritically humble, docile and incapable of controlling family affairs while his wife assumes personal freedom at the family's expense. Her husband Ngonyama, like Tobias, is highly sensitive to all the needs of his family. The family does not lack anything but Patricia is not contented. She diverts family resources to buy pleasure, living life to its fullest; drinking, smoking, shopping extravagantly and worse still sleeping with other men. The new colonial culture did not only affect African fatherhood, but also motherhood. While the African family thrived in a village setting with its structures supported by the agro-pastoral economy, its transfer to the urban areas where it was to depend on a weekly or monthly wage, upset African family values which are now being exploited by Patricia for her own personal interests. Patricia diverts family income to buy pleasure through exploiting the traditional view that as head of the family her husband should adequately provide for it. In spite of our sympathy towards Ngonyama's passivity against his domineering and wayward wife, in the eyes of the public he is not a good father. He symbolises the dismal and socially embarrassing demise of fatherhood. The name, 'Ngonyama' which in Ndebele means 'lion', is a satire upon its bearer's character as father. He is a tamed lion stripped of its power, courage and aggression. A woman neighbour to the Ngonyamas observes when she remarks:

> *'A-a, laye uNgonyama lo yindoda ngamabhulugwe oqotho. Kungowakwamu aluba umuntu sowabuyisela kibo wayalaywa kabili...'* (67).
>
> ('It's really amazing, Ngonyama is only a man because he puts on trousers. Had it been my husband, I could have long been sent back to my parents for re-education' (i.e. on proper motherhood) ...).

While many men failed to attain and/or maintain fatherhood as a result of their rural wives who deceived them by having extra-marital affairs, in the urban areas fatherhood greatly lost its social purposefulness as men engaged in cohabitation, prostitution and nomadic fathering.[6] In Paul Chidyausiku and Charles Mungoshi's respective novels, *Nyadzi dzinokunda rufu* [Shame transcends death] (1962) and *Ndiko Kupindana Kwemazuva* [How time passes] (1975) young men abuse their fatherhood lured by money, alcohol and prostitutes. As we saw Rudo and Patricia abusing their motherhood by indulging in extra-marital affairs, the same applies to what these men do with their fatherhood. They share it between their wives and urban prostitutes. In *Nyadzi dzinokunda rufu* the new urban culture in Bulawayo of alcohol and prostitutes titillates Nyika to the extent of forgetting not only his wife but also his family roots. He wastes money, buying prostitutes beer, clothes and food. He even connives with the prostitutes to have his wife killed. Similarly Rex in *Ndiko Kupindana Kwemazuva* is not portrayed as an ideal father either. He abandons Rindai, an ideal and ever-committed wife in the rural areas. In Harare he cohabits with and impregnates a prostitute, Magi, ironically Rindai's friend. Like Nyika, Rex is being transformed significantly by the urban environment, which puts him into a frenzy and consequently losing him his awareness of social identity. The way urbanisation alienates African men is aptly captured by Mungoshi who writes:

> Pane chimwe chinhu chinoita kuti wava muHarare ukanganwe twese twawabva wakaronga kumusha kwako. Pane nyemwe rinongouya, nyemwe rinenge shavi rourombe, rinongokuti kwindi waera wati kwiti chete paMusika weHarare.... Harare inokupa wara rinokupa mavara kuti uri nhingi kana kuti uri ngana, vausiri. ... Kusanduka vara sorwaivhi (135-36).
>
> (There is something that makes you forget everything you planned while back home in the rural areas. There is a certain excitement which just fills you from nowhere, an excitement triggered by a spirit of irresponsibility, which completely takes control of you once you disembark from the bus at the Harare bus terminus ... Harare fills you with frenzy giving you this or that identity, which in reality you are not. ... Changing your identity like a chameleon).

It is only after a tragedy in the family which vigorously shakes their false consciousness that painfully awakens them to realise the depth of their alienation. Nyika does so after discovering that his wife whom he thought was dead was actually alive. As for Rex he regains his consciousness as father after his daughter, Rangarirai is knocked down by a car and dies.

The acquisition of education by Africans and their pursuit of various professions were key factors in initiating them into western cultural sensibilities and in the process disorienting many of them from African fatherhood. With its promise of entry into the (colonial) African educated elite, colonial education was not a process of the acquisition of neutral knowledge; it entailed the assimilation of cultural values of the imperial power (Billington, et.al., 1991: 67). Because most educated men could now pay bridewealth on their own unlike in the past when their fathers were responsible, the economic independence gave them the freedom to practice fatherhood according to their own liking. While some preferred to marry educated women, others delayed marriage in pursuit of pleasure and still others avoided committing themselves but resorting to mobile fathering. Thomson Tsodzo's *Pafunge* [Think of it] (1972) and Aaron C. Moyo's *Uchandifungawo* [You will think of me] (1975) focus on these issues. Against the wishes of his parents, Smart in *Uchandifungawo* jilts and eventually divorces his rural, loyal and morally upright wife, Rumbidzai, and marries Noster, a nurse. Smart thinks that an uneducated wife is only there to be fed and looked after without complementing his roles as husband.

'Chete zvokuroora mukadzi asina kudzidza zvakafanana nokuroora chirema chisina mitezo yose, munhu anongopedza mazimari angu akangoti parukukwe zete' (50).

(Marrying an uneducated woman is like marrying a cripple with deformed body parts, someone who will just squander my money idly).

In the same way that Rex and Nyika only realise much later and after some devastating consequences about how urban life destroys marriage, Smart's belated reawakening only serves to illustrate to him how true his parents' advice was. Contrary to Ngonyama, his salary was not adequate to meet the demands of urban life and Noster's insatiable consumerist tendencies. It is also demeaning on Smart's fatherhood that he does not father a child with Noster but gives in to Noster's demands that her child with a previous husband is adequate for them and Smart should look after it. After Smart had lost his job Noster asserts more of her freedom; she brings her boyfriends into their matrimonial home and orders Smart to perform domestic chores. Smart's attempt to reassert the very patriarchal fatherhood which his father had wanted him to inherit is futile. He tries ordering Noster to stop her unbecoming behaviour arguing that he paid bridewealth for her, but Noster divorces him and chases him out of her house.

Josiah, Ozias and Phainos in *Pafunge* are condemned for their socially destructive manhood. Instead of being faithful to the girls they court, the act of impregnating and jilting girls has become their hobby. While the sedentary nature of Zimbabwean society in the past made it difficult for men to impregnate women and flee, the physical fluidity and cosmopolitan nature of colonial Zimbabwe enabled people to move much faster to other places than before. While impregnating a girl, let alone denying responsibility was a serious crime in the traditional past, increased mobility during this time meant that a man could easily escape the crime and go to another place. Besides, the high status a man acquired in traditional society for fathering many children obliged him to take responsibility of all his children. With modern values emphasising the nuclear family and/or staying single among the educated Africans, having many children was considered too burdensome in an economy now based on money, a scarcity to most Africans. The brotherhood of the unscrupulous conmen, Josiah, Ozias and Phainos is based on nothing but the pleasure of luring girls into relationships which immediately end once the girls confess pregnancy. Their abuse of manhood is satirically described by Tsodzo as:

Iwo machinda matatu aya akati hamutizivi. Vanasikana

vomaSadzajena novokune dzimwe nzvimbo vakazvimbiriswa vakazvirega. Musikana ainge angoita pamuviri chete aibva arambwa (34).
(These three gentlemen said to themselves these girls were foolish. They impregnated the girls of Sadzajena and other places with impunity. Any girl who fell pregnant was immediately rejected).

However, it is Josiah who seems to practise this reckless manhood to exaggerated levels. He ends up having children in almost every city and town of the country. While traditionally mobile and urban women were viewed as prostitutes, Josiah has extended this to believe that every woman is a prostitute. It is this fallacious and arrogant justification of his unchecked fathering which results in him marrying his own daughter, Rudo, he had fathered with Annatoria many years ago. Like Rex and Nyika, Smart's alienated fatherhood has tragic consequences. While Rex and Nyika's restoration of their fatherhood left them with permanent psychological scars, unfortunately Smart's is irretrievable. Rumbidzai refuses to reconcile with him after so many years. He is spat out and ostracised by both the new and traditional worlds. In an Electral fashion, Josiah is punished by one of the products of his reckless fathering, his daughter Rudo who kills him with sleeping tablets after realising that he was the culprit behind her mother's suicide. Josiah's attribution of his nefarious fathering to an evil spirit (*mweya wakaipa*, 106), testifies to the intricate colonial processes' causation of the destruction of the social consciousness of African men's awareness of themselves and their social responsibilities to account for their actions.

In Chenjerai Hove's *Bones* (1989) we discern that Africans' socio-economic disempowerment under the colonial capitalist order is another major contributor to the dearth of fatherhood and manhood among African men. Marume, Chiriseri and Chisaga and indeed all other men at Manyepo's farm are entrapped in a socio-economic quagmire constantly militating against their awareness as men and the desire to be free men in control of their families. Although *Bones* largely thematises female struggles as seen through the large space and loud voice Hove gives to Marita, a close examination of its male characters reveals the tragic conditions in which fatherhood makes futile and infinitesimal struggles to liberate itself. Marume's tragedy is that his potential authority as father from a traditional sense, has been destroyed/usurped through enslavement by Manyepo, the settler capitalist farm owner. The way in which Manyepo has taken control of his male labourers' manhood is thorough to the effect that Marita ridicules the men at Manyepo's farm as being 'castrated'. Marume, whose name ironically means 'man', a derivation from the Shona word, 'murume' (meaning, male/man) is a satirical critique of its owner who is dominated by his wife, Marita. Marita regards him with pity and sometimes talks to him as if talking to her son. Like African-American slaves during slavery, Marume, Chisaga, Chiriseri and other man labourers at Manyepo's farm have been reduced to agent fathers, who father children which they have no social rights over, but do so on behalf of the white farm owner. Orlando Patterson (1993: 11) gives us similar experiences among African-American men whose 'pre-existing patterns of work and gender roles' were altered by the institution of slavery. Men lost rights over their children and hence their 'recognised roles as fathers ...' Thus besides the physical and mental control of African men, capitalist labour relations went further to control their sexuality. In desperation Marume notices this when he laments their conditions saying:

Do you think we are children with all this beard on our faces?
Have we the men not made our wives pregnant and have the
wives not become pregnant after we slept with them? (22)

True is Albert Memmi's (1965: xii) observation that '... the deprivations of the colonised are the almost direct result of the advantages secured to the coloniser .... To observe the life of the coloniser and the colonised is to discover rapidly that the daily humiliation of the colonised, his objective subjugation, are not merely economic'. From Marume's words we realise how the colonial system left little space for African manhood and fatherhood's social praxis. African men can only claim the ability to impregnate a wife and can do nothing else before and after that. As Paulo Freire (1970: 107) argues, 'in order to dominate, the dominator has no choice but to deny true praxis to the people, deny them the right to say their own word and think their own thoughts'. The unrelenting pathological fear of being a small man which grips Marume and his co-male labourers, is testimony to the deliberate and brutal colonial shattering of the African men's pride, making them socially invisible. These men have been 'thoroughly domesticated by the ideology of colonialism' (Rino Zhuwarara, 2001: 222) as a result of their loss of land, the basis of their socio-economic system. Their subsequent conversion into low-wage labourers is the underlying factor for their pitiful and tragic fatherhood.

Conclusion

The chapter has argued that a close scrutiny of Zimbabwean literature illustrates that the concept of fatherhood and its attendant roles of manhood and fathering were conditioned by the socio-economic system and worldview dominant in pre-colonial and colonial Zimbabwe. While the commonest fatherhood open to every man was achieved through marriage, at its highest level fatherhood assumes national connotations where the leader of kingdom/chiefdom is also father. In their depiction of all these forms of fatherhood, Zimbabwean writers analysed in this chapter largely concur that fatherhood loses its relevance to the family, community and nation at large if a father consciously or otherwise disregards his mandate. Thus Nyamombe and Mjaji are ideal fathers while Ndyire, Chirisamhuru and Pfumojena are not ideal fathers under this criterion. However, it is clear in Zimbabwean texts that for a man to attain celebrated fatherhood, he requires unconditional and constant backing from his wife, children, kinsmen and kinswomen and as leader from his people. The colonial context which saw the radical transmutation of Zimbabwean cultures and their economic and thought systems, greatly disoriented African fatherhood and manhood resulting in feminised and agent fatherhoods, nomadic fathering and in some cases surrogate fatherhood. Whatever form it took, Zimbabwean texts largely mirror it as an alienated, beleaguered and tragic fatherhood. It is subtly controlled by the powerfully alluring urban pleasures and the physically and mentally enslaving capitalist economy which took away African men's traditional power and authority to exercise their mandate as fathers.

ENDNOTES
1. The definitions have been elaborated from those in the Webster's *Third New International Dictionary* (1986) and *The Oxford English Dictionary* (1989).
2. Mwari is the Shona High God.
3. Mabweadziva (the Stones of Dziva) are the Matopos Hills housing the shrines of Mwari. For many centuries during the pre-colonial period, the Mwari oracle was quite active among the Karanga, Venda, Kalanga and Ndebele.
4. An annual festival, also known as The First Fruits Ceremony, was presided over by the king and its chief functions were spiritual regeneration, re-confirmation of loyalty to the king, fertility of the land and national unity (Pathisa Nyathi,
Traditional Ceremonies of the AmaNdebele. Gweru: Mambo Press, 2001: 29 – 33).
5. The terms, *ngano* and *inganekwan*e are Shona and Ndebele terms for folktales respectively.
6. We use the term, 'mobile fathering' to refer to the wanton impregnation and abandonment of women by men who do not even care about how the women and the children they will bear will survive.

13

Intricate space: The father-daughter relationship in Zimbabwean literature and culture

ANNA CHITANDO AND ANGELINE M. MADONGONDA

Introduction

The father-daughter relationship has been given little attention in scholarly work on Zimbabwean literature. Rarely do critics explore this relationship in instances that can demonstrate the caring and gentle nature of the man in regard to his womenfolk. Critics tend to emphasise the antagonism – even war – between the male and the female through which patriarchy asserts its dominance. In this chapter, however, we largely deal with the positive father-daughter nexus as portrayed in Zimbabwean fiction. We begin by giving some background conceptions of fatherhood, offering insights into different father figures from traditional culture through to contemporary social mores. Our main focus is, therefore, one that attempts to identify alternative masculinities; ones which work to society's best advantage; ones where responsible fatherhood seeks to use its power positively so as to empower rather than violate its own children – daughters in particular.

We explore the position of daughter vis-à-vis that of father, as she, like her mother and grandmother before her, falls within the hierarchy of patriarchal power exercised within society. As gender inequalities extend to the daughter, it is presumed she finds herself on the bottom rung of the ladder of social hierarchy (Morrell, 2001); ironically, however, the daughter (for whatever reasons) still occupies a special place in the life of her father.

Background: defining fatherhood in Zimbabwean society

Although this is subject to much debate, the father plays a crucial role in bringing up the family. The traditional role of the father is to provide for the family and to oversee its general welfare. The mother is relegated to the confines of the kitchen and looking after the children. Because of this division of labour, the gender roles that are assigned to the sexes do not allow much interaction between a father and his daughter; it is thus difficult to perceive open acts of affection within the traditional father-daughter relationship. The father and the boys were/are restricted to the confines of the *dare* [traditional village council/meeting place for men] (Gelfand, 1973) and the mother and the girl to the kitchen. This situation is aggravated by the importance that is placed on the boy child even in contemporary society (Mukonoweshuro, 2000).

The girl child appears to occupy the lowest position in social rankings, especially in traditional and conservative communities. However, the mature or married daughter has a reserved space at the *dare* as the *tete vemusha* [the aunt of the family] especially at important family functions such as marriage ceremonies. This demonstrates a close relationship between the father and his daughter as the latter could sit amongst the men and take part in family decisions. Hers is a position that is assigned by patriarchy, in which the father is supreme. She rises even beyond her mother who cannot play the same role, except when amongst her own people. The question, however, still remains about how much power she exercises in the decision-making process.

However, before we go further, there is need to define fatherhood in Shona society as it takes several diverse forms. Apart from the conventional biological father there are other 'fathers' whose contributions to 'their' children's lives cannot be taken for granted. In the traditional context, the term father is broad and can include any male elder in the village/community and the extended family within which the brother of one's father becomes one's father as well. This has its roots in the communal nature of Shona society where in the event of the real father dying or being absent for some time, then the brother takes over the economic role of father (Bourdillon, 1982). Even in the presence of one's actual father, a daughter (or son) has to acknowledge the fatherhood of her various uncles. This relationship is still very much alive even in contemporary society, for example in the works of Tsitsi Dangarembga (*Nervous Conditions* and *The Book of Not*) where Tambudzai's relationship with Babamukuru is analogous to the real father-daughter one. Mungoshi's 'Sacrifice' (1997) also demonstrates this relationship through Tayeva who, even in the presence of her own father, has to recognise the existence of her *babamukuru* [uncle] as her 'real' father. Such fathers, even today, take a pivotal role in ceremonies such as funerals and marriages that reach out to broader family relationships.

Within the contemporary Zimbabwean context, the term 'father' has mutated in line with changes in society since the inception of colonialism. This accords with what Morrell (2001: 4) underlines as the volatility an fluidity of gender, that masculinity 'can and does change and ... is therefore not fixed ...' The patriarchal role of the male still persists but the relationship to the daughter has become complex. Interaction has improved with the father being prepared to face any challenge to protect his daughter. A non-governmental organisation such as Padare/ Enkundleni [men's fora on gender issues that explore male relationships with women] has received international acclaim for advocating that values and practices that have been detrimental to the welfare of the girls and women should be banished. Padare thus mirrors other international fora for men whose '[i]nitiatives involve working with men to develop policy on paternity leave and promoting fathers' involvement with childcare' (Morrell, 2001: 5). They signify a movement and transformation of the traditional *dare* to a modern one.

Acts of defiance by a father in order to protect his daughter can be found in traditional society (as portrayed in fiction). These acts challenged or interrogated patriarchal traditions or beliefs from within. Mutasa's protagonist (Mutumwa) in *Mapatya* [twins] (1978) defies traditional conventions and decides to keep both his twin daughters, Miriro and Mirirai, although this was considered an abomination in Shona society. Similarly Mungoshi's Chizema (in a more contemporary situation) opts for death rather than have his only daughter Tayeva offered as sacrifice to appease an avenging spirit ('Sacrifice' in *Walking Still*, 1997). The feeling of love and devotion is mutual because Tayeva decides that she will obey the wishes of the clan in order to save further bloodshed and pain, not least that of her father.

The father can also act philanthropically by deciding to adopt a child and keep him/her as his own as in *Chipo Changu* [My Gift] (Chingono, 1978). Even in traditional society a man could marry a woman with children from a previous marriage, a phenomenon referred to as *kudhonza sanzu nemarara aro* [dragging a branch and all its leaves]. The rising divorce rates have also seen a proliferation of stepfamilies, and the role of stepfathers should not be overlooked. Westerhof (2005) demonstrates this phenomenon where a father can lay claim and display an attachment and affection to his stepdaughters. This chapter however, focuses on the conventional biological father as well as the uncle, *babamudiki* or *babamukuru's* role.

Fatherhood, a significant feature of masculinity, should not be considered out of (historical) context. According to Morrell (2001: 7)

[Masculinities] are socially and historically constructed in a process, which involves contestation between rival understandings of what being a man should involve. [Masculinity] is so culturally variable and so context dependant .... [that] the challenge is to identify what forces operate to effect change in masculinities, when, where and how such changes occur, and what the effects are.

This chapter captures largely the transitional periods of pre-colonial, colonial and post-colonial experiences of the characters involved as well as their movement from the traditional to a modernised paradigm.

The daughter, in her own right, recognises how invaluable a father is to her. It is, after all, through the father that girls gain their first reflection of themselves as female. Rosen-Grandon (1995) has pointed out how knowledge of and closeness to one's father prepares one for knowing one's husband through 'compromise, commitment and consideration'. Thus fathers can play pivotal roles in their daughters' lives.

Traditional oral folklore

Folklore in African orature provides a valuable source of cultural history and socialisation, relaying and fortifying values that are primary in a particular society. As alluded to by Finnegan (1970: 27), 'oral literature in particular possesses vastly more aesthetic, social and personal significance'. Gender roles, for instance, are shown in folk-tales, riddles and proverbs. This is clearly demonstrated in Furniss and Gunner's (1995) collection of essays that primarily focus on power, gender and marginalisation in African oral literature. A close analysis of these essays depicts African oral narratives as tools for shaping gender expectations. Values such as subservience and the importance of getting a hard-working man for a husband were inculcated into young girls through oral tradition. The girl child was socialised into believing in feminine subservience. Boys are often portrayed as strong and full of energy, while girls are objects of beauty to be adored or, ironically, violated and abused. Haralambos (1980: 531) provides a western version of how young boys and girls are socialised into adult behaviour when he says:

differences are achieved through 'canalization' involving the direction of boys and girls towards different objects. This is particularly obvious in the provision of toys for girls, which encourage them to rehearse their expected adult roles as mothers and housewives. Girls are given dolls, soft toys, and miniature domestic objects and appliances to play with. Boys, on the other hand, are given toys, which encourage more practical, logical, and aggressive behaviour, for example bricks and guns.

Zimbabwean folk stories play a similar role in preparing youngsters for adulthood. It becomes clear that, whilst folklore has a role to play in society, it is often influenced by the gender ideologies of the day.

When we look at the functional role of African orature from another perspective, we find that certain folk-tales may be viewed as subversive, when they appear to question or challenge prevailing social ideals or values. For example, conservative tales would portray a traditional society that worships strength and power, where subversive tales endow virtue to those assumed weak in society. For example the story 'The Prince and the Leper' (Mungoshi, 2000), in which Mapezi the outcast is rewarded and marries the prince Sangare.

In conventional folk-tales, powerful animals such as lion and elephant are commonly depicted using their power to oppress or bully weaker animals. Weaker animals are portrayed succeeding in ventures that the so-called stronger animals fail to accomplish. This is a fundamental challenge to society's tendency to privilege strength and power. However, folk-tales generally propagate different social values and different values can co-exist, for example, strength and humility. Similarly concepts of power may be used to interrogate the notion of fatherhood in oral folklore. A good father entails being responsible, caring for the family, and fulfilling all duties expected from the head of a household. Such positive qualities are lacking in Kuruta, the father in Mungoshi's 'The Spirit of the Ashpit' (1999: 41-55). Here we have a father who is insensitive to the needs of his family. Kuruta keeps honey for himself while his wife and children suffer from unbearable hunger. His traditional role as provider is compromised by selfishness.

The father in this folk-tale, often does not recognise the value and potential of his daughter(s). Kuruta's daughter was just as much a victim of his negligence as his other children. This position, however, is often reversed when the daughter comes of age. Then the father becomes aware of her value particularly if she's beautiful: '... [with] her ankles, wrists and neck decked in bronze and copper bangles, bracelets and necklaces .... [on] her forehead ... a moon-white shell, her hair ... plaited in circular braids knotted at the top of her head,' Mungoshi ('The Lazy Man and his Dog', 2000: 57) transforming the daughter into a trophy of some kind, a beauty to be won not given away.

In some folk-tales, when a daughter is ripe for marriage, the father plays a significant role in selecting a suitor for her. In most cases, prospective candidates are put on trial to prove their worth. While the father may be said to be safeguarding his daughter in this way, such an approach also implies some degree of male dominance and materialism; the father continues to exert his control over matters that do not directly involve him. In the contemporary context the more liberated girl child challenges the authority resulting in such clashes as that between Nyasha and Babamukuru. The folk-tale, 'The Lazy Man and his Dog' (Mungoshi, 2000: 53-62), is about a poor, lazy young man who cannot clothe himself and has to kill his dog in order to have something to wear in his quest for a wife. His motive in marrying is to find a wife who will 'do all the work' so that he can go on 'listening to his mother's stories,' (55). The idea that a wife has 'to do all the work' denotes abuse of females by their male counterparts. The father in the story seeks to safeguard his daughter against men who have such a mentality. He proposes some trials/tests that a future son-in-law has to accomplish before marrying his daughter. These tests sought to establish the suitor's qualities, especially the need for patience and love. While this clearly indicates a father who wants to hold onto his daughter for as long a he possibly can, these tests may be interpreted as safeguarding the interests of the daughter.

In his search for such a wife, the lazy young man arrives at a certain village where the chief has a daughter who is deaf and mute. Every year, 'the chief arranges a contest in which young men compete to try and make her talk' (Mungoshi, 2000: 57). The man who succeeds will win the daughter regardless of her feelings. The same scenario exists in the folk-tale, 'Baboon wants a Wife' (Makina, 1983: 1), where the father Badza 'only wanted the cleverest person in the country to marry [his most beautiful daughter]'. In these situations, tasks that are set for the suitors are almost impossible to achieve in the real world. This indicates that most fathers are protective and unwilling to let go of their daughters to incompetent sons-in-law. Although marriage proceedings in such folk-tales do not leave room for mutual love between the daughter and her suitor, they register the commitment that a father may have towards his daughter's welfare.

The father however continues to have influence over his daughter's life, with positive results for his child. When the son-in-law is invited to the chief's court ('The Lazy Man and His Dog'), this could be read as a gesture of kindness, but it also works in the interest of the father, (the chief), who will continue to live with his daughter for a stipulated number of years; ensuring her security and at the same time testing his son-in-law's commitment and capabilities. This is tantamount to the practice of *kutema ugariri*, where the son-in-law pays bride-price through provision of free labour to his in-laws for a stipulated period of time. However, after this period, the husband takes his wife to his own homestead. These provide examples of good fathers who use their influence to protect and empower their daughters. The daughter is still, however, portrayed as a fragile, helpless asset that has to be handled with utmost care. She seems vulnerable without her father's guardianship. This is not the case, however, in Hanson's *Takadini* (1997), which reads well as a folk-tale. Takadini is an albino, and no father is willing to have him for a son-in-law. One daughter rebels against her father's wishes and marries Takadini. All social myths associated with albinism are disproved when the couple gives birth to a child who is not an albino. The story of Takadini thus conveys a moral message, particularly to fathers who continue to make decisions for their mature daughters, as if they were unable to make their own decisions.

Female-male relationships in a traditional milieu bolster women's subservient status. The latter are not supposed to complain at any time in their interaction with a male figure. This is why it takes so long a time for Zhizha (Vera, 1996) to reveal that her father has raped her. The writer speaks to the problem of incest, recurrent, for example, in the Zimbabwean press. By negatively portraying Muroyiwa, Zhizha's father, the author seems to suggest that it is imperative to promote positive fatherhood, where fathers do not violate women and girls in society. Literary works, as well as the media, therefore, chronicle cases where minors are violated even by their own fathers. It is the same thematic concern that is explored in Toni Morrison's novel *The Bluest Eye* (1970) when Pecola is raped by her biological father. She is never the same thereafter and her life becomes meaningless as a result of the experience. Here is a problem of socialisation where men tend to associate masculinity with conquest that knows no boundaries.

Yvonne Vera's *Under the Tongue* displays a society whose moral decay has reached alarming levels. Her work demonstrates the challenges facing society. Incest is now a rampant phenomenon owing to the disintegration of value systems that combated such practices. The same theme of moral decadence is depicted in Tsodzo's *Pafunge* [think of it] (1970). *Under the Tongue* and *Pafunge* were published after a gap of 26 years, confirming that the problem of incest is an enduring one, brought on by the changing make-up of modern society. Joe Rugare, (Joe Rug) is a male chauvinist who goes around liberally sowing his wild oats. A daughter, Rudo is born to Joe Rug as a result of his immoral activities. A vicious cycle develops, however, when father and daughter meet later in life, and fall in love, without being aware of their biological relationship. Rudo is made pregnant and dumped by her own father. What is important is the authorial voice which suggests that fathers ought to be more accountable citizens – and specifically in their dealings with their daughters.

Contrary to what is happening today, traditionally incest was dealt with severely and had spiritual implications whose repercussions were greatly feared. *Makunakuna* [incest] could spell banishment of the perpetrator from the kingdom and everyone feared the punishment of angered spirits who could retaliate by withholding the rains unless the perpetrator confessed. In the face of AIDS and the economic pressures confronting many Zimbabweans today, the incestuous father becomes a vampire feeding off the blood of its offspring. There have been numerous reports of fathers who take their virgin daughters as antidote for HIV/AIDS and prescription for economic well-being. Such fathers destroy the trust and bond that should be shared by the two as illustrated by Vera.

Moving with the times: the father in contemporary Zimbabwean society

The oppressive nature of patriarchy does not end with the inception of colonialism but manifests itself in the transforming society. Literary works of and about the sixties and seventies reveal some oppressive patriarchal characteristics. Girls are deprived of the opportunity to go to school unlike their male siblings. Betty in Mungoshi's *Waiting for the Rain* (1975), stays at home while her brother Lucifer goes to school. Similarly, Tambu in Tsitsi Dangarembga's *Nervous Conditions* has to drop out of school while the available funds are put towards her brother Nhamo's education. In a more contemporary setting, Chizema's brothers 'advise' him that educating girls is an act synonymous to 'money thrown into Munyati River' (Mungoshi, 1997: 123). Babamukuru (*Nervous Conditions*) inculcates the value of education about which Mai (Tambu's mother) is sceptical. He makes his brother Jeremiah realise that like Nhamo, Tambu is capable of 'lift[ing] ... the family out of ... squalor.' (*Nervous Conditions*, 4). Tambu's biological father refutes this when he says, 'Can you cook and feed [books] to your husband?'(*Nervous Conditions*, 15). Dangarembga traces the development from a traditional father (Jeremiah) to a modern one (Babamukuru). By juxtaposing two fathers, Dangarembga offers us opportunities to compare and contrast the qualities of both men in the roles they play in the life of Tambu.

Although Babamukuru still possesses elements of traditional patriarchy, he represents those more progressive fathers who realise the value of giving their daughters an education in a swiftly modernising society. Ironically, however, he may also be empowering Tambu to defy the oppressive nature of patriarchy and the traditional 'deficient' gender roles that the woman has been assigned by society (Bourdillon, 1982). Through the adolescent Tambu, Dangarembga (*The Book of Not*) demonstrates how puberty marks a period of rebellion embodied by breaking the rules at the Sacred Heart School. Her defiance becomes a symbol depicting her unhappiness with the old patriarchal world as well as the western system, although both worlds contain challenges too powerful for her to grapple with. Babamukuru's reprimand as well as her letter of apology force her to conform, just as she had had to do as a small child. She abandons her rebelliousness and revisits the more harmless principles of unhu (decorum) (observed from Babamukuru) and vows to work harder in order to please him. Nyasha however is different and she openly defies her father and her rebellious nature is given a masculine flavour, as suggested by Holland (2005: 133) when she says, 'Ultimately the most powerful masculine figure in the novel, male or female, is Nyasha. She turns determinedly from multiple markers of femininity through her statements and actions, particularly her starvation.'

Tambu who tries by all means to please her father by excelling in her studies reciprocates Babamukuru's generosity. She represents those daughters who cannot wait to go home to receive praise from their fathers. But patriarchal conventions stipulate that fathers should not show open elation particularly over their daughters' success, a position aptly captured by Dangarembga (*The Book of Not*, 59) at the Sacred Heart prize-giving ceremony where '[f]athers folded their arms to pretend it was a women's affair, but beamed complacently.' Incidentally, daughters do not seem to value the response of their respective mothers. Arguably this shows that daughters have in fact implicitly, if subconsciously, bought into the patriarchal system. In *The Book of Not*, Tambu refers very little to her mother (*Mai*) who in most cases would pull her down with disparaging remarks over her education. Her antagonism and lack of affection is evident in her remarks upon Tambu's failure at A-level, which drive a nail in the coffin of their relationship. Instead of encouraging her daughter, she is full of derision and scorn, as well as showing ingratitude towards Babamukuru for providing her child with an education. She says this of Tambudzai's teaching profession,

... *Tambudzai! Spending all that time with all those Europeans only to rot in a school that doesn't have form four! And not even youngsters who have an intellect, just any old idiot! ....at a craft school, where people work just with their hands, without any thinking!* (195).

Dangarembga seems to depict the disharmony that exists between mother and daughter. Tambudzai herself admits her shame in Mai (228) and she finds her mother's perception of herself 'terribly revolting' (195) and would have expected solace in the words, 'Get on with it my daughter! Pull yourself together! Do something for yourself' (195) after her failure at A-level. In a similar manner, Tambu's mother is associated with the betrayal of Babamukuru. Dangarembga dramatises Babamukuru's beating emphasising Mai's hatred for him in her 'catches of satisfaction' at the blows being delivered on Babamukuru. Mai's froth and 'sinews [in the neck] that shivered and trembled' from the chorusing along with the others for the final crucifixion of Babamukuru, translates her hatred into a physical phenomenon. Tambu's hatred for her mother thus mirrors that of her mother's towards Babamukuru. Mai's double standards are, however, exposed when she blackmails Tambu and attempts to coerce her into admitting her existence as a mother and insinuate her personal contribution to Tambu's present status. This is revealed in the following statement, '...are you aware who gave birth to you? ... sitting in that Harare of yours, enjoying knowing you were borne by someone!' (226) The bottom line is, she wants a share of the same success she has failed to acknowledge and has been scornful of.

Babamukuru thus becomes a role model, a position exemplified in *The Book of Not* where Tambudza's life continues to be shaped by her uncle. She reveals the paradoxes and contradictions that bedevil the educated elite. While the guns are being fired in the bush, Babamukuru and indeed Tambudzai build careers for themselves. Babamukuru is jubilant in Tambu's success at O-level and equally angered by her later failure (*The Book of Not*). However, his bitterness is misdirected and should have been aimed at the education system that did not allow African children equal access to educational opportunities. Tambu is not allowed to attend lessons at Umtali Boys High school because of the colour of her skin, but has to make do with notes from a third party, Angela. Any reader can understand Tambu's distress when she is unable to excel. Dangarembga does not openly criticise the racist white system but allows the reader to speculate on the part played by the colonial government in Tambu's destiny.

Tambu and Babamukuru are both victims of the system; the latter serves the Smith regime as headmaster of the mission school and thus inculcates the ideology of the coloniser in the younger generation. He is unable to openly criticise the colonial system; instead, he can only show his displeasure by listening to the Voice of Zimbabwe (nationalist radio station broadcast from Mozambique) at night. His powerlessness represents the emasculation of the Zimbabwean man in the face of colonialism. He cannot openly defy the system but can only do so under the cover of darkness. His spinelessness is evident in Jeremiah within his own household, which loses him his daughter's allegiance which is won over by Babamukuru's economic stability as Berndt (2005: 104) puts it,

[Babamukuru's] seems to be the predominant influence in Tambudzai's life, shaping her values and directing her desires. She respects and admires him as father figure, partly because her real father Jeremiah, a ridiculous figure, cares neither economically nor emotionally for his family.

Since Babamukuru is Tambu's role model, she becomes a member of the educated elite, a class that was treated with suspicion by the nationalists. His weakness lies in his inability to actively fight against the incumbent government. Tambu, for her part, provides knitwear for the Rhodesian forces. It is therefore not by coincidence that Dangarembga 'punishes' Babamukuru. He is unable to enjoy the fruits of independence from a wheelchair. Similarly, Tambu's frustration at finding employment of her choice could be interpreted as punishment for her act of complicity with the Smith regime. The two are victims of the white government and their acts of 'allegiance' go unrecognised. They stand accused of being *tshombes* [sellouts] and Babamukuru pays heavily through the beating by the guerrillas at the *pungwe* [all night vigil] and 'the stray bullet' that 'ricocheted off a flag post during the twenty-one gun salute which was sounded as the Zimbabwean flag was raised at the Independence celebrations' (*The Book of Not*, 197-8).

In spite of Babamukuru's misfortunes, his father figure role should not be taken for granted as demonstrated by Dangarembga. Westerhof, whose work we highlighted in the section on defining fatherhood in Zimbabwean society, also highlights the bond that grows between her children and their (step)father, Horst, who would oversee their welfare in spite of the irreconcilable differences with his wife. Nyasha and Tambu benefit from Babamukuru tremendously but this does not mean, however, that all fathers and uncles are like Babamukuru. The reverse is manifest in other works of literature. The greedy and covetous uncle Phineas in the film *Neria* assumes the role of father for material gain not the welfare of the surviving family. He literally strips Neria (his brother Patrick's wife) of their material possessions. There is a similar situation in Shimmer Chinodya's *Tale of Tamari* where Tamari's uncle assumes the partriarchal role because he hankers after the monthly rentals leaving Tamari and her brother to vend for a living.

Traditional ideas have survived in the conviction that daughters are commodities. Today, some fathers of educated daughters, display characteristics of selfishness and materialism, revealing a contradiction inherent in the father-daughter relationship. Daughters are considered cash cows. Jeremiah in *Nervous Conditions* feels that once a girl gets education she 'will meet a young man and I will have lost everything' (30) which points at the greed apparent in such fathers. Yet marriage does not mean losing one's daughter as Tayeva (in 'Sacrifice') stresses; a cordial relationship can exist between maternal in-laws and the married couple (Mungoshi, 'Sacrifice' 1997). Education is an investment in the future, not for the daughter alone but for the whole family. Jeremiah, for example, thinks only of personal gain not the happiness of his daughter. Conversely, a daughter who falls pregnant and does not get an educational qualification is 'written off as a bad investment' ('Of Lovers and Wives' in Mungoshi, 1997: 106). Rowesai's father, Mutandawachingama, in *Rudo Ibofu* only attempts to get his daughter out of the convent so he can be assured of a bride price (Chakaipa, 1966). It can thus be concluded that a daughter of marriageable age, in a contemporary context, is free to marry whomever she wishes, provided her prospective husband can pay the required *lobola*. Chakaipa's *Rudo Ibofu* underlines this; that way the conflict between father and daughter, with regards to marriage, is resolved.

Conclusion

The relationship between a father and his daughter is thus fraught with contradictions, with the father being caught between the patriarchal role of power and authority and that of a loving father. A good father according to his wife is socially deemed 'under petticoat government', for instance Patrick in *Neria* as well as Chizema in Mungoshi's 'Sacrifice'. A good father according to his children is considered weak or *muKristu* [gentle Christian man] a phenomenon looked down upon by many Zimbabwean men. A man is supposed to be respected and feared in his household. In this chapter, good fatherhood has been measured in light of the actions that the father displays towards his daughter and vice-versa.

This chapter demonstrates that the father-daughter relationship in Zimbabwean literature is doubly complex. It varies from the highly protective father in *Mapatya* (twins), to the abusive father who rapes his own daughter in *Under the Tongue*. The rigidly patriarchal father figure and submissive daughter dominate traditional oral folklore. In some instances however, this is modified when daughters become assertive, and fathers relent as they learn to appreciate the former's actions. With the passage of time there is a movement away from the rigid, intolerant and oppressive father to a more flexible, accommodating and liberated one.

Bibliography

Introduction – – Kizito Z. Muchemwa and Robert Muponde

Dolan, Chris (2002). 'Collapsing Masculinities and weak States: A case study of Northern Uganda' in *Masculinities Matter! Men, Gender and Development*, Frances Cleaver (ed.). London: Zed Books; Claremont: David Philip. 57-83.

Epstein, Julia and Kristina Straub (1999). *Body Guards: The Cultural Politics of Gender Ambiguity*. New York and London: Routledge.

Fine, Michelle and Peter Kuriloff (2006). 'Forging and Performing Masculine Identities within Social Spaces'. *Men and Masculinities*, 8 (3): 257-261.

Mamdani, Mahmood (2002). 'Making Sense of Political Violence in Postcolonial Africa'. *Identity, Culture and Politics*, 3 (2) December: 1-24.

Marechera, Dambudzo (1978). *The House of Hunger*. London: Heinemann.

Mendible, Myra (1999). High 'Theory/Low Culture: Postmodernism and Politics of Carnival'. *Journal of American Culture*, 22 (2): 71-76.

Muponde, Robert (2006.) Men mild as milk: trapped masculinities and girl child rape in Zimbabwean literature. Paper presented at Postcolonial Sexualities: Politics and Discourses. The Graduate School of International Development Studies, May 3rd-6th, Roskilde University, Denmark.

Vera, Yvonne (2002).*The Stone Virgins*. Harare: Weaver Press.

Chapter 1: **'Why don't you tell the children a story?': Father figures in the Zimbabwean short story** – Kizito Z. Muchemwa

Benjamin, Walter (1973, 1992). *Illuminations*, ed. and trans. by Hannah Arendt. London: Fontana.

Boje, David M. (2001). 'Carnivalesque Resistance to Global Spectacle: A Critical Postmodern Theory of Public Administration'. *Administrative Theory & Praxis*, 23 (3): 431-458.

Boone, Joseph A. (1997). 'Creation by the Father's Fiat: paternal narrative, sexual anxiety, and the deauthorizing designs of *Absalom, Absalom*!' in *Feminisms: an anthology of literary theory and criticism*, Robyn R. Warhol and Dianne Price Herndl (eds). Basingstoke: Macmillan Press. 1069-1086.

Chimhundu, Herbert (2006). 'Mutauro, Rudzi, Norusarura' (Language, Race, Ethnicity, and Discrimination). Public Lecture delivered on 17 May. Masvingo State University, Zimbabwe.

Debord, Guy (1994). *The Society of the Spectacle*, trans. Donald Nicholson-Smith. New York: Zone.

Doctorow, E.L. (1994). *The Waterworks*. London: Picador.

Hobsbawm, Eric (1983). 'Introduction: Inventing Traditions' in *The Invention of Tradition*, Eric Hobsbawm and Terence Ranger (eds). Cambridge: Cambridge University Press.

Kanengoni, Alexander (1997). *Echoing Silences*. Harare: Baobab Books.

Madanhire, Nevanji (2003). 'The Grim Reaper's Car' in *Writing Still: New stories from Zimbabwe*, Irene Staunton (ed.). Harare: Weaver Press. 127-136.

Marechera, Dambudzo (1978). *The House of Hunger*. London: Heinemann.
Mungoshi, Charles (2003). 'The Sins of the Fathers' in *Writing Still*, op.cit.137-160.
——— (1972). *Coming of the Dry Season*. Harare: Zimbabwe Publishing House.
——— (1975). *Waiting for the Rain*. London: Heinemann.
Muponde, Robert (2004). 'The Worm and the Hoe: Cultural politics and reconciliation after the Third Chimurenga' in *Zimbabwe: Injustice and Political Reconciliation*, Brian Raftopoulos and Tyrone Savage (eds). Cape Town: Institute for Justice and Reconciliation. 176-192.
Nyamubaya, Freedom (2003). 'That Special Place' in *Writing Still*, op.cit. 217-228.
Ranger, Terence (2005). 'Rule by historiography; the struggle over the past in contemporary Zimbabwe' in *Versions of Zimbabwe: New approaches to literature and culture*, Robert Muponde and Ranka Primorac (eds). Harare: Weaver Press. 217-243.
Vera, Yvonne (1994). *Without a Name*. Harare: Baobab Books.
——— (2002). *The Stone Virgins*. Harare: Weaver Press.

Chapter 2: **Killing fathers** – Robert Muponde

Chirasha, Ben (1985). *Child of War*. Harare: College Press.
Dangarembga, Tsitsi (1988). *Nervous Conditions*. Harare: Zimbabwe Publishing House.
——— (2006). *The Book of Not*. Oxfordshire: Ayebia.
Donald, Bridget (2000). 'Circling Back on the Road to Independence: Models of History and National Identity in Irish Children's Literature' in *Text, Culture and National Identity in Children's Literature*, Jean Webb (ed.). Helsinki: NORDINFO: 24-33.
Gillis, John R. (2000). 'Marginalization of Fatherhood in Western Countries'. *Childhood*, 7 (2): 225-238.
Green, Maureen (1976). *Goodbye Father*. London/Henley: Routledge and Kegan Paul.
Harris, Wilson (1992). 'The Fabric of the Imagination' in *From Commonwealth to Post-Colonial*, Anna Rutherford (ed.). Sydney: Dangaroo Press. 18-29.
Jameson, Fredric (1981). *The Political Unconscious: Narrative as a Socially Symbolic Act*. London: Methuen.
Jensen, Robert (1998). 'Patriarchal Sex' in *Feminism and Men: Reconstructing Gender Relations*, Steven P. Schacht and Doris W. Ewing (eds). New York: New York University Press. 99-118.
Katiyo, Wilson (1976). *A Son of the Soil*. Essex: London.
Koselleck, Reinhart (1985). *Futures Past: On the Semantics of Historical Time*, trans. Keith Tribe. Cambridge/Massachusetts: The MIT Press.
Kunene, Daniel P. (1985). 'Journey as Metaphor in African Literature' in *African Literature Studies: The Present State/L'etat Present*, Stephen Arnold (ed.). Washington: Three Continents Press. 189-215.
Lassen-Seger, Maria (2000). 'The Fictive Child in Disguise: Disempowering Transformations of the Child Character' in *Text, Culture and National Identity in Children's Literature*, op. cit. 186-196.
Lesejane, Desmond (2006). 'Fatherhood from an African Cultural Perspective' in *Baba: Men and Fatherhood in South Africa*, Linda Richter and Robert Morrell

(eds). Cape Town: Human Sciences Research Council. 173-182.
Marechera, Dambudzo (1978). *The House of Hunger*. London: Heinemann.
Miller, Alice (1990). *The Untouched Key: Tracing Childhood Trauma in Creativity and Destructiveness*. London: Virago Press.
Morrell, Robert (2006). 'Fathers, fatherhood and masculinity in South Africa' in *Baba: Men and Fatherhood in South Africa*, op. cit. 13-25.
Mungoshi, Charles (1975). *Waiting for the Rain*. London: Heinemann.
——— (1980). 'The Mount of Moriah' in *Some Kinds of Wounds and other St*ories. Gweru: Mambo Press.
Nyota, Muchadei Alex (2006). 'The Supernatural in Mungoshi's Works' in *Charles Mungoshi: A Critical Reader*, Maurice Vambe and Memory Chirere (eds). Harare: Prestige Books. 198-205.
Parke, D. Ross (1981). *Fathering*. Glasgow: Fontana.
Rahman, Najat (2003). 'The Trial of Heritage and the Legacy of Abraham'. *Men and Masculinities*, 5 (3): 295-308.
Rutherford, Anna (ed.) (1992). 'Introduction: The Essential Heterogeneity of Being' in *From Commonwealth to Post-Colonial*, op.cit. iii-ix.
Sithole, Ndabaningi (1977). *Roots of a Revolution: Scenes from Zimbabwe's Struggle*. Oxford: Oxford University Press.
Taitz, Laurice (1999). 'Knocking on the door of the *House of Hunger*: Fracturing Narratives and Disordering Identity' in *Emerging Perspectives on Dambudzo Marechera*, Anthony Chennells and Flora Veit Wild (eds). Trenton NJ: Africa World Press. 23-42.
Zhuwarara, Rino (2001). *Introduction to Zimbabwean Literature in English*. Harare: College Press.
Zimunya, Musaemura, B. (1982). *Those Years of Drought and Hunger: The Birth of African Fiction in English in Zimbabwe*. Gweru: Mambo Press.
——— (1985). *Country Dawns and City Lights*. Harare: Longman.

Chapter 3: **Of fathers and ancestors in Charles Mungoshi's *Waiting for the Rain*** – Neil ten Kortenaar

Dangarembga, Tsitsi (1988). *Nervous Conditions*. London: Women's Press.
Freud, Sigmund (1957). 'Mourning and Melancholia' in *The Standard Edition of the Complete Psychological Works of Sigmund Freud*, Vol. XIV. London: Hogarth Press. 237-258.
Geschiere, Peter (1997). *The Modernity of Witchcraft*, trans. Peter Geschiere and Janet Roitman. Charlottesville: University of Virginia Press.
Hammond-Tooke, W. D. (1985). 'Descent Groups, Chiefdoms and South African Historiography'. *Journal of Southern African Studies*, 11 (2): 305-319.
Malaba, Mbongeni Z. (1997). 'Traditional Religion or Christianity? Spiritual Tension in the African Stories of Charles Mungoshi'. *Word & World*, 17 (3): 301-307.
Mungoshi, Charles (1975). *Waiting for the Rain*. Harare: Zimbabwe Publishing House.
Radcliffe-Brown, A.R. (1950). 'Introduction' in *African Systems of Kinship and Marriage*, A.R. Radcliffe-Brown and Daryll Forde (eds). London: Oxford University Press. 1-85.

Stratton, Florence (1986). 'Charles Mungoshi's Waiting for the Rain'. *Zambezia*, 13 (1): 11-24.
Vambe, Maurice Taonezvi (2004). *African Oral Story-telling Tradition and the Zimbabwean Novel in English*. Pretoria: University of South Africa Press.
Veit-Wild, Flora (1992). *Teachers, Preachers, Non-Believers: A Social History of Zimbabwean Literature*. London: Hans Zell.
Werbner, Richard (1991). *Tears of the Dead: The Social Biography of an African Family*. Edinburgh: Edinburgh University Press.
Zhuwarara, Rino (2001). *Introduction to Zimbabwean Literature in English*. Harare: College Press.

Chapter 4: 'Sins of the Fathers': Revealing family secrets in Mungoshi's later fiction – Pauline Dodgson-Katiyo

Coetzee, J.M. (1987, 1986). *Foe*. London: Penguin.
Gagiano, Annie (2006). 'Mourning, Betrayal and "Dark" Epiphanies in *Walking Still*' in *Charles Mungoshi: A Critical Reader*, Maurice Vambe and Memory Chirere (eds). Harare: Prestige Books. 132-145.
Marechera, Dambudzo (1980). *Black Sunlight*. London: Heinemann.
McCulloch, Jock (2000). *Black Peril, White Virtue: Sexual Crime in Southern Rhodesia, 1902-1935*. Bloomington: Indiana University Press.
Muchemwa, Kizito Z. (2006). 'Constructions of Identity in *Coming of the Dry Season* and *Waiting for the Rain*' in *Charles Mungoshi: A Critical Reader*, op. cit.37-53.
Mungoshi, Charles (1975). *Waiting for the Rain*. London: Heinemann.
────── (1997). *Walking Still*. Harare: Baobab Books.
────── (2003). 'The Sins of the Fathers' in *Writing Still: New Stories from Zimbabwe*, Irene Staunton (ed.). Harare: Weaver Press, 137-160.
────── (2004). 'It Is the Old Story, Isn't It?' [Interview with Mai Palmberg]. http://www.nai.uu.se/forsk/current/stateofthearts/literature/mungoshisve.html
Musiyiwa, Mickias and Tommy Matshakayile-Ndlovu (2005). 'Ethnicity in Literature of Shona and Ndebele Expression' in *Versions of Zimbabwe: New approaches to literature and culture*, Robert Muponde and Ranka Primorac (eds). Harare: Weaver Press, 75-88.
Primorac, Ranka (2006). 'The Circularity of the Perverse: Zimbabwean Post Independent Masculinity in Charles Mungoshi's "The Hare"' in *Charles Mungoshi: A Critical Reader*, op. cit.124-131.
Ranger, Terence (2004). 'Nationalist Historiography, Patriotic History and the History of the Nation: The Struggle Over the Past in Zimbabwe'. *Journal of Southern African Studies*, 30 (2): 215 -234.
Werbner, Richard (1991). *Tears of the Dead: The Social Biography of an African Family*. Edinburgh: Edinburgh University Press.
White, Luise (2003). *The Assassination of Herbert Chitepo: Texts and Politics in Zimbabwe*. Bloomington and Indianapolis: Indiana University Press.
Williams, Stephen (1991). 'Art in Zimbabwe: From Colonialism to Independence' in *Cultural Struggle and Development in Southern Africa*, Preben Kaarsholm (ed.). London: James Currey, 61-73.
Zhuwarara, Rino (2001). *Introduction to Zimbabwean Literature in English*.

Harare: College Press.

Chapter 5: **The strong healthy man: AIDS and self-delusion** – Lizzy Attree

Chennells, Anthony (2006). 'The Grammar of Alienation in *Waiting for the Rain*' in *Charles Mungoshi: A Critical Reader*, Maurice Vambe and Memory Chirere (eds). Harare: Prestige Books. 21-36.

Chiweza, David, Brigadier General (Retired) (2006). 'The doctrine of necessary force': *The Herald* 27 July. 10.

Epprecht, Marc (2004). *'Hungochani': the History of a Dissident Sexuality in Southern Africa*. Montreal: McGill-Queen's University Press.

Gagiano, Annie (2006). 'Mourning, betrayal and "dark epiphanies" in *Walking Still* in *Charles Mungoshi: A Critical Reader*, op.cit. 132-145.

Gunduza, Lovemore and Maurice Vambe (eds) (2001). *We Are the Herb*. Gweru: Mambo Press.

Kanengoni, Alexander (1993). *Effortless Tears*. Harare: Baobab Books.

Kruger, Steven F. (1996). *Aids Narratives – Gender and Sexuality, Fiction and Science*. New York and London: Garland Publishing.

Leiner, Marvin (1994). *Sexual Politics in Cuba: Machismo, Homosexuality, and AIDS*. Boulder: Westview Press.

Muchemwa, Kizito (2006). 'Constructions of identity in *Coming of the Dry Season* and *Waiting for the Rain*' in *Charles Mungoshi: A Critical Reader*, op. cit. 37-53.

Mungoshi, Charles (1997). *Walking Still*. Harare: Baobab Books.

Rasebotsa, Nobantu, Meg Samuelson and Kylie Thomas (eds) (2004). *Nobody ever said AIDS: Stories and poems from Southern Africa*. Cape Town: Kwela Books.

Sacks, Oliver (1986). *The Man who Mistook his Wife for a Hat*. London: Picador.

Shaw, Drew (2006). '"Deviant" Innovations in Zimbabwean Writing: From the Racial Divide to Same Sex Desire' in *The Round Table: Special Issue: Zimbabwe and the Space of Silence*, Ranka Primorac and Stephen Chan (eds). Abingdon: Routledge Journals, Taylor & Francis. 273-281.

Sontag, Susan (2002). *Illness as Metaphor and AIDS and Its Metaphors*. New York: Penguin Classics.

Truffaut, François (1961). *Jules et Jim*, a film based on the novel by Henri-Pierre Roché.

www.unaids.org AIDS Epidemic Update. December 2006. (accessed on 21/11/06)

Vambe, Maurice and Memory Chirere (eds) (2006). *Charles Mungoshi: A Critical Reader*, op.cit.

Worton, Michael (2004). 'Behold the (Sick) Man' in *National Healths – Gender, Sexuality and Health in a Cross-Cultural Context*, M. Worton and N. Wilson-Tagoe (eds). London: UCL Press. 151-165.

Chapter 6: **Fatherhood and nationhood: Joshua Nkomo and the re-imagination of the Zimbabwe nation** – Sabelo J. Ndlovu-Gatsheni

Anderson, Benedict (1993). *Imagined Communities: Reflections on the Origins and Spread of Nationalism*, Revised Edition. London: Verso.

Alexander, Jocelyn, Joan McGregor and Terence Ranger (2000). *Violence and Memory: One Hundred Years in the 'Dark Forests' of Matebeleland*. Harare: Weaver Press.

Brickhill, James (1995). 'Daring to Storm the Heavens: The Military Strategy of ZAPU, 1976-1979' in *Soldiers in Zimbabwe's Liberation War*, N. Bhebe and T. Ranger (eds). Harare: University of Zimbabwe Publications.

Catholic Commission for Justice and Peace and Legal Resources Foundation (1997). *Breaking the Silence: Building True Peace: Report on the Disturbances in Matebeleland and the Midlands, 1980-1988*. Harare: CCJP and LRF.

Renan, Ernest (1990). 'What is a Nation?' in *Nation and Narration*, H. Bhabha (ed.). New York: Routlege.

Kriger, Norma J. (2003). *Guerrilla Veterans in Post-War Zimbabwe: Symbolic and Violent Politics, 1980-1987*. Cambridge: Cambridge University Press.

———— (1995). 'The Politics of Creating National Heroes: The Search for Political Legitimacy and National Identity' in *Soldiers in Zimbabwe's Liberation War*, op. cit.

Mandaza, Ibbo and Lloyd Sachikonye (1991). *The One Party State and Democracy: The Zimbabwe Debate*. SAPES Trust: Harare.

Mugabe, Robert (2001). *Inside the Third Chimurenga*. Harare: Ministry of Information and Publicity.

Ndlovu-Gatsheni, Sabelo (2006). 'Puppets or Patriots! Nationalist Rivalry Over the Spoils of Dying Settler Colonialism in Zimbabwe, 1977-1980' in *Nationalisms Across the Globe: An Overview of Nationalism in State-Endowed and Stateless Nations:* Vol. 2. W. J. Burszta, T. Kamusella and S. W.Wojciechowski (eds). Pozna: Poland.

———— (2003). 'The Post-Colonial State and Matebeleland: Regional Perceptions of Civil-Military Relations, 1980-2002' in *Ourselves to Know: Civil-Military Relations and Defence Transformation in Southern Africa*, R. Williams, G. Cawthra and D. Abrahams (eds). Pretoria: Institute for Security Studies.

Nkomo, Joshua (1984). *Nkomo: The Story of My Life*. London: Methuen.

Ranger, Terence (2004). 'Nationalist Historiography, Patriotic History and the History of the Nation: The Struggle Over the Past in Zimbabwe'. *Journal of Southern African Studies*, 30 (2): 215-234.

———— (1999a). 'Joshua Nkomo: A Cultural Nationalist'. Public Lecture: Bulawayo Natural History Museum.

———— (1999). *Voices from the Rocks: Nature, Culture and History in the Matopos Hills of Zimbabwe*. Harare: Baobab Books.

Raftopoulos, Brian (1996). Race and Nationalism in a Post-Colonial State, Seminar Series No. 10. Harare: SAPES Trust.

Sithole, Masipula (1999). *Zimbabwe: Struggles within the Struggle*. Harare: Rujeko Publishers (2nd ed).

White, Louise (2003). *The Assassination of Herbert Chitepo: Text and Politics in Zimbabwe*. Bloomington: Indiana University Press.

Yap, Pohjolaine K. (2001). Uprooting the Weeds: Power, Violence, Ethnicity and Violence in the Matebeleland Conflict, 1980-1987. Ph.D. thesis: University of Helsinki.

Newspapers

The Herald, 4 July 1980.
The Herald, 7 November 1980.
The Herald, 6 July 1999.
The Chronicle, 11 November 1981.

Horizon, March 1993.
The Financial Gazette, 28 January 1993.
The Financial Gazette, 8 July 1999.
The Zimbabwe Mirror, 5-9 July 1999.
Zimbabwe News, 30 (6) July 1999.
Zimbabwe *Independent*, 9 July 1999.

Chapter 7: **Mai Mujuru: Father of the nation?** – Lene Bull Christiansen

Amadiume, Ifi (1987). *Male Daughters, Female Husbands: Gender and Sex in an African Society*. London: Zed Books.
Berger, Guy (2005). 'When spies spoil news media'. *Mail and Guardian*, South Africa, 17 August. Data on the internet. Posted 18 August, 2005. Accessed 18 August, 2005 at <www.zwnews.com>
BBC News (2004). 'Cheers as Mugabe slaps down Moyo'. Data on the internet. Posted 6 December, 2004. Accessed 16 August, 2006 at <www.news.bbc.co.uk>
Campbell, Horace (2003). *Reclaiming Zimbabwe: The Exhaustion of the Patriarchal Model of Liberation*.Trenton: Africa World Press.
Chadya, Joyce M. (2003). 'Mother Politics: Anti-colonial Nationalism and the Woman Question in Africa'. *Journal of Women's History*, 15 (3): 153-157.
Christiansen, Lene Bull (2005a). 'Yvonne Vera: Rewriting Discourses of History and Identity in Zimbabwe' in *Versions of Zimbabwe: New approaches to literature and culture*, Robert Muponde and Ranka Primorac (eds). Harare: Weaver Press.

––––––– (2005b). *Tales of the Nation: Feminist Nationalism or Patriotic History? Defining National History and Identity in Zimbabwe*. Uppsala: Nordic Africa Institute.
Frank, Liz (2002). Zimbabwe women call for new elections. Interview with Everjoice Win. Data on the internet. Accessed 8 August, 2006 at <www.kit.nl/gcg/assets/images>
Hammar, Amanda (2003). 'Making and Unma(s)king of Local Government in Zimbabwe' in *Zimbabwe's Unfinished Business: Rethinking Land, State and Nation in the Context of Crisis*, Amanda Hammar, Brian Raftopoulos and Stig Jensen (eds). Harare: Weaver Press.
Holst Petersen, Kirsten (1995). 'First Things First: Problems of a Feminist Approach to African Literature' in *The Post Colonial Studies Reader*, Bill Ashcroft, Gareth Griffiths and Hellen Tiffin (eds). London: Routledge.
Kwinjeh, Grace (2004). Mujuru: a worm in a fish pond. Data on the internet. Posted 7 December, 2004. Accessed 23 March, 2005 at <www.newzimbabwe.com>
Lyons, Tanya (2004). *Guns and Guerilla Girls: Women in the Zimbabwean Liberation Struggle*. Trenton: Africa World Press.
Makuni, Mavis (2004). 'Mujuru needs to look East for inspiration'. *The Financial Gazette* 16 December. Harare. Data on the internet. Posted 16 December, 2004. Accessed 23 August, 2005 at <www.fingaz.co.zw>
Mama, Amina (1997). 'Sheroes and Villains: Conceptualizing Colonial and Contemporary Violence Aganinst Women in Africa' in *Feminist Genealogies, Colonial Legacies, Democratic Futures*, Alexander and Mohanty (eds). New

York: Routledge.
Misihairabwi, Priscilla and Grace Kwinjeh (2005). 'MDC: a better deal for Zimbabwean women'. Data on the internet. Posted 8 February, 2005. Accessed 23 March, 2005 at <www.newzimbabwe.com>
Moyo, Jonathan (2006a). 'Tsholotsho saga: the untold story'. Data on the internet. Posted 9 May, 2006 at <www.newzimbabwe.com>
─────── (2006b). 'Tsholotsho saga: the untold story 2'. Data on the internet. Posted 9 May, 2006 at <www.newzimbabwe.com>
─────── (2006c). 'Tsholotsho saga: the untold story 3'. Data on the internet. Posted 9 May, 2006 at <www.newzimbabwe.com>
Muleya, Dumisani (2005). 'Mediagate deepens'. The *Independent*, 19 August. Data on the internet. Posted 20 August, 2005. Accessed 20 August, 2005 at <www.zwnews.com>
Nagel, Joane (1998). 'Masculinity and Nationalism: gender and sexuality in the making of nations'. *Ethnic and racial studies*, 21 (2): 242-269.
─────── (2000). 'Ethnicity and Sexuality'. *Annual Review of Sociology*, 26: 107-133.
New African (2005). 'Maybe I came out of the Guinness Book of Records'. Interview with Joyce Mujuru 11 May, 2005. *New African*, June 2005, (441).
New Zimbabwe (2005). 'Our Shouts!!! Zimbabwe women: a struggle within a struggle'. Data on the internet. Accessed 23 March, 2005 at <www.newzimbabwe.com>
Nhongo-Simbanegavi, Josephine (2000). *For Better Or Worse? Women and ZANLA in Zimbabwe's Liberation Struggle*. Harare: Weaver Press.
Niehaus, Isak (2005). 'Masculine domination in sexual violence: Interpreting accounts of three cases of rape in the South African Lowveld' in *Men Behaving Differently: South African Men since 1994*, Reid and Walker (eds). Cape Town: Double Storey Books.
Njovana, Eunice and Charlotte Watts (1996). 'Gender Violence in Zimbabwe: A Need for Collaborative Action'. *Reproductive Health Matters*, (7): 46-55.
Rooney, Caroline (1991). 'Mothers of the Revolution: Zimbabwean Women in the Aftermath of War'. *African Languages and Cultures* 4 (1): 55-64.
Rukuni, Charles (2005). 'Mujuru is here to stay'. *The Financial Gazette*, 20 January. Harare. Data on the internet. Posted 20 January, 2005. Accessed 23 August, 2005 at <www.fingaz.co.zw>
Staunton, Irene (ed.) (1990). *Mothers of The Revolution: The War Experiences of Thirty Zimbabwean Women*. London: James Currey; Harare: Baobab Books.
Thomas, Sylvia (2005). 'Mujuru, you have failed us!' Data on the internet. Posted 18 July, 2005. Accessed 23 August, 2005 at <www.genderlinks.org.za>
Walby, Sylvia (2000). 'Gender, nations and states in a global era'. *Nations and Nationalism*, 6 (4): 523-540.
Weiss, Ruth (1986). *The Women of Zimbabwe*. Harare: Nehanda Publishers.
White, Luise (2003). *The Assassination of Herbert Chitepo: Texts and Politics in Zimbabwe*. Bloomington: Indiana University Press.
Win, Everjoice (2004a). 'Are there any people here?' Violence against women in the Zimbabwean conflict. *Agenda* 59, (17). Data on the internet. Accessed 10 December, 2004. at <www. kubatana.net>
─────── (2004b). 'Joyce Mujuru is a man, and can stay with the boys'. Data on the

internet. Posted 15 December, 2004. Accessed 23 March, 2005 at <www.newimbabwe.com>

Zimbabwe Women Writers (2000). *Women of Resilience: The Voices of Women Ex-combatants*. Harare: Zimbabwe Women Writers.

Chapter 8: **Masculinities, race and violence in the making of Zimbabwe** – Jane L. Parpart

Alexander, Jocelyn (1996). 'Things Fall Apart, the Centre can Hold: processes of post-war political change in Zimbabwe's rural areas' in *Society in Zimbabwe's Liberation War*, N. Bhebe and T. Ranger (eds). Oxford: James Currey.

Alexander, J. and J. McGregor (2005). 'Hunger, violence and the moral economy of war in Zimbabwe' in *Violence and Belonging*, V. Broch-Due (ed.). London: Routledge.

Barnes, Theresa (1995). 'The Heroes' Struggle: life after the liberation war for four ex-combatants in Zimbabwe' in *Soldiers in Zimbabwe's Liberation War*, N. Bhebe and T. Ranger (eds). London: James Currey.

────── (2002) '"We are afraid to command our children": responses to the urbanisation of African women in colonial Zimbabwe, 1930-44' in *Sites of Struggle: essays in Zimbabwe's Urban History*, B. Raftopoulos and R. Yoshikuni (eds). Harare: Weaver Press.

Bond, Geoffrey (1977). *The Incredibles: the story of the 1st battalion, the Rhodesian Light Infantry*. Salisbury (Harare): Sarum Imprint.

Bull, Theodore (1967). *Rhodesian Perspective*. London: Michael Joseph.

Catholic Commission for Justice and Peace and Legal Resources Foundation (1997). *Breaking the silence, Building True Peace: a report on the disturbances in Matabeleland and the Midlands, 1980-1988*. Harare: CCJP/LRF.

Caute, David (1983). *Under the Skin: the death of White Rhodesia*. London: Penguin.

Chan, Stephen (2005). 'The Memory of Violence'. *Third World Quarterly*, 26 (2): 369-382.

Chinodya, Shimmer (1989). *Harvest of Thorns*. Harare: Baobab Books.

Chiumbu, Sarah (2004). 'Redefining the National Agenda: media and identity – challenges of building a new Zimbabwe' in *Media, Public Discourse and Political Contestation in Zimbabwe*, H. Melber (ed.). Uppsala: Nordic Africa Institute.

Cockburn, Cynthia (2004). 'The continuum of violence: a gender perspective on war and peace' in *Sites of Violence: gender and conflict zones*, W. Giles and J. Hyndman (eds). Los Angeles: University of California Press.

Cocks, Chris (1988). *Fireforce: one man's war in the Rhodesian Light Infantry*. Alberton, S.A.: Galago.

Cowderoy, Dudley and Roy Nesbit (1987). War in the Air: Rhodesian Air Force, 1935-1980. Alberton, S.A.: Galago.

Ellert, H. (1989). *The Rhodesian Front War: counter-insurgency and guerrilla war in Rhodesia, 1962-1980*. Harare: Mambo Press.

────── (1995). 'The Rhodesian Security and Intelligence Community 1960-1980' in *Soldiers in Zimbabwe's Liberation War*, op.cit.

Enloe, Cynthia (1993). *The Morning After: sexual politics at the end of the Cold War*. Los Angeles: University of California Press.

———— (1995). 'Feminism, Nationalism and Militarism: wariness without paralysis?' in *Feminism, Nationalism and Militarism*, C.R. Sutton (ed.). New York: American Anthropological Association.

Fuller, Alexandra (2004). 'Letters from Zimbabwe: The Soldier'. *The New Yorker*, 1 March: 54-67.

Hancock, I. (1984). *White Liberals, Moderates and Radicals in Rhodesia, 1953-1980*. New York: St. Martin's Press.

Harold-Barry, David (2004). 'One country, two nations, no dialogue' in *Zimbabwe: the past is the future*, D. Harold-Barry (ed.). Harare: Weaver Press.

Holland, Kathyrn (2005). 'The Troubled Masculinities in Tsitsi Dangarembga's *Nervous Conditions*.' in *African Masculinities*, L. Ouzgane and R. Morrell (eds). London: Palgrave.

Hughes, Richard (2003). *Capricorn: David Stirling's Second African Campaign*. London: Radcliffe Press.

Itano, N. (2003). 'Sex Assault now a Political Act' in Zimbabwe <womensenews.com/ article.cfm. 09/05/03>

Jacobs, Susie (1995). 'Gender Divisions and the Formation of Ethnicities in Zimbabwe'. in *Unsettling Settler Societies*, D. Stasiulis and N. Yuval-Davis (eds). London: Sage.

Kaarsholm, Preben (2005). 'Coming to Terms with Violence' in *Versions of Zimbabwe: New approaches to literature and culture*, R. Muponde and R. Primorac (eds). Harare: Weaver Press.

Kanengoni, Alexander (1997). *Echoing Silences*. Harare: Baobab Books.

Kaulema, David (2004). 'The Culture of Party Politics and the Concept of the State' in *Zimbabwe: the past is the future*, op.cit.

Kriger, Norma (1995). 'The Politics of Creating National Heroes: the search for political legitimacy and national identity' in *Soldiers in Zimbabwe's Liberation War*, op.cit.

———— (1991). *Zimbabwe's Guerrilla War: peasant voices*. Cambridge: Cambridge University Press.

Lotter, Chris (1984). *Rhodesian Soldier and others who Fought*. Alberton, S.A.: Galago.

Lovett, John (1977). *Contact*. Salisbury, Rhodesia: Galaxie Press.

MacBruce, James (1983). *When the Going was Rough: a Rhodesian Story*. Pretoria, S.A.: Femina Publishers.

Maxwell, David (1999). *Christians and Chiefs in Zimbabwe: a social history of the Hwesa People*. Westport, Conn.: Praeger.

McCulloch, Jock (2000). *Black Peril, White Virtue: sexual crime in Southern Rhodesia, 1902-1935*. Bloomington, IN.: Indiana University Press.

Moore, David (2005). 'ZANU-PF and the Ghosts of Foreign Funding'. ROAPE 103 (March): 156-162.

Moore-King, B. (1988). *White Man Black War*. Harare: Baobab Books.

Morrell, Robert (2001). *From Boys to Gentlemen: settler masculinity in colonial Natal*. Pretoria: University of South Africa.

Muzondidya, James (2005). *Walking a Tightrope: towards a social history of the Coloured people of Zimbabwe*. Trenton, N.J.: Africa Research and Publications.

Ndlovu-Gatsheni, S. (2005). 'The Last Days of Rhodesia and the Politics of Transition to Independence in Zimbabwe, 1977-1980' (mimeo).
Nhongo-Simbanegavi, Josephine (2000). *For Better or Worse? Women and ZANLA in Zimbabwe's Liberation Struggle*. Harare: Weaver Press.
Pongweni, Alec (ed.) (1982). *Songs that Won the Liberation War*. Harare: College Press.
Raeburn, Michael (1978). *Black Fire*. London: Julian Friedmann Publishers.
Raftopoulos, Brian (1999). 'Nationalism and Labour in Salisbury, 1953-1965' in *Sites of Struggle*, op.cit.
Ranchod-Nilsson, Sita (2006). 'Gender Politics and the Pendulum of Political and Social Transformation in Zimbabwe'. *Journal of Southern African Studies*, 32 (1): 49-67.
Ranger, Terence (1979). *Revolt in Southern Rhodesia 1986-7*. London: Heinemann.
———— (1995). *Are We Not also Men?: the Samkange family and African politics in Zimbabwe 1920-64*. London: James Currey.
Reeler, A.P. (2004).' Sticks and Stones, Skeletons and Ghosts' in *Zimbabwe: the past is the future*, op.cit.
Reid-Daly, Lt. Col. Ron, as told to Peter Stiff (1982). *Selous Scouts Top Secret War*. Alberton, S.A.: Galago. Also 1999. *Pamwe Chete: the legends of* the *Selous Scouts*. Weltervreden Park, S.A.: Covos-Day.
Scarnecchia,Timothy, (1999). 'The Mapping of Respectability and the Transformation of African Residential Space' in *Sites of Struggle*, op.cit.
Schmidt, Elizabeth (1992). *Peasants, Traders and Wives: Shona women in the history of Zimbabwe, 1870-1939*. Portsmouth, N.H.: Heinemann.
Shire, Chenjerai (1994). 'Men don't go to the Moon: language, space and masculinities in Zimbabwe' in *Dislocating Masculinity*, A. Cornwall and N. Lindisfarne (eds). London: Routledge.
Sithole, Ndabaningi (1977). *Roots of a Revolution*. Oxford: Oxford University Press.
Skimin, Robert (1977). *The Rhodesian Sellout*. New York: Libra Publishers.
Staunton, Irene (ed.) (1990). *Mothers of the Revolution*. Harare: Baobab Books.
Streets, Heather (2004). *Martial Races: the military, race and masculinity in British imperial culture, 1857-1914*. Manchester: Manchester University Press.
Summers, Carol (2002). *Colonial Lessons: Africans' Education in southern Rhodesia, 1918-1940*. Portsmouth, N.H.: Heinemann.
Tredgold, Robert (1968). *The Rhodesia That was my Life*. London: George Allen and Unwin.
Tosh, John (1999). *A Man's Place: masculinity and the middle class home in Victorian England*. New Haven, Conn.: Yale University Press.
Tshabangu, O. M. (1977). *The March 11th Movement in ZAPU*. York, UK: Tiger Papers.
Vambe, Lawrence (1976). *From Rhodesia to Zimbabwe*. London: Heinemann.
Vera, Yvonne (2002). *The Stone Virgins*. Harare: Weaver Press.
Weiss, Ruth (1994). *Zimbabwe and the New Elite*. London: Taurus Publishers.
———— with Jane Parpar (2001). Sir Garfield Todd and the Making of Zimbabwe. London: British Academic Press.
Werbner, R. (1991). *Tears of the Dead: the social biography of an African family*.

Edinburgh: Edinburgh University Press.
West, Michael (2002). *The Rise of an African Middle Class: colonial Zimbabwe, 1898-1965.* Bloomington: Indiana University Press.
White, Luise (2005). 'Precarious Conditions: a note on counter-insurgency in Africa after 1945' in *Violence, Vulnerability and Embodiment*, Shani D'Cruze and A. Rao (eds). Oxford: Blackwells.
―――― (2003). *The Assassination of Herbert Chitepo.* Bloomington and Indianapolis: Indiana University Press.

Chapter 9: **It couldn't be anything innocent: Negotiating gender in patriarchal-racial spaces** – Ane M. Orbo Kirkegaard

Aarmo, Margrete (1999). 'We are uniquely gay' An exploratory study of the lives and experiences of black gays and lesbians in Harare, Zimbabwe. Ph.D. Thesis. Oslo: University of Oslo.
Barnes, Teresa (1999). 'We women worked so hard' *Gender, urbanisation and social reproduction in colonial Harare, Zimbabwe, 1930-1956.* Oxford: James Currey Publishers.
Butler, Judith (1993). *Bodies that matter: on the discursive limits of 'sex'.* New York: Routledge.
Cawthorne, M. (1999). 'The third Chimurenga' in *Reflections on gender issues in Africa*, P. McFadden (ed.). Harare: SAPES Books.
Connell, R. W. (1999). *Masculinities.* Cambridge: Polity Press.
Godwin, Peter (1996). *Mukiwa – a white boy in Africa.* London: Picador.
―――― and Ian Hancock (1995). *Rhodesians Never Die: The Impact of the War and Political Change on White Rhodesia, c. 1970-1980.* Harare: Baobab Books.
Handwerker, W. Penn (1990). 'Politics and Reproduction: A Window on Social Change' in *Birth and Power: Social Change and the Politics of Reproduction*, W. Penn Handwerker (ed.). Boulder: Westview Press.
Jacobs, Susie (1995). 'Gender divisions and the formation of ethnicities in Zimbabwe' in *Unsettling settler societies: Articulations of gender, race, ethnicity and class*, Daiva Stasiulis and Nira Yuval-Davis (eds). London: Sage Publications.
Kirkegaard, Ane M. Ørbø (2004). A matter of difference? Family planning and gendered discourses on sexuality and reproductive decision-making among black and white Zimbabweans. Ph.D. Thesis. Göteborg: Göteborg University.
Laqueur, Thomas (1995). *Making sex – body and gender from the Greeks to Freud.* Cambridge, Mass.: Harvard University Press.
Lowry, Donal (1997) '"White woman's country" – Ethel Tawse Jollies and the making of white Rhodesia'. *Journal of Southern African Studies,* 23 (2): 259-281.
McFadden, Patricia (2000). 'Cultural practice as gendered exclusion: experiences from Southern Africa' in *Power, resources and culture in a gender perspective*, Ian Christopolos and Anna Liljelund (eds). Uppsala: The Collegium for Development Studies, Uppsala University
Yuval-Davis, Nira (2002). *Gender and nation.* London: Sage Publications.
Schmidt, Elisabeth (1996). *Peasants, Traders and Wives – Shona women in the history of Zimbabwe.* Harare: Baobab Books.
Smith, Ian Douglas (1997). *The Great Betrayal: The Memoirs of Africa's most Controversial Leader.* London: Blake Publishing Ltd.

Stasiulis, Daiva and Nira Yuval-Davis (eds) (1995). *Unsettling settler societies: Articulations of gender, race, ethnicity and class*. London: Sage Publications.
Weeks, Jeffrey (1989). *Sex, Politics and Society: The Regulation of Sexuality since 1800*. London: Longman Group.

Chapter 10: 'Boys': Performing manhood in Zimbabwean drama – Praise Zenenga

Bowker, H. Lee (ed.) (1998). *Masculinities and Violence*. Thousand Oaks: Sage Publications.
Carnes, C. Mark and Clyde Griffen (eds) (1990). *Meanings of Manhood: Constructions of Masculinity in Victorian America*. Chicago. The University of Chicago Press.
Chitauro, Moreblessings, Caleb Dube, and Liz Gunner (1994). 'Song, Story and Nation: Women as Singers and Actresses in Zimbabwe' in *Politics and Performance: Theatre, Poetry, and Song in Southern Africa*, Liz Gunner (ed.). Johannesburg: Witwatersrand UP.
Connell, R. W. (1995). *Masculinities*. St Leonards: Allen and Unwin.
———. (2000). *The Men and the Boys*. St Leonards: Allen and Unwin.
Dangarembga, Tsitsi (1987). *She No Longer Weeps*. Harare: College Press.
Dudink, Stefan, Karen Hagemann and John Tosh (eds) (2004). *Masculinities in Politics and War: Gendering Modern History*. Manchester: Manchester University Press.
Edwards, Tim (2006). *Cultures of Masculunity*. London: Routledge.
Fanon, Frantz (1963). *The Wretched of the Earth*, trans. Constance Farrington. Harmondsworth: Penguin.
Frederikse, Julie (1982). *None But Ourselves: masses vs. media in the making of Zimbabwe*. Harare: Anvil Press.
Gramsci, Antonio (1996). *Prison Notebooks* Vol. 1, trans. Joseph A. Buttigieg and Antonio Callari. New York: Columbia UP.
Howson, Richard (2006). *Challenging Hegemonic Masculinities*. London: Routledge.
Hunter, G. Andrea and James Earl Davis (1992). *Constructing Gender: An Exploration of Afro-American Men's Conceptualization of Manhood*. Gender & Society, 6 (3): 464-479.
Kimmel, S. Michael (2006). *Manhood in America: A Cultural History*. New York: Oxford University Press.
——— (ed.) (1995). *The Politics of Manhood: Profeminist Men Respond to the Mythopoetic Men's Movement (and the mythopoetic leaders answer)*. Philadelphia: Temple University Press.
Louie, Kam (2003). *Theorising Chinese Masculinity: Society and Gender in China*. Cambridge: Cambridge University Press.
Morrell, Robert (ed.) (2001). *Changing Men in Southern Africa*. Pietermaritzburg: University of Natal Press.
Msengezi, H. Gonzo (1984). *The Honourable MP*. Mambo Press: Gweru.
Reese, Renford (2004). *American Paradox: Young Black Men*. Durham: Carolina Academic Press.
Rohmer, Martin (1999). *Theatre and Performance in Zimbabwe*. Bayreuth: University of Bayreuth.
Sinclair, Ingrid (1996). *Flame*. Harare: ZimMedia.

Sinha, Mrinalini (1995). *Colonial Masculinity: The 'Manly Englishman' and the Effeminate Bengali' in the Late Nineteenth Century*. Manchester: Manchester University Press.

Spivak, Gayatri, Chakravorty (1988). 'Can the Subaltern Speak?' in *Marxism and the Interpretation of Culture*, Carrey Nelson and Lawrence Grossberg (eds). Urbana: University of Illinois Press.

Staunton, Irene (ed.) (1990). *Mothers of the Revolution*. Harare: Baobab Books.

Zinyemba, Ranga (1986). *Zimbabwean Drama: A Study of Shona and English Plays*. Gweru: Mambo Press.

Chapter 11: 'A man can try': Negotiating manhoods in colonial urban spaces in Dambudzo Marechera's *The House of Hunger* and Yvonne Vera's *Butterfly Burning* – Grace A. Musila

Arnfred, Signe (ed.) (2004). *Re-thinking Sexualities in Africa*. Uppsala: Nordic Africa Institute.

Barnes, Terri (1999). *'We Women Worked so Hard': Gender, Urbanization and Social Reproduction in Colonial Harare, Zimbabwe, 1930-1956*. Portsmouth, N.H.: Heinemann.

Basch, Francoise (1974). *Relative Creatures*. New York: Schocken Books.

Brittan, Arthur (2001). 'Masculinities and Masculinism' in *The Masculinities Reader*, Whitehead and Barrett (eds). Cambridge: Polity Press.

Brown, Carolyn (2003). 'A "Man" in the Village is a "Boy" in the Workplace' in *Men and Masculinities in Modern Africa*, Stephan Miescher and Lisa Lindsay (eds). Portsmouth: Heinemann.

Bryce, Jane (2002). Interview with Yvonne Vera in *Sign and Taboo: Perspectives on the Poetic Fiction of Yvonne Vera*, Robert Muponde and Mandi Taruvinga (eds). Harare: Weaver Press; Oxford: James Currey.

Chikwava, Brian (2003). 'Seventh Street Alchemy' in *Writing Still: New Stories from Zimbabwe*, Irene Staunton (ed.). Harare: Weaver Press.

Cleaver, Frances (ed.) (2002). *Masculinities Matter! Men Gender and Development*. London: Zed Books.

Coetzee, J.M. (1999). *Disgrace*. London: Secker and Warburg.

Connell, Robert (2005). *Masculinities*. Berkeley and California: University of California Press (2nd ed.).

Fanon, Frantz (1967). *The Wretched of the Earth*. Harmondsworth: Penguin Books.

Gagiano, Annie (2000). *Achebe, Head, Marechera: On Power and Change in Africa*. Boulder, Colo: Lynne Rienner Publishers.

Gurnah, Abdulrazak (1995). '"The Mid-point of the Scream" The Writing of Dambudzo Marechera' in Essays on *Contemporary African Writing* Vol.II: Contemporary Literature, Abdulrazak Gurnah (ed.). Oxford: Heinemann.

Holland, Kathryn (2005). 'Troubled Masculinities in Dangarembga's *Nervous Conditions*' in *African Masculinities: Men in Africa from the Late Nineteenth Century to the Present*, Robert Morrell and Lahoucine Ouzgane (eds). New York: Palgrave Press.

Jones, Eldred (1985). 'A Man Can Try' in *African Short Stories in English: An*

Anthology, J. De Grandsaigne (ed.). London: Macmillan.
Marechera, Dambudzo (1978). *House of Hunger*. London: Heinemann.
Mda, Zakes (2002). *The Madonna of Excelsior*. Cape Town: Oxford University Press.
McClinotck, Anne (1995). *Imperial Leather: Race, Gender and Sexuality in the Colonial Context*. New York: Routledge.
Miescher, Stephan and Lisa Lindsay (eds) (2003). *Men and Masculinities in Modern Africa*. Portsmouth: Heinemann.
Morrell, Robert (2000). 'The Times of Change: Men and Masculinity in South Africa' in *African Masculinities: Men in Africa from the Late Nineteenth Century to the Present*, op. cit.
―――― and Lahoucine Ouzgane (eds) (2005). *African Masculinities: Men in Africa from the Late Nineteenth Century to the Present*, op. cit.
Morrison, Toni (1987). *Beloved: A Novel*. New York: Signet.
Muponde, Robert and Mandi Taruvinga (eds) (2002). *Sign and Taboo: Perspectives on the Poetic Fiction of Yvonne Vera*a, op.cit.
Nelson, Nici (2001). 'Representation of Men and Women, City and Town in Kenyan Novels of 1970's and 1980's' in *Readings in African Popular Fiction*, Stephanie Newell (ed.). Bloomington: Indiana University Press; Oxford, James Currey. 108 -116.
Ngugi, James (1965). *The River Between*. London: Heinemann.
Said, Edward (1995). *Orientalism*. London: Penguin.
Segal, Lynne (1990). *Slow Motion: Changing Masculinities, Changing Men*. London: Virago Press.
Schmidt, Elizabeth (1992). 'Race, Sex and Domestic Labor: The Question of African Female Servants in Southern Rhodesia, 1900-1939' in *African Encounters with Domesticity*, Karen T. Hansen (ed.). New Brunswick, N.J.: Rutgers University Press. 221-241.
――――(1992). *Peasants, Traders and Wives: Shona Women in the History of Zimbabwe, 1870 – 1939*. Portsmouth: Heinemann; Harare: Baobab Books; London: James Currey.
Sideris, Tina (2001). 'Rape in War and Peace: Social Context, Gender, Power and Identity' in *The Aftermath: Women in Post-conflict Transformation*, Sheila Meintjes, Anu Pillay and Meredith Turshen (eds). London and New York: Zed Books. 142-157.
Taitz, Laurice (1996). Where once our Heroes Danced there is Nothing but a Hideous Stain: Nationalism and Contemporary Zimbabwean Literature. M.A. dissertation, University of the Witwatersrand.
Veit-Wild, Flora (1992). *Teachers, Preachers and Non-Believers*. London: Hans Zell Publishers.
Vera, Yvonne (1994). *Without a Name*. Harare: Baobab Books.
Whitehead, Stephen and Frank Barrett (eds) (2001). *The Masculinities Reader*. Cambridge: Polity Press.
Wood, Katharine and Rachel Jewkes (2001). 'Violence, Rape and Sexual Coercion: Everyday Love in a South African Township in *The Masculinities Reader*, op. cit.

Chapter 12: **The nature of fatherhood and manhood in Zimbabwean texts of pre-colonial and colonial Settings** – Mickias Musiyiwa and Memory Chirere

Achebe, Chinua (1958). *Things Fall Apart*. London: Heinemann.
Beach, David N. (1980). *The Shona and Zimbabwe, 900 – 1850*. Gweru: Mambo Press.
Billington, Rosamund, et.al. (1991). *Culture and Society*. London: The Macmillan Press.
Chakaipa, Patrick (1959). *Pfumo reRopa*. Salisbury: Longman.
Chidyausiku, Paul (1962). *Nyadzi Dzinokunda Rufu*. London: Oxford University Press.
Fortune, George (1982). *Ngano* Vol. 2. Harare: Mercury Press.
Freire, Paulo (1970). *Pedagogy of the Oppressed*. New York: Continuum.
Hove, Chenjerai (1988). *Bones*. Harare: Baobab.
Kawara, James (1982). *Ruchiva*. Harare: Longman.
Khiyaza, G. (1978). *Ukuthunjwa kukaSukuzukuduma*. Gwelo: Mambo Press.
Machimbira, Julius (1975). *Gondoharishari*. Salisbury: Longman.
Makhalisa, Barbara (1983). *Impilo Yinkinga*. Harare: Longman.
Memmi, Albert (1965). *The Colonizer and the Colonized*. Boston: Beacon Press.
Moyo, Aaron, C. (1975). *Uchandifungawo*. *Gwelo:* Mambo Press.
Mungoshi, Charles (1975). *Ndiko Kupindana Kwamazuva*. Gwelo: Mambo Press.
Mutasa, Norbert (1991). *Misodzi, Dikita neRopa*. Gweru: Mambo Press.
Mutswairo, Solomon (1956). *Feso*. Cape Town: Oxford University Press.
Ndhlala, Geoffrey (1979). *Jikinya*. London: Macmillan.
Ndlovu, B.D. (1999). *Laphuma Elinye Lingakatshoni*. Harare: College Press.
Nyathi, Pathisa (2001). *Traditional Ceremonies of AmaNdebele*. Gweru: Mambo Press.
Patterson, Orlando (2000). 'Backlash', *Transition* Vol 62.
P'Bitek, Okot (1986). *Artist the Ruler*. Nairobi: Heinemann.
The Oxford English Dictionary, Second Edition (1989). Oxford: Clarendon Press.
Tsodzo, Thomson (1972). *Pafunge*. Salisbury: Longman.
Webster's Third New International Dictionary, Vol. II (1986). Chicago: Encyclopedia Britannica, Inc.
Weinrich, Aquina.K. (1982). *African Marriage in Zimbabwe*. Gweru: Mambo Press.
Zhuwarara, Rino (2001). *Introduction to Zimbabwean Literature in English*. Harare: College Press.
Zvarevashe, Ignatius (1976). *Kurauone*. Salisbury: College Press.

Chapter 13: **'My father – the hero?' The father-daughter relationship in Zimbabwean literature and culture** – Anna Chitando and Angeline M. Madongonda

Berndt, Katrin (2005). *Female Identity in Contemporary Zimbabwean fiction*. Bayreuth: Bayreuth University.
Chakaipa, Patrick (1966). *Rudo Ibofu*. Gwelo: Mambo Press.
Chingono, Julias (1978). *Chipo Changu*. Salisbury: Longman.

Chinodya, Shimmer (2004). *Tale of Tamari*. Harare: Weaver Press.
Dangarembga, Tsitsi (1988). *Nervous Conditions*. London: The Women's Press.
—— (2006). *The Book of Not*. Oxfordshire: Ayerbia Clarke Publishing Ltd.
Finnegan, Ruth (1970). *Oral literature in Africa*. London: Oxford University Press.
Furniss, Graham and Liz Gunner (1995). *Power, Marginality and African Oral Literature*. London: Cambridge University Press.
Holland, Kathryn (2005) 'Troubled Masculinities in Tsitsi Dangarembga's *Nervous Conditions*' in *African Masculinties: Men in Africa from the Late Nineteenth Century to the Present*, Lahoucine, Ouzgane and Robert Morrell (eds). Hampshire: Palgrave Macmillan. 121-136.
Gelfand, Michael (1973). *The Genuine Shona*. Gweru: Mambo Press.
Hanson, B.J. (1997). *Takadini*. Harare: Fidalyn Productions (pvt) Ltd.
Haralambos, Michael and Martin Holborn (1980). *Sociology: Themes and Perspectives*. London: Unwin Hyman Limited.
Makina, Rewaizvenyu (1983). *Baboon Wants a Wife and Other Stories*. Gweru: Mambo Press.
Mawuru, Godwin, (1993) *Neria* (a film). Harare: Media for Development Trust.
Morrell, Robert (2001). 'The Times of Change: Masculinity in South Africa' in Robert, Morrell (ed.) *Changing Men in Southern Africa*. London: Zed Books.
Morrison, Toni (1970). *The Bluest Eye*. New York: Penguin Books.
Mukonoweshuro, Sharai (2000). *Days of Silence*. Harare: Wonder Book Publishers.
Mungoshi, Charles (2000). *One Day, Long Ago*. Harare: Baobab Books.
—— (1999). *Stories from a Shona Childhood*. Harare: Baobab.
—— (1997). *Walking Still*. Harare: Baobab Books.
—— (1975). *Waiting for the Rain*. London: Heinemann.
Mutasa, Norbet, M (1978). *Mapatya*. Salisbury: Longman.
Rosen-Grandon, Jane, R. (1995). Father Daughter Relationships. Accessed 27 January, 2007 at <www.dr Jane.com/chapters/Jane.125.html>
Tsodzo, Thompson, K. (1972). *Pafunge*. Salisbury: Longman.
Vera, Yvonne (1996). *Under The Tongue*. Harare: Baobab Books.
Westerhof, Tendai (2005). *Unlucky in Love*. Harare: Public Personalities Against Aids Trust.

www.ingramcontent.com/pod-product-compliance
Lightning Source LLC
Chambersburg PA
CBHW011744290426
44113CB00017BA/2646